Make It Yours!

SMALL BUSINESS BOOKS FROM WILEY

Make It Yours!

HOW TO OWN YOUR OWN BUSINESS

- *Buy a Business*
- *Start a Business*
- *Franchise a Business*

Louis Mucciolo

John Wiley & Sons, Inc.
New York • Chichester • Brisbane • Toronto • Singapore

Publisher: Stephen Kippur
Editor: Katherine S. Bolster
Managing Editor: Ruth Greif
Editing, Design & Production: G&H SOHO, Ltd.

This publication is designed to provide accurate and authoritative information
in regard to the subject matter covered. It is sold with the understanding
that the publisher is not engaged in rendering legal, accounting, or other
professional service. If legal advice or other expert assistance is required,
the services of a competent professional person should be sought. FROM A
DECLARATION OF PRINCIPLES JOINTLY ADOPTED BY A COMMITTEE OF
THE AMERICAN BAR ASSOCIATION AND A COMMITTEE OF PUBLISHERS.

Library of Congress Cataloging-in-Publication Data

Mucciolo, Louis.
  Make it yours!

  1. Small business—Management. I. Title.
HD 62.7.M79 1987   658.1'141   87-8168
ISBN 0-471-62585-X(pbk.)
ISBN 0-471-62582-5

Printed in the United States of America

87 88 10 9 8 7 6 5 4 3 2 1

To my wife, Mary, who once again has
recorded it all . . . a triple salute
to a wonderful partner.

To the many others who have contributed
their thoughts and experiences, my
sincere thanks.

Preface

This is a beginner's book. Its purpose is to get you to begin the *actuality* of becoming your own boss, running your own business, trying out for the best job you may ever have.

Some of you will look to small business ownership because of a desire to control your own destiny and chart your personal success. Others are being forced to consider the real feasibility of a small business for survival and job security.

You may be unemployed or suddenly insecure in your present job. Perhaps you are about to graduate from college and your career prospects are not overly bright. Or the whirlwinds of change may be putting your company into a no-growth or merger state, and you are looking for a new job opportunity.

Whatever the motivation, there's a great deal to research and evaluate, especially if this is the first time you are seriously considering the idea of going it alone.

This is a time when many of your long-held beliefs are coming apart. Security in government jobs, big business, and union-intensive industries is no longer written in stone. Unemployment, recession, inflation, and interest rates have not willingly gone into any politically ordered submission. Instead they've seesawed and erupted in highly volatile cycles, with devastating results in different regional areas.

Does this uncertainty mean this isn't the time for organizing and running a small business? Not on your life! These very frustrations are exactly the kick-in-the-pants kind of motivation many of us need to get started. And getting started is what this book is all about. Perhaps, then, today is the time for you to begin to *create your own job*, to start at the top and be the boss!

Why not? After all, what is it you really want from a job? Usually it's an opportunity to contribute your skills and enthusiasm in return for the chance to achieve career growth. Along the way, that includes earned promotions, additional responsibilities, increasing salaries, and an honest recognition of worth and ability.

It sounds logical, but it doesn't always work that way. There are too many unhappy tales of dead-end jobs, one-way communication, squelched ideas, and nonrecognition of individual contributions.

For those who create their own jobs as entrepreneurs, however, everything changes. Challenges abound. To be a success, you must forever be increasing your responsibilities, enlarging your horizons, creating solutions, and growing. With success come wonderful rewards, both personal and financial.

Of course, running your own business is not for everyone; only a small percentage have what it takes. But if you do join the entrepreneurial ranks, you'll be joining well over 10 million other small businesses actively operating across the country. Today entrepreneurship is a growth industry with millions of successful winners—winners who have ensured their own career developments, increased their financial net worth, and created their best tax shelter.

Although there's a lot to learn, the first order of the day is to *keep it simple!* The information you require should be easy to read and absorb. It should cover the elementary as well as the more advanced, but without the necessity for a now-do-you-understand-it translation. This book is an attempt to provide the preliminary information that's needed by a great number of enterprising people who want to consider the possibility of being on their own for the first time.

David Birch, a well-known researcher of business marketplace dynamics, has classified small businesses into two classes: the entrepreneurial venture that aims for growth in the high multiples, and the "income substitution" business that will generate a very comfortable income for the owner and his or her family. This book relates to the latter, which is the category that comprises the great majority of all small businesses in the country.

For starters, make sure you analyze and understand all the options available for beginning a business of your own. Evaluate yourself and promise to devote ample time to following through after the preliminary preparations. Keep in mind that the magic carpet exists only in fairy tales. You and your abilities, plus a strong commitment, are the primary forces that can propel you into the winner's circle.

After you have read this guide, if you think you have what it takes, then go for it and make it yours! Running a business of your own really can be the *best job you ever had!*

L.M.

Contents

Make It Yours!

Introduction

STARTING OUT

To be quite candid, becoming an entrepreneur and starting at the top isn't always all peaches and cream. For one thing, there's no guarantee of success. Additionally, you may never be able to achieve the complete freedom to do whatever it is you want to do.

In fact, initially your wonderful small business will tie you up in knots and overwhelm you with more responsibilities than any job ever did. And your reward? Much less time for yourself, family, friends, sports, and favorite social activities.

But oh what a wonderful feeling it will be to use your own ideas, to be your own boss.

This is especially true if you are blessed with enthusiasm, a definite hankering to be on your own, lots of energy and inquisitiveness, and if you aren't afraid of new and exciting experiences. Those are only a few of the personal resources necessary for a successful entrepreneurship.

Just recently, I interviewed a new entrepreneur, one who had purchased an ongoing business about six months ago. He thoroughly enjoyed talking about it. This was his first business and it was an area he had no experience in. Apprehensive? Yes, but at the same time fairly confident that he would learn quickly and, in fact, had already done so.

Both his attitude and his confidence were definite pluses when it came to having the required personal characteristics so necessary for success. So was his willingness to take a risk and that's possibly the most important attribute you must have.

Experts in the field would like you to be fortified with a few other pluses: having a parent who owned a business, being an only child or the firstborn, having childhood experience selling lemonade or delivering

1

newspapers or selling pollywogs door to door, and so on. Fortunately, my own observations indicate you still have a good chance to succeed even if none of these were part of your upbringing.

At this point, however, it isn't my intention to list all the required personal traits for becoming a successful small business owner. I don't want to get overly involved with the "personality appraisal chart" that is so often the initial kickoff of every book, seminar, or course on starting and managing a small business. Sure it's important! And if you haven't already looked over and successfully completed one of the many recommended self-appraisal checklists of personal resources, turn to Appendix B and take a run-through of the "personal characteristics" review.

FIRST THINGS FIRST

There are a number of ways to get into the small business arena, ranging from starting a part-time operation on the kitchen table all the way up to inheriting a successful, ongoing family venture. Within that range, however, the dominant method still seems to be some variation of the following:

- buying an established business
- starting from scratch
- joining a franchise family.

The pros and cons for each method will fill numerous pages of this book. So will the probing and analyzing of their complexities and their individual start-up procedures. Are there similarities as well as differences? Which will be best for you, and for your skills?

The following chapters will explore each small business entry category from the standpoint of a fairly modest venture, operated by an active owner-manager.

Because of the present economic and societal turmoil, there are new forces affecting lifestyles, education, product acceptance, urban needs, marketing, even demographics. With changes come new opportunities and new approaches to existing ventures. Whether you take part in the whirlwind innovations of technology and futuristics or take firm hold and refresh a tried-and-true venture is up to you and what you have to offer.

The road to successful entrepreneurship is still pitted with innumerable sinkholes that swallow up, into oblivion, the great majority of new start-up ventures—no matter how they started. The entrepreneurs who do succeed usually have these characteristics:

- the required personality characteristics
- some knowledge of the business they selected
- a determination to prepare beforehand
- a beginning knowledge of basic management practices
- an awareness of the need for marketing and promotion.

GETTING THERE

Since entrepreneurship is your goal, let's check some definitions of "entrepreneur" that may apply:

Webster's Third New International Dictionary: *1: the organizer of an economic venture; esp: one who organizes, owns, manages, and assumes the risks of a business. . . . 2: one that organizes, promotes, or manages an enterprise or activity of any kind.*

The American Heritage Dictionary: *a person who organizes, operates and assumes the risk for business ventures, especially an impressario.*

Webster's New World Dictionary: *a person who organizes and manages a business undertaking, assuming the risk for the sake of the profit.*

All the definitions are fairly specific, and the last one doesn't neglect the vital aspect of profit. Without profit, the entrepreneur's existence would be a short one. Note also that the word "risk" appears in all the definitions.

What may prove more informative than the authoritative sources and their very precise, highly impersonal, matter-of-fact definitions are the short, on-target phrases often used by others to describe entrepreneurs they know or work with:

- "a self-starter and doer"
- "an innovator, always thinking ahead"
- "one who sees value where others don't"
- "a risk-taker, but not a gambler"
- "a leader as well as an owner"
- "a real problem-solver"
- "it's his baby and that's the way he wants it"
- "the boss."

There's a lot more imagery in those comments, and rather than defining what an entrepreneur is, they highlight what characteristics he or she should possess. The majority have to do with personal characteristics and resources—we're back to that again. And it bears repeating. Your self-analysis evaluation should indicate a *positive* outlook. If not, your entry into entrepreneurship will be an out-and-out gamble, rather than a calculated risk—one where the odds are with you.

THE AWARENESS FACTOR

Most of your initial knowledge about the operational procedures of a small business will come from on-the-job training. For the first-time entrepreneur, this confrontation with reality can either be a successful adventure or a disastrous failure.

Since your experience as a new entrepreneur is extremely limited, it's imperative that you acquire some familiarity with what lies ahead before you ever start. You won't become a successful owner-manager overnight, but you can develop some awareness of the jolting realities that you are sure to encounter.

The best way to cushion those business surprises is to spend your spare time actively pursuing the initial homework procedures that every beginner-entrepreneur should be following. One aspect of that is *reading*. Reading about all the different facets of small business: what it means, what it entails, what it requires, how problem-solving is achieved, and what elements help to ensure success.

If you are unfamiliar with the basics of business management, for example, maximize that kind of reading by taking courses in management. In most areas, there are ample opportunities for attending small business management classes or seminars in community colleges, universities, adult education courses, or sessions sponsored by the Small Business Administration (SBA).

Don't start your venture without some basic management knowledge. Historically, bad management practices account for over 90 percent of small business failures.

Another aspect of your preparation should involve *talking*. Just getting together with a variety of owner-managers and simply talking with them about their actions in running a business is an education in itself. Most entrepreneurs enjoy discussing the usual and unusual problems of cash flow, locations, buying and pricing, competition, capital investments, and, above all, customers.

Analyzing those common areas of on-line ventures serves to give real-life emphasis to your text reading. In fact, the odds are great that you'll learn a great deal that doesn't show up in any "how to" book or business course.

When you have laid the foundation through that kind of realistic preparation, *reading* and *talking*, you can evaluate and examine the varied start-up options that most closely match your own objectives and your ability to accomplish them. That will be the main thrust of the subsequent chapters.

FULL SPEED AHEAD

The material that follows is divided into three sections: buying a business, starting a business from scratch, and joining a franchise. Within that structure, there will be a concentration on basic information for beginners, from my own observations and those of authoritative sources in the field.

Additionally, the owners of many and diverse small businesses will explain why they chose their particular form of start-up in owning their own business. The reasons may vary considerably, or we may be able to detect some obvious commonalities that motivated their choices. In some cases, their reasonings may match your own feelings exactly.

This book isn't meant to be a blueprint for guaranteed success, or the most comprehensive last word on small business entrepreneurship. Instead, it's an expanded overview that will help you evaluate the options available within the three best ways to get started in the business arena. From this wealth of basic material, both actual and advisory, each reader should be able to match up his or her individual needs and attributes for a personal decision and determination of the best way to go.

If this is to be your first venture, *read the entire book*! No matter which option you ultimately choose, each section can contribute specific success strategies for your final selection.

Buy a Business

One of the high points in life is buying your first house.

Many prefer to purchase it from a previous owner—one who has already completed the landscaping, built the patio, finished the basement, and installed all the extras inside.

Fuel charges and utility costs will have been documented for many years. Property taxes and assessments are a matter of record.

Most everything is visible and verifiable. Is that the key to buying a business?

1

The Buying Option

THE EASY WAY TO GO?

Among the many Dun & Bradstreet reports, one statement that may have significance in the area of buying a business was extracted and underlined as follows:

"Every year, hundreds of thousands of firms are started, almost an equal number discontinued, and even more transfer ownership or control."

A review of any major newspaper or special-interest trade magazine will reveal an ample number of business opportunity ads that relate to businesses for sale. The reasons to sell are too numerous to list, but most seem to involve "illness," "retirement," "other interests," or "relocating." It's important to evaluate the truth of these reasons when you begin to analyze the dozens of factors that affect the "buy-no-buy" decision.

Keep in mind that the opportunities to purchase an existing business are not confined to retail stores. Although those stores abound, the businesses for sale also include manufacturing, mail order, distribution, varied services, and even professional practices. Buying a business is certainly an attractive way to become an entrepreneur, one that can be open to everyone: those with specific skills and experience, as well as those with no background but plenty of heart and determination.

In too many instances, however, the prospective entrepreneur has chosen to buy a business because he or she thinks it is the simplest way to start. After all, in an already established situation, everything is all laid out for inspection and evaluation. Unfortunately, such is not the case. Buying a business involves a complicated and demanding investigative process. In some ways it requires more preparation and concentrated study than if you were to start from ground zero.

THIS ONE IS A REAL STEAL

As a buyer, you are eager to begin and you can easily visualize yourself in the *setting* of the business you are considering for purchase. Within that emotional framework, you are vulnerable to inadequate preparation and simple misevaluation. This is one area where the familiar "let the buyer beware" is most applicable, and the negative consequences when you don't investigate thoroughly are almost certainly disastrous. Many a life savings have gone down the drain because insufficient time was devoted to proper evaluation and too much attention was given to emotional appeals like "It's a wonderful opportunity and you can't afford to let someone else grab it."

Most businesses are on the seller's block for the same reason that many good-looking cars are on the used-car lot: somewhere along the line there's been trouble! With used cars, however, the defects may be a lot easier to spot than they are in a business for sale. In both cases, the additional factor of fraud may also rear its ugly head. So "caveat emptor" doesn't only apply to your observation of normal business practices, it also relates to being wary of a superslick rip-off. Although you should be careful, don't make the mistake of thinking that all businesses for sale are duds.

Professional assistance in buying a business is mandatory. An accountant and lawyer familiar with the field you have chosen will be invaluable in checking the many financial and legal aspects that have to be evaluated. Depending on the size and character of the business, experts in the areas of inventory, machinery and equipment, land and facilities, and so on may also be needed for qualified appraisals. Even a modest retail store will require professional consultancy to help determine the present worth of the business and its future potential.

PUTTING THE CART BEFORE THE HORSE

Let's look at first things first. If your interest is attuned to buying an established business, there are some initial factors to be defined.

- type of business you prefer
- size of operation you can handle
- relevant skills and experience

- geographical location you prefer
- capital you have available or can raise
- sources of business opportunities to investigate

Almost all these factors interlace and affect each other. Your skills and previous experience ought to determine the type of business you should concentrate on. Available capital will influence both the type and size of the enterprise; it may also target your sights and search toward a realistic goal. Your personal feelings can come into play in many areas. Do you prefer an urban, suburban, or rural location? Does your temperament comfortably allow you to work with and supervise employees? Are you unenthusiastic about face-to-face customer relations, or sales contacts with all the attendant rejections?

The point is that you must give ample thought and consideration to the preliminaries *before* you start the search for that star-studded business opportunity of your dreams.

This doesn't exclude those who have no particular skills or experience that might relate to the problems of running your own business. In actual fact, that may be one reason for your decision to purchase an ongoing and already successful enterprise, rather than starting from the bottom rung.

But in all cases, the need to clearly define those initial factors is an essential ingredient of the search. Perhaps the requirement of "skills and experience" will have to be replaced with "likes and dislikes" in the case of the inexperienced beginner. Then the type of business selected should be one you can be comfortable with and one in which you have some expertise as a hobbyist or even as a consumer. All in all, inexperience will mean complete on-the-job training while you are actually running the business. It's a double dose of problems and certainly not the easiest way to become a small business owner.

A better solution, of course, would be to work for someone else in the field that interests you, or at the very least to try to become as familiar as possible with the business you are considering before any purchase is finalized.

WHERE ARE THE BARGAINS?

Classified Ads

The most frequently used sources of businesses for sale are the classified ads in the newspapers. Since ads do not always appear in competitive newspapers, it pays to peruse all the papers that service the region in which you wish to concentrate your search. With many sellers, the type or size of the business being offered may dictate in which specific paper it will appear. The opportunity ads are usually fairly explicit as to the nature of the business and oftentimes carry initial information of gross sales and purchase price. If so, this may help you to concentrate on those offerings that bear some relationship to your objectives, finances, and capabilities.

You must be able to follow up on an ad, and it's a lot easier if there's a phone number, rather than a box number. In all cases, however, what you see in the ad is only the very beginning of your informational search.

Personnel Agency: For sale, fully equipped, very attractive office in central business area. Owner retiring. Cash & terms negot. Call ------ bet. 10 AM and 1 PM

Plant & Gift Shop: Colorful South Shore seaside village. Estab. 6 yrs. Unique oppty. Take over now for tourist season. $22,000. After 5 PM, call ------

---

Mail Order: Service business, estab. over 15 yrs.; immed. sale, 15M cash + . Due to illness. Will train qual. buyer. Box # ------

---

Light Manufacturing: $8,000 @ month net. Exlnt. terms. Seller has other interests. Estab. 10 years. 65K down, principals only. Call for details ------

---

Pie Route: Suburban, exclusive territory Net $425/wk., 5½ days. Can expand. Owner will train. Full price $18,500—$11,500 cash, includes panel truck. PO Box # ------

Business Brokers

A source that can give you an immediate response to a request for additional details is the business broker. Some brokers are residential realtors who also deal in the buying and selling of commercial properties, others are specialists who concentrate on this field. Brokers usually handle a variety of offerings and can give you a great deal of information and background about what to expect when buying a business. In fact, a prediscussion with a business broker can result in a quick-study awareness of the cash down/notes payable norms, the nonnegotiable items, bank loan probabilities, and contract clauses.

Brokers' for-sale ads also appear in the classified section of the newspapers, but their office doors are always open for you to drop in and ask about availabilities. Their commissions come from the seller, but at the same time they want to complete a deal that will be successful for both parties. It isn't in their interest if you purchase a business you can't handle, whether due to lack of capital or lack of knowledge. In dealing with local brokers, the purchaser becomes a part of the broker's own community, and a record of failures won't rate any shiny gold stars for that broker's future buy-sell activities.

Of course the brokers would like to close their deals as quickly as possible, and they are quite expert at arousing your enthusiasm. But when you do find something of interest, cool your emotional responses and bring in your own attorney and accountant to take over. Then any pressure or urgency advocated by the broker can be put into the correct perspective.

Many broker ads are more detailed than a seller's offering because the broker does not want to be besieged by unqualified buyers or just plain browsers. Other ads are of the "variety" type to indicate the scope of ventures the office is handling and the assurance that they have just what you are looking for.

Suburban TV, radio, appliances. Sales & serv. Estbld. 50 + years. Vehicle and small parts incl. $75M + stock. Terms avail. 9,000 sq. ft. w/apt. & ofc. space in addition to bus. ------ (Rltr.) Call ------

Clean Profit $45,000 yr.!!
Vending—62 machines. A-1 accounts. Estbld. 20 years. Will teach. Dodge van incl. 30 hrs./wk. $35,000 nec. Exclusive w/------. Call ------

Businesses for Sale

Employment agencies
Clock mfg.
Car washes
Wholesale dist. stationery
Sportswear store
   plus many more
Call ------

Looking for a Business?

Dry cleaner	Make offer
Light mfg.	Nets 90M
Candy/nut	Nets 30M
Dry stat'y	Nets 60M
Kitchen design ctr.	Low $ down
Phone------	

Bankers, Accountants, Lawyers

There are those who believe that more businesses are bought and sold through contacts and word-of-mouth then any other way, and that these businesses are the "better ones." Although such beliefs have not been verified, the potential of these professional sources should be explored.

If you know or can arrange contacts with any of the bankers, accountants, or lawyers in the area of your search, try them. They are among the first to know if a present owner has some yearning for "another place" or a hankering to "do some other things." A visit to the local banker may strike paydirt via one of the bank's own commercial depositors, or you may be put in direct contact with an accountant whose clients relate to the bank's services.

Accountants are certainly aware of their clients' future intentions: whether they intend to expand, retrench, or sell out. It's to the advantage of both parties for the accountant to talk up a possible sell situation with the other accounts he or she serves. This can result in motivating a merger or acquisition offer, or it may simply serve to pass the word around—"If you know of someone who may be interested, give me a buzz."

Lawyers who are working on new business setups are especially aware of their clients' need for additional capital. This information may very well be passed on through the grapevine, and you may want to consider it with relation to a partnership arrangement. The banker also is very often given this initial information, and that's how the whole circle gets started—one of the best word-of-mouth sources in action.

Another often overlooked source is yourself. If you're interested in buying an established business, have you let people you work with or deal with know about your intentions? Are they aware of any persons who are considering selling their ventures?

It may be a longshot, but have you thought of approaching a business you know about and simply asking the owner if there's any thought of selling? He or she may surprise you with a yes, or may be able to suggest someone else in the same field who does want to sell.

Trade Associations

Trade associations, trade magazines, supplier representatives, and manufacturers are good sources to explore because they relate directly to a specific type of business. In many cases, if there is a limited market for a unique type of venture, the seller tends to make greater use of the contacts in that field and, at the same time, give consideration to a business opportunity ad in the trade publication.

There seems to be an official association for almost every type of business imaginable. In addition to being good sources, these associations offer the new or existing entrepreneur much information about all the goings-on in that particular industry. Some of this information will be useful to you in evaluating any businesses you may be considering. Are their operating ratios in line with the average statistics in the industry? What about rule-of-thumb formulas for buy-sell situations in this field?

Other information can help determine what the size of a profitable marketing area should be and the demographics that must accompany it. Whatever acceptable guidelines exist in that field should become a part of your knowledge and expertise.

How do you check on whether there's an association in the field you intend to enter? The best source is your public library. Go to the reference desk and ask for the *Encyclopedia of Associations*. Look up the section for Trade, Business, and Commercial Organizations. Here is a sampling of the kind of listings you will find. These have been condensed to just the bare essentials of description.

American Bottled Water Association
Washington, D.C.

Founded 1959. Members 225. Owners and operators of bottled water plants; dealers, distributors and suppliers to the industry.

Society of American Florists and Ornamental Horticulturists
Alexandria, Va.

Founded 1884. Members 7,856. Growers, wholesalers, retailers, and allied tradesmen in the floral industry.

Souvenier and Novelty Trade Association
Philadelphia, Pa.

Founded 1965. Members 15,000. Manufacturers, wholesaler-distributors, re-tailers, publishers, and others associated with the industry.

National Retail Hardware Association
Indianapolis, In.

Founded 1900. Members 18,000. Federation of 23 state and regional associa-tions of independent hardware retailers.

National Pest Control Association
Vienna, Va.

Founded 1933. Members 2,500. Firms engaged in the control of insects, ro-dents, birds, and other pests in or around structures.

Retail Floorcoverings Institute
Chicago, Ill.

Founded 1973. Members 1,600. Retail floorcovering owners and managers; floorcovering distributors and manufacturers.

National Retail Merchants Association
New York, N.Y.

Founded 1911. Members 35,000. Department, chain, and mass merchandise and specialty stores retailing men's, women's, and children's apparel and home furnishings.

Retail Tobacco Dealers of America
New York, N.Y.

Founded 1932. Members 5,000. Retailers of tobacco products, candy and
sundry products; also candy and stationery stores, independent cigar stores,
drug stores.

National Restaurant Association
Washington, D.C.

Founded 1919. Members 13,000. Restaurants, cafeterias, clubs, contract
feeders, drive-ins, caterers, institutional food services.

American Booksellers Association
New York, N.Y.

Founded 1900. Members 5,500. Retail book stores.

The above excerpts tell only part of the story. The listings also indicate a variety of meaningful activities for an association's members and
industry, such as conducting seminars, distributing educational materials, participating in research programs, and publishing newsletters and
industry statistics.

What About Luck?

Luck sometimes rears its wonderful head and thrusts an opportunity
at you when you least expect it. In fact, one woman recently complained
to me that she wasn't fortunate enough to frequent any of the areas or
groups where business opportunities often arise. She may have been
right, but some instances come to mind that really had nothing to do
with a special group or situation. The new owner of a retail shop, for
example, informed me of the luck that got him to buy his present
enterprise.

As a pipe smoker, he often dropped in to his favorite tobacconist for a
special blend, a cup of coffee, and some general conversation. His
ambition, which he had previously mentioned to the proprietor, was to
find a good photography shop, buy it, and run it, for that was one of his
professional capabilities. Much searching, however, had not produced
anything that felt right to him.

During one of his visits to the tobacco shop, the elderly proprietor
said, "Why don't you buy *this* store? I'm ready to retire soon."

Well, that was a new thought and at first he simply shrugged it off.

But later, after discussing the pros and cons, the feasibility factors seemed a lot more promising and finally the deal was made. Now he loves it.

A marketing director who was released because of a merger had this tale of luck and opportunity. To offset the trauma of nonemployment, he took off for a favorite fishing camp in New England. While he was there, the proprietor mentioned this would be the last season because her arthritis wouldn't allow her to continue.

The director's ability to size up things quickly and his disenchantment with corporate politics came immediately into play. He called a friend to come up and help with a serious appraisal of the advantages and disadvantages. Their combined evaluation indicated the camp had great potential. When they negotiated a very favorable price, the deal was set.

Without question, the buyer's take-home pay will be much less than his former executive compensation, and the initial work in sprucing up the fishing camp will be a lot harder. But he's opted for a different lifestyle that he feels will be more satisfying.

Luck? Serendipity? Right place at the right time? Yes, all of those and a lot more, especially the willingness to both *recognize* and *consider* the potential of a sudden opportunity. That's exactly why lifestyles and personal preferences, in addition to skills and experience, can enter into your evaluation of an established business. A pipe smoker who used special blends rather than a brand-name, packaged tobacco is now in an environment that he is comfortable with and really enjoys. A fishing enthusiast who frequented a "pure" fishing camp rather than a vacation resort is now extending his hobby to the highest degree—his own business.

Keep your ears open and your options flexible. This book is designed to alert you to the choices that exist in starting at the top by becoming your own boss.

2

What's Buying All About?

ADVANTAGES OF BUYING A BUSINESS

Many small business experts, and even owners, say "It's better to buy" when asked about the best way to get started. Usually it's a quick, off-the-cuff answer. But on the surface it certainly seems like the right way, and that's also where the immediate advantages show up best.

1. The location has already been determined.
2. Leases, fixtures, and equipment exist.
3. Inventory, supplies, or raw materials are there.
4. Suppliers and sources are on the books.
5. Experienced employees are available.
6. Customers and accounts are established.
7. Business records are there to guide you.
8. Previous owner experience may be called on for the transition period.
9. An actual cost to get into business can be determined.
10. A past profit picture and a possible return on investment may be calculated.
11. A favorable price may be negotiated because of owner's retirement or ill health.
12. A long waiting period to establish the new business is omitted and customers are immediate.
13. Initial financial outlay may be less than a new start-up if seller accepts down payment and notes.

With all that going for you, it's not difficult to understand why buying an established business is so often recommended. It also seems a much safer way to go for the first time owner-manager who doesn't have any previous experience or skills to bring to the small business arena.

Of great importance is the acknowledged fact that you immediately become an established business, even to the extent of drawing a salary. Most new started-from-the-bottom ventures require a few years of all-consuming effort before the owner can afford a reasonable take-home stipend.

DISADVANTAGES

As in the purchase of a used car, not very many businesses for sale can be considered a perfect buy. There will be cases where problems exist or, at the very least, improvements can be made. One frequent problem is that owner-sellers are unable to accept a reasonable price because they confuse the value of the business (return on investment) with their income (return on investment plus salary).

These are some of the disadvantages that may show up, sometimes negating the benefits. Often the purchase price can be adjusted accordingly for specific negatives in the cost/value areas.

1. Lease may be expiring and negotiations are required.
2. Premises may require redecoration or enlargement.
3. Inventory may be unbalanced and/or outdated.
4. Equipment may require replacement or repair.
5. Existing location may be in a declining area.
6. Employees may be unionized, to your possible disadvantage in contract terms.
7. Present owner's relationship with customers and suppliers may have deteriorated.
8. Present or incoming competition may be too strong for a continuing profit potential.
9. Small business financial records are usually not a true reflection of value (have your accountant check).
10. Your own urgency to get started may cause a premature purchase.
11. Overall purchase price is much higher than the initial costs of a new start-up.

Buying a business is truly a complicated and demanding investigative process. The probable disadvantages you will discover are a direct result of investigating and are a caution to avoid rushing in too quickly. If you miss one opportunity because you took too much time to evaluate, don't despair, there will be another one coming up in a few days.

What good are advantages if an overlooked or sloughed-off negative neutralizes the benefits of buying an established venture? After all, the records do show that successful, ongoing businesses have been purchased that failed *after* the new owners took over and ran them for a while. What went wrong?

Were the new owners incompetent in management practices?

Did the new owners misinterpret the potential?

Was the competition underevaluated?

Was the location undergoing changes?

Was most of the capital used for purchase and was the business now undercapitalized?

Were professional services used, and were the new owners knowledgeable in the field?

Did the new owner institute radical changes to an already successful business?

Was the success of the business primarily due to the previous owner's skills?

Such questions simply take the so-called advantages and put them under the magnifying glass of veracity and value. If everything checks out fairly well, then the purchase of that existing business may actually be a true opportunity. But keep in mind that even after you check everything out, you cannot be absolutely sure. Small business is *not* an exact science, and there's always an element of risk.

But even the better opportunities must have their advantages and positive aspects *maximized*. Sometimes this doesn't happen and the new owner becomes one of the statistics in the failure column.

A retiring owner of a modest auto repair shop sold his operation to a buyer who bought it for his son. The son was a good mechanic, and the repair shop had been established for many years, with ample activity and income. Within a year, however, the business went downhill. The due notes weren't met and the former owner was forced to take the business back.

What went wrong? A number of things. First, the new owner immediately changed the name of the business. Then, after a short while, he decided to close at noon on Saturday—normally the best day for car owners who work all week. Perhaps he didn't want to pay his mechanics overtime for Saturday, or he considered his personal needs more important than the business. Later he tried to put his major emphasis on repairing sports cars—something he really enjoyed doing.

Ego, personal likes and dislikes, lifestyle, and inexperience all came into play in this situation. Whatever advantages had previously existed in this business were gradually dissipated by the changes. During the initial investigation, not enough attention was paid to the *character* of the existing operation, or the personal reaction to this factor.

In another case, an executive of a publishing company gave up his position and used the funds from his vested pension to purchase a printing company from two partners. Since he had always purchased a great deal of multi-color print runs and was responsible for color separations and controls, he felt this experience gave him the capabilities to handle the new venture.

It was a tough challenge. In addition to understanding the complex equipment and skilled personnel that were involved, his own assumption of the sales and administrative functions were quite time consuming. Then, before all the on-the-job training could be completed, illness struck and he had to be hospitalized. His wife could contribute very little to this highly technical situation, and the employees were technicians, not management oriented.

Trying to hold everything together from a hospital bed, and then from home while he recuperated, proved to be impossible. No one could fill his shoes in sales and administration, finance, and job control. The business suffered a fatal blow, and finally it was resold to the previous owners.

Aside from the illness, did he initially bite off more than he could chew? The original partners were professionals in the printing business and were able to split responsibilities as well as fill in for one another. It was the type of operation that demanded this kind of highly skilled, highly technical management.

Investigation is important, but assessing the information is mandatory. That brings us to the initial inquiry of the investigative process: What kind of information do you require to make an evaluation?

WHAT TO LOOK FOR

When buying a business, you should evaluate all the facts you would normally have checked out if you were starting a new venture from scratch. In addition, evaluate all you can find about the established business.

After a surface perusal of a number of opportunities, a *specific* business-for-sale will arouse your interest. Now the time you devote to on-site investigation and personal evaluations will be of great importance, and the need for the professional assistance of an accountant and lawyer will become evident.

The business records, financial structure, potential returns, leases, liens, contracts, and many other factors, as outlined in the next few pages, are *their* targets. Since established businesses are not restricted to retail stores, you can select the factors that pertain to your own venture.

YOU AND THE BUSINESS CHARACTER

It will be important to be realistic and fully aware of your parameters, of what *you* can handle financially, emotionally, and in relation to previous experience and skills. The initial investigation concerns both the operational actualities themselves and your own personal reaction to them, and sometimes the reactions of your family.

Are you prepared:

For a six-or seven-day week?
For evening hours or multiple shifts?
To supervise personnel?
To be a part of the everyday scene?

If there are employees, consider the following:

Are they experienced?
How long were they employed?
Are they under contract?
Are they members of a union?
Do they relate well to the present owner?
Can you judge their caliber and morale?
Is there a pension/benefits plan?

Evaluate the character of the business:

Does it generate excessive paperwork?

Does it involve a multitude of colors and sizes, inventoried or manufactured?

Are the products or services of heavy or bulky units?

Are most sales in the low or medium-cost range?

Are the products durable, fragile, or perishable?

Is it a cash or credit operation?

Are permits or licenses necessary?

Do any federal regulations apply?

Is it too highly technical for your skills?

Does it require delivery vehicles, parking facilities, or specialized or costly equipment?

There are plenty of questions. Fortunately, this is the kind of data you can validate during the early information-gathering discussions with the present owner. Buying an established business doesn't get you off the hook. You will have to do a great deal of work and make a number of difficult decisions. Don't expect someone else to make your decisions or do this preliminary work for you. In this way you can disqualify a number of prospects *before* you call in the heavy and expensive talent— your accountant and lawyer.

Additionally, if you have operational skills, you must ascertain if the proposed business is management-intensive or not. Many individuals have tried to expand a single skill, or a sole administrative experience, into a business of their own and it simply wasn't enough. An accurate appraisal and awareness of this deficiency, however, could help create a workable solution through an extra effort to learn from existing experienced personnel, or by joining with a qualified partner.

LOCATION

The existence of a business in a specific location does not necessarily mean the location is a good one. Your personal observation of location and the areas within its reach will be meaningful:

What is the local competition?

Is there any regional competition?

Is the area well kept or deteriorating?

What is the income level of the area?

Is the marketing area large enough?

If you manufacture, is there an available labor pool?

If you distribute, what about loading platforms and transportation?

Talk to other business owners, the local bankers, and even the residents of the locality. Check if the consensus points to business growth or simply the status quo. If it's a retail or service situation, is it in a shopping center or neighborhood group of stores? Are the parking facilities satisfactory for both customers and your supplier deliveries?

PREMISES

Does the store, manufacturing plant, or service business have enough room for the present operation, and is there room for internal expansion? Is there too much space? Can you sublease? Is the building owned? Can it be sold to generate working capital in a leaseback arrangement?

Furnishings and fixtures, including lighting, shelving, counters, shipping equipment, refrigeration where necessary, and lavatories are all part of the physical evaluation of the premises. They will also relate, in part, to asset value and worth when determining purchase price.

A retail store may need an attractive, smart, contemporary look.

A service business may have to radiate a trim, organized, feeling that says "We know what we're doing."

The manufacturer may require a well-lit, amply heated, functionally laid-out, efficient type of operational premises.

It's essential to detemine what the particular business you're looking at needs. If it lacks these requirements, you must decide:

Will the business require relocation?

Are extensive changes called for?

Must you redecorate?

Must you enlarge the premises?

Is additional space available for expansion?

Will equipment require replacement?

Are furnishings to be revamped?

Can operations continue during renewal activities?

If you are still interested, will it make sense to call in an expert who knows the field for experienced guidance? If costs are involved in these areas, this should be a factor when negotiating purchase price.

When relating to premises, don't forget to check on the lease and its present status. What are the rent and the extra charges? What are the costs of heat, electricity, air conditioning, maintenance, labor increases, and so on? An occupancy lease can seem simple, but have your attorney look it over. Since it is an existing lease, the terms, length, options, and ability to transfer to the buyer are key factors in the final transaction.

BUSINESS RECORDS

Admittedly, for a beginner, it's terrific to know for certain about many of the areas he or she would normally be apprehensive about. How much inventory for start-up? What about correct pricing? How can I reach customers best? Who are the best suppliers? It's all there in an ongoing business, and that's a definite plus!

But when it comes to knowing where that business has been and where it's going, you have to thoroughly examine the business records. That present owner is going to paint wonderful word pictures of the fantastic opportunity you will be acquiring and the real regrets he or she has, for one reason or another, in having to give it up.

Naturally there's a purchase price involved. It's one, the owner says, that you won't have any problems with because the future potential of the business is great and you get back your money in no time. Maybe so, but that's exactly why you want the records. They are one of the real keys to opening up those areas that help you determine the validity of the owner's glowing story.

In many instances, the seller will only give you as much statistical information as he or she feels is necessary for a preliminary evaluation. Then a demand for earnest money may be made if you wish your accountant to inspect the books, financial statements, tax returns, and inventory. Otherwise curiosity seekers or competitors may come in to look over the books, and the seller wants some protection against that kind of nonproductive merry-go-round.

Discussions with business brokers have verified this practice of requesting earnest money and then mentioned a number of versions of the method used. It's somewhat similar to buying a house, where a tentative contract and deposit are used to take the house off the market and give your experts a chance to check the structure, termite control, mortgage availability, and so on.

A southwestern broker mentioned that his request for earnest money is made a part of the actual sales contract. It usually involves 10 percent or thereabouts, and the contract allows the buyer a few weeks to "qualify" the business. The accountant and lawyer can check out and verify all the facts as stated by the owner. Should anything be not as stated, the buyer has the right to back out and take the earnest money back.

In the Northeast, another broker indicated that he requests $1,000, which is held in his office as part of a binder agreement. It protects the buyer in temporarily taking the business off the market and gives the seller a rationale for opening his or her books to scrutiny. The binder stipulates that the sale is subject to the business doing what the broker advertised and if it doesn't, the deal is off and the binder money is returned.

Obviously, if the binder or earnest money stage has been reached, the buyer's interest is sincere and the initial observations and preliminary discussions have been of a positive nature. Thus there will also be situations where the seller, when convinced that the buyer is a genuine prospect, may be willing for an accountant to check the records without a binder arrangement. In the closing stages you should not finalize any transaction without the assistance of your accountant and lawyer. This is the time of verification, and that's when you need professional assistance.

Since this is the buyer's first business venture, the odds are great that he or she is unfamiliar with perusing and understanding the normal financial records that have to be examined. For a thorough review of the records to determine accuracy and help establish a picture of profit potential, this is the data your accountant will initially request and analyze:

- annual balance sheets
- profit and loss statements
- federal and state income tax returns
- sales tax returns
- general records of sales, production, inventories, and so on
- a twelve-month projected profit and loss statement.

It is important to understand that most small businesses do not maintain their books in accordance with generally accepted accounting procedures (GAAP). They do not accrue liabilities, expenses are accelerated, and income is deferred at the end of every tax year. The owner takes out as much salary as the business can afford, regardless of the value of his or her services. There are many other differences between their books and those of large corporations.

Your accountant should be familiar with the operations and records of small business so that these differences will be taken into account. If records exist for the past three or more years, that will be a plus in estimating the annual growth or dropoffs in sales, expenses, inventories, and the profit picture. Has the earning trend been consistent, going up, or starting to head downhill?

The seller's projected statement of profit and loss for the next twelve months will be compared with your accountant's projections to determine working capital needs and profit potential. These are only estimates, not facts.

If accounts receivables are to be included in the purchase, they must be aged and reviewed to determine collectibility. As a general rule, it is better not to buy them. Let the seller structure them at face value and then deduct them from the purchase price.

3

Checking Out the Business

WHAT ARE YOU BUYING?

Each purchase of an established venture has its own identity and set of conditions. One factor within all the varieties of deals, however, remains the same. The seller tries to get as high a price as possible and the buyer seeks to purchase the business for the most reasonable outlay that can be negotiated.

There are some transactions that involve all the assets, both tangible and intangible:

- cash and securities
- inventory
- furniture and fixtures
- equipment and vehicles
- accounts receivables
- supplies
- building and land
- lease
- contracts
- patents and trademarks
- clients and mailing lists
- permits and licenses
- goodwill
- trained personnel
- supplier contacts.

And, occasionally, the liabilities as well may be included in the purchase:

- accounts payable
- mortgages
- back taxes (all types)
- liens upon assets
- pending suits
- loans (long and short term)
- employee benefits (vacation pay, and so on)
- contingent liabilities (unexpired warranties, and so on).

Too often, an inexperienced buyer is not aware that only a portion of an inventory may be current and viable. The shelf life may have been exceeded, with spoilage a possibility. Slow movers may abound. What will the loss ratio be if these factors exist?

This was exactly the case for a beginning entrepreneur who purchased a small cheese shop as a starter operation to gain some retail experience. After the purchase, she was amazed to find boxed chocolates on the shelves that must have been there for many months. Another on-the-job lesson she absorbed was the realization that too many items were too generously stocked. The store was in a suburb of New York City and the suppliers were a mere twenty-five miles away. Any replenishment of inventory could be accomplished in two days—why overstock and deprive herself of needed shelf space?

Great lessons for a new owner! One of her first acts was to clean out the store with heavily marked-down inventory sales. This got rid of the slow movers, the overstock, and some almost overaged shelf goods. Yes, it did cost her, but it also gave her a chance to introduce herself as the new owner to the store's regular customers.

BRING IN THE PROS

In all cases, professional assistance is needed if you are purchasing your first venture. The realistic value of the assets must be added up, and the actual total of whatever liabilities you assume must be subtracted. The resultant figure will be the net worth of the business, not the purchase price.

The correct net worth figure may only be a starting point for your accountant. Other factors to determine the value of the business may be more meaningful when it comes to evaluating if the business is the one for you. What is its "marketplace" value? How much cash will you need? What is a reasonable rate of return? What is the estimated income from the business? After your payments, what is left for you and your services? Will you earn enough to make ownership worthwhile?

In conjunction with the business records, you will require a what's-it-worth-today evaluation of inventory, supplies, furniture and fixtures, equipment, building, vehicles, and so on by a knowledgeable and qualified appraiser. Appraisals, however, should be considered as guesstimates of value and they can be off as much as 25 percent. Nevertheless, they are necessary.

Incidentally, this appraisal problem isn't restricted to any one type of business. If products are being manufactured, what is the state of the raw materials that go into the finished product? How about the dies and molds? Do they have to be replaced or refinished? Equipment must be checked for age and effectiveness. If the equipment is old, are parts readily available and repair costs reasonable? In the event any of these assets are obsolete, replacements will be required and costs for the new units will be at today's prices. An appraisal will help to estimate current value and its effect on the total purchase price you will pay.

Another aspect is the furniture and fixtures. Are they suitable for the business at hand? They may be outmoded, well used, and, at this stage, of definite secondhand quality. Needless to say, if this were the case, it would mean replacement, and that simply translates itself to dollars. Since a surface inspection can determine this situation, make sure you observe these factors early on, before your enthusiasm takes hold and causes a slough-off in this and similar areas.

In the meantime, your accountant can be working on the following:

- verifying assets
- aging accounts receivables
- checking depreciation schedule
- reviewing tax accruals
- determining key ratios
  assets/liabilities
  cash sales/credit charges
  return on investment
  inventory turnovers
- analyzing past balance sheets, tax returns, statements, and accounting methods.

All this, of course, is to verify what exists now, and to project future profit potential.

Your attorney, coordinating with the accountant, will be involved in still other areas. Some of these are preliminary examinations and others are in consideration of an actual contract of purchase. Initially, then, the attorney will review:

- existing lease terms
- patents or exclusive rights
- franchisor or distributor contracts
- union agreements and pension programs
- permits and licenses.

That's sufficient for the initial once-over. An important facet of those items is whether they are transferable to the new owner. Must new or more costly terms be negotiated for existing exclusive rights, or any of the favorable contracts that are an essential part of the business you may be purchasing? If so, will this affect the purchase price and the profit potential?

When and if agreement has been reached, the buy-sell contract will assume center stage. Then the attorney will be concerned with the following, and more:

- what you are actually buying
- specific assets and liabilities, if any
- terms of payment and price
- verification of clear title
- takeover date
- prorating of insurance, taxes, and fees
- existence of liens, if any
- the state's Bulk Sales Act requirements
- amount of escrow funds
- noncompete restrictions
- indemnification against future lawsuits or tax liabilities relating to activities before the sale and the time period for the escrow arrangements.

Although the last stage regarding contract terms represents the culmination of the evaluation process, the emphasis in this chapter is directed to the need for professional assistance once you've opted to buy a business. Just a general outline of what this assistance covers indicates that these complex areas are no place for amateurs!

YOUR OWN ONCE-OVER RESEARCH

Lest you forget, however, the value of a prospective business also relates to the external factors lightly touched upon earlier. Your initial investigation of the premises, location, and market at the time you established your initial interest, in conjunction with the internal financial and legal findings, can help determine overall value and profitability, as well as the validity of the suggested purchase price.

That research on your part will be doubly valuable. Past performances may check out superbly, but, once again, the major concern in these transactions has to be: "If I buy this business, what is the *future* potential of profits and return on investment?"

Too many established businesses have folded because of some changes that affected their existing location. An urban renewal program may radically change the surrounding neighborhood and vitally alter the character of the shopping area. The same kinds of changes could affect a manufacturing entity if the renewal involved a leased building it was renting, or if an essential highway access might be terminated.

Not only a deteriorating neighborhood or an urban renewal can affect location. What about the simple factor of no-growth, or an exceedingly costly move—either could create a completely new and insufficient profit picture. The moral is to check everything about location.

This checking should also apply to premises, for the same reasons. If a personal observation of retail premises, plant layout, distribution facilities, or operational efficiencies indicates any negatives, they should be weighed with relation to their effect on present value and future profit potential.

Both location and premises can play a part in market analysis. How many competitors exist in the area? What are their sales and their advertising efforts? How do their premises shape up? Visit competitors and make comparisons; it may alter your decision to buy. This will require outside investigation—local bankers, other merchants, Chamber of Commerce, trade associations, and so on.

That external investigation should also take in other aspects of the market, such as size of area, population, recent population changes, family sizes, age groupings, purchasing power, and employment. The same sources, plus the federal, state and/or county census figures should be reviewed for this information. Local banks or newspapers often have current statistics of this type available.

This personal research should enable you to look over numerous opportunities, weeding out the unsuitable ones and, at the same time, further sharpening your developing judgment of various aspects of business. When you finally come up with a genuine possibility, call in the professionals to help handle the areas you have no expertise in. Where you can function, do so yourself.

Since the evaluation process is a complex one, it's worth reviewing some advice offered by other sources.

SMALL BUSINESS ADMINISTRATION (SBA)

Let's take a page from the Small Business Administration's publication, "Buying and Selling a Small Business." It lists a series of build-up questions that may chart the future course of the business you intend to purchase.

Analysis

The word "predict" is important. The buyer should be able to follow through the steps listed below and predict with some confidence the future of the business.

What factors affect sales?
 How will these factors behave?
  Therefore, what sales can I expect?

What makes up the cost of sales?
 How will these cost factors apply to expected sales?
  Therefore, what gross profit can I expect?

What expenses are required to run this business?
 How will expenses develop under my ownership?
  Therefore, what net profit can I predict?

What assets will the business need and possess?
 What is the condition of these assets?
  Therefore, what assets improvements will I have to make?

What credit does the business assume?
 What is the condition of the credit position?
  Therefore, what changes, if any, can occur in the debt
   structure?

How much cash do I have?
 How much cash will the business generate?
  Therefore, what will be my available-cash position?

What immediate cash outlay must I make?
What will the cash needs of the business be?
Therefore, what cash outgo will be necessary?

What will be my net cash position as things now stand?
What additional cash resource, if any, must I have?
Therefore, what financing plan shall I use?

The SBA also has a few questions that relate to the value of the business—the future potential.

Value

A business has a purpose. That purpose is to provide a satisfactory return on the owner's investment. Consequently, determining value involves measuring the future profit of the business being sold.

What am I buying? A business, or a building full of equipment and inventory?

What return would I get if I invested my money elsewhere—in stocks, bonds, or other business opportunities?

What return ought I get from an investment in this business?

The Small Business Administration has approximately a hundred field offices throughout the nation. It is the federal government's main avenue of assistance for the small entrepreneur and those wishing to become entrepreneurs. The SBA provides information in many areas—seminars, small business counseling, loans, special women's programs, and numerous relevant publications.

In addition to the "Buying and Selling a Small Business" booklet, many other SBA publications cover the basic and more advanced requirements necessary to achieve success in your own small business. In fact, every area is touched upon, and it would be well worth your while to contact the nearest SBA office (check the phone book) to obtain their listings of available publications. These listings—SBA Forms 115-A and 115-B—include both costs and ordering information.

COUNTRY BUSINESS, INC. (CBI)

For another point of view, it is appropriate to check over a business broker's outlook and advice in buying a business. Country Business is unique in this field because it is an organization that offers a multi-level service to prospective entrepreneurs.

CBI'S weekend seminars in country inns stress this method-outline for small business acquisition:

- good match of buyer and business
- proper price and terms
- reasonable and complete business plan
- proper capitalization
- effective use of information sources
- analysis of business strengths and weaknesses
- basics of good management
- follow-through and adjustment to changes in the business environment.

Their message to the prospective buyer is simple—if you address yourself studiously to each of the points of the method, your success in a small business will virtually be assured.

What is really interesting is their recommendation that you prepare a reasonable and complete business plan. Although this is a normal procedure for the new start-up, not many people relate to it for an ongoing business that is to be purchased. CBI feels this is so important that a "Business Planning Guide" is an integral part of the materials provided at the seminars. They describe this aspect as follows:

> *"The Business Planning process is the most important activity you will conduct in looking for a small business. It will force you to check all of the data required to understand the business and make projections. It is extremely likely that if there are incurable weaknesses in the business, they will show up in the course of preparing the Business Plan.*
>
> *"The Business Plan will serve as the basic document required to obtain any outside financing. But, more important, it will serve as your 'bible' in measuring your own progress in actually running the business you buy. Most successful owners refer constantly to their plans, and amend or expand them as time goes by."*

Country Business ads are often seen in the *Wall Street Journal*. The New England area is their primary sphere of operations, and they have offices in Vermont, Maine, New Hampshire, Massachusetts, and New York. Their corporate headquarters are in Burlington, Vermont.

4

Making the Deal

WHAT ABOUT PURCHASE PRICE?

Because buyer and seller see things from different perspectives, setting a fair price can often involve some complex give-and-take negotiations. As indicated earlier, the buyer strives to acquire the business at the lowest price possible, while the seller seeks to sell it for the highest figure attainable.

But the situation need not become a standoff. What is important is to determine the seller's real needs so that your discussions will achieve a mutual accord. It's possible to accomplish this if you work at it and negotiate a deal by some combination of the four ingredients that make up the majority of purchases: price, down payment, interest rate, and monthly payments. Fortunately, in most cases, a legitimate compromise can be worked out.

Since purchasing a business is our main concern, attention should be focused on the *proper* buying price. Within certain lines of businesses, sale price ratios have been used as general guidelines, subject, of course, to various adjustments for special factors in each venture. In most cases, the price is based on the value of tangible assets, less the costs of all known liabilities—the net worth. Additionally, there are the evaluative factors of goodwill and the estimation of what the return on investment will be.

Goodwill means the intangibles, and they, of course, are where the problems of price negotiation will appear. If there is an approved listing of the liabilities you are to assume and an up-to-date *appraisal* of equipment, inventory, furniture and fixtures, and so on, there will be no major problems. Admittedly, that appraisal is only a rough estimate of value that both seller and buyer are willing to accept, even though its accuracy may be very questionable.

In certain situations, this two-step valuation may very well prove to be the basis of a final price agreement. Other ventures that show good earnings at present and excellent future profit potential are more complex. They may involve varying multiples of investment return or earning power, and although there are many formulas, there's plenty of room for interpretation of "earnings."

INVESTMENT RETURN

What can the business earn? Both the present owner and your accountant can contribute projections that may help chart this potential. But there are no guarantees, of course. Your focus on investment return, however, simply means comparing the potential profits of the business with the amount of money you could earn if you decided to invest that same capital in stocks, bonds, money funds, or other similiar investments.

When dividends, interest rates, or capital gains are in the annual range of 7 to 10 percent, does the proposed business give you an equivalent return?

In real fact, the business will have to give you more. Don't forget that an investment in securities or banks doesn't require your presence or your labor. What about risk? Small business entrepreneurship is admittedly one of the riskiest investments around—ask a banker about that statistic. On that basis alone, your return on investment from a business should be higher than what you could earn from bonds, stocks, or banks, especially if you invest in the safer, low-risk securities.

Taking over a business means giving up your present job and salary. Will the new venture enable you to earn the same amount, although you will be working much harder? Even if, as often happens, you contemplate a lower take-home amount, your projections should indicate that the business can earn the anticipated profits *plus* a reasonable owner-operator salary. The estimated net profits will help determine whether you can recover the cost of your capital investment in three, five, or seven years, for example, and that's an important factor in determining a fair price for a going business.

Once I was sitting in a broker's office listening to a seller explaining his operation. It was a small retail store in a medium-to-low-income shopping strip. The annual gross was approximately $80,000, and he was able to earn $10,000 or so a year. The broker's eyebrows shot up and he said, "But that's only a modest salary in today's economy, and your store is operating six days a week plus one night for late shopping. Why would anyone want to leave their job for that kind of a risky, demanding setup, with such a minimal return?"

Why indeed? Perhaps that isn't the type of operation that may interest you, but it does indicate how in some small ventures the entrepreneurs are just barely scraping by. No doubt that's why this owner wanted to sell; he had already indicated his intention to get a job that paid more and had fewer responsibilities.

For some others, however, there are definite tax-shelter advantages or personal satisfactions in owning a business that may influence and even tolerate a seemingly marginal operation. Make sure there is sufficient return on both your capital investment and your personal labor when you are evaluating the purchase of a specific venture.

GOODWILL

There are those who believe goodwill relates primarily to the established reputation a present owner enjoys with customers. There's more to it than that.

Many other professionals lump all intangibles under that same category. One commonality that relates to both groups, however, is the accepted fact that most intangible assets rarely show up on a balance sheet.

In line with these thoughts, let's review a listing of the business valuables that could fit into this fairly open category of goodwill:

- excellent location
- customer lists
- mailing lists
- favorable lease
- complete inventory records
- past sales record
- good supplier relationships
- good bank credit line
- qualified employees
- exclusive contracts and/or lines
- franchise arrangements

- seller's excellent reputation
- seller's willingness to consult
- seller's noncompete agreement.

Many of these intangibles can be the catalysts that help to provide greater profit and income-producing potential. As such, they are extremely valuable. Many professionals tend to target an actual value on goodwill only when there is a definite *plus* relationship to the earning power of the business.

A buyer's decision may also be influenced by other intangibles that relate to personal likes and dislikes. Is the character of the business easygoing or frenetic? Does it have the desired ambiance? Is it in urban or rural surroundings? Does it involve small unit sales requiring large volume or high unit sales with low volume and little paperwork? Is it part of a new growth industry or one of the staples? Does it have image and stature? Any one of these factors may be extremely important to a buyer and will definitely influence the negotiating process.

As you can see, the goodwill factor has plenty of room for varied interpretations of worth and value, and that's why it causes the most controversy in sales negotiations. In many cases, it is discarded completely insofar as listing a dollar value for it in the final sales contract.

PRICE AND OTHER FACTORS

Whatever is paid for a business over and above the adjusted tangible net worth usually reflects one or more of the many goodwill intangibles. In a true sense, this additional payment is often indicative of other very simple non-balance sheet values.

1. The business exists.
2. The business does not have to be started from scratch.
3. The business has proved it can survive.
4. The business has a track record of profitability.
5. Because of these factors, the business has greatly lessened the chance of failure.

The seller's asking price—which may or may not fairly reflect the actual value of the business or its real worth to you—serves as more than just a starting point. Instead, it should force you to take all the evaluative steps previously discussed in order to make a fairly accurate appraisal of the business and the asking price.

Admittedly there is no simple or single definitive method of appraising a small business that has the general acceptance of all the parties involved: buyers, sellers, accountants, bankers, lawyers, brokers, and so on.

There's reason enough for the lack of agreement. Unlike large corporations the small ventures are usually privately held and their records may be somewhat less than perfect. Often they are quite unique in their approach to managerial techniques, and in many cases success results from a highly personal, owner-dominant stance. The emotional aspect is also more evident in the small business arena. The seller's long-term, all-encompassing involvement and the buyer's highly individual likes and dislikes, lifestyle, background, and skills can be important factors.

This was clearly demonstrated by someone I interviewed in the Southwest a few years ago. He had purchased a small motel, even though the mom-and-pop records of the seller were insufficient for his accountant to establish the worth of the business. In the long run, it was the buyer's own judgment, superficial analysis, background, and gut feeling that closed the deal.

His reasoning encompassed many aspects to suit both his personal and his entrepreneurial needs:

- a desire for a small-town lifestyle for his young family
- a business that did not require specific skills
- a venture that did not require a long wait to win the local townspeople's confidence
- a business he and his wife could operate
- new ownership not adversely affecting transient clientele
- a large assumable mortgage at a very reasonable interest rate
- modest initial refurbishment required
- competitiveness even with a slight increase in rates
- an opportunity to increase services by personal labor and attendance
- increasing land values and additional footage next to the motel included in the purchase
- an owner's apartment on the premises.

For many months, the young owner was very apprehensive about the "real value" of his purchase. Had the $262,000 price been too high, had he been too anxious? A reasonable formula of four times annual rental income was considered to provide an acceptable price, but what had the mom-and-pop uncorroborated income really been?

Fortunately, this story has a happy ending. One year later, after keeping scrupulous records, both the actual annual income and the growth in land values indicated that his purchase had been a real buy. A good deal of luck, learning, and hard work also helped to achieve this positive end result. It has gotten even better since.

Keep in mind that there really had been some degree of careful analysis in his prepurchase stage. There was an effort to evaluate personal needs and previous background, plus a well-considered judgment value on the visible aspects of the motel and its special characteristics. The evaluative process, in this case, fell somewhat short of perfection, but each small business is a unique entity, and both the seller's and buyer's needs—financial and nonfinancial—will strongly influence the negotiation.

For small businesses, buying and selling is a process of give-and-take between two parties, with an eye toward a satisfactory conclusion for both sides. Some imperfect standards can assist in determining a fair price, and it's important for all to be aware of them and to apply them wherever they fit. Let's review some of the more common terminologies, keeping in mind that all of them are used with some sort of modification.

POTENTIAL

Many sellers have stressed "the fabulous potential that exists here" in answer to why the asking price seems so high. It's important to clarify what potential the seller is talking about.

The probable future earning power of the business is going to be determined by delving and probing into the figures. It can and will be estimated by checking the records of past profits, sales and operating ratios, owner's income, tax returns, sales and purchase data, and a projection of operations for the next year or two. With the professional assistance of an accountant, this analysis is one of the most important in the valuations of what the purchase price should be.

Often, however, the seller's push and supersell relates to how much *more* you can do with the business. That means you, the buyer, with your fresh energy, new ideas, and terrific enthusiasm, will be the one responsible for this wonderful vision of increased potential.

That may very well be true. If you have the knowledge and experience that enable you to see areas that can be productively improved or more successfully marketed, this can readily improve earnings. But that will be a result of *your* contribution, and you shouldn't pay the seller extra for that! Don't confuse the present performance of the business with what effect your actions may have in the future.

It's not at all unusual for a buyer to be so anxious to get started and to incorporate his or her own ideas into an existing venture that this kind of capability is mistakenly factored into the price. Don't get carried away.

There's another kind of potential that's worth watching out for. Quite often you will run across businesses that show very small tax payments, or none at all. The owner may tell you that the business really earns a lot more than the books show. Since small business owners often run a cash-basis set of books with the goal of keeping taxable income to a minimum, this may very well be a legitimate situation. If the business is really one that attracts your interest, your accountant can verify the actualities.

On the other hand, you may run across a cheating seller who confides that there are two sets of books—one for him or her and one for the government. This seller guarantees the business has a lot more potential than is shown—it's a real honey! A little fudging here, some cash sales there, and so on and so on. Two-book businesses are not the best avenues of approach for the new entrepreneur. Take a walk before the seller cheats you too!

FORMULA VALUES

Not all kinds of business fall into this price/value category, but when they do, formulas or ratios can only serve as initial guidelines. Business brokers, trade associations, accountants with buy-sell experience, and other professionals can be good sources for alerting you to established industry norms.

For example, the motel buyer in the Southwest had called a number of motel brokers in that area to get the approximate purchase price formula of four times the annual rental income.

Other types of business have multiples of varying aspects common to their own industry. Trade associations are excellent sources for this kind of information. They are aware of industry changes and influences that might affect the so-called norms in the rule-of-thumb, buy/sell formulas.

The Associated Telephone Answering Exchanges in Virginia noted that the high technology changes in their industry have completely invalidated any thought of a formula value. At one time, an approximate ratio of twelve to eighteen months' revenues was somewhat accepted. In the past ten years, however, differences in technology, equipment, and tariffs in effect have negated any type of sales formulas.

When it comes to the purchase of an established locksmith venture, one of their association members indicated that two rule-of-thumb evaluations were in common use: approximately one year's gross revenues or five times one year's net. Naturally, he cautioned, many other factors could come into play in order to arrive at a final price. But, generally, if the business was run correctly, the final negotiation would fit somewhere in one or both of the indicated parameters.

A member of the Arizona Licensed Beverage Association, with lots of experience in retail package stores, indicated how new legislation affected the entire industry. Prior to 1975, business was consistently good for *all* liquor stores. After repeal of the Fair Trade legislation, however, competition was intense and the smaller package stores were put into a tight profit squeeze and a much more marginal operation. Today the purchase price formula has undergone many downward changes and might follow along these lines:

- a good price for the liquor license, but not as much as pre-1975
- a fair price for fixtures, but often at a bargain price to sweeten the deal
- a full cash price for the inventory
- a highly negotiable figure for goodwill; the seller will try for one or two year's wages.

Changes do occur in various industries, and the trade associations are usually able to monitor the trends. Some of the larger organizations are gold mines of information and have reams and reams of statistics pertaining to their members' operations.

All in all, however, the following bears repetition: if a formula value does exist for the business you are considering, use it only as *one* of the tools for your evaluation. Never use it as the sole determination.

Among the other methods may be one that will fit your needs. If not, use guidelines from a variety of methods that seem most appropriate to your particular purchase to arrive at a possible figure.

ASSET APPRAISAL

Many small ventures are purchased on the simple basis of their asset value. The tangible assets can include real estate, equipment, inventory, furniture and fixtures, and office and production supplies. These are not difficult to evaluate, but if they are complex or extensive, it's advisable to call in a professional for an accurate appraisal. This will be especially useful in inventory and equipment valuations.

After totaling the tangible assets, check all liabilities and subtract them from the assets to arrive at the net worth of the business. To this, the seller will be adding an additional amount for goodwill.

As has been explained, the asset value of goodwill and the intangibles that fit into that category is more difficult to determine. But it can usually be negotiated to a modest percentage of the total value of the tangible or physical assets.

Many intangibles are completely subjective in both value and lifestyle. As a buyer, if you strongly prefer the lively activity and excitement of an urban environment, you would certainly give that location more value than a similar profit-making venture in an easygoing, small-town atmosphere. I know entrepreneurs who abhor the thought of running any business that involves a great deal of paperwork and an inventory with a profusion of sizes and colors. That intangible characteristic would have no value and would be a complete turnoff in their estimation. To others, however, it would be a neutral factor because their interest focuses on the bottom line only and the type of business doesn't matter.

Country Business, Inc., indicates that the familiar asset purchase is the most common form of purchase and is often the best way to structure a buy and sell of a small business. As indicated above, there will usually be some modifications for the applicable goodwill items. CBI also advises you to obtain complete operating records and existing promotional materials in the overall purchase package.

EARNINGS VALUE

Numerous approaches can characterize the earnings value method of purchase. Some variations are capitalization of future earnings, multiples of excess earning power, return on investment (ROI), return through profits, and times earning power.

Each category differs somewhat in approach or specific emphasis. In general, however, the best sense of them seems to be a two-step analysis, involving the factors of owner salary and investment income. Examining both these items also forces you to consider profitability—excess earnings or future earnings—as well.

As noted earlier, any business should be profitable enough to pay for both personal labor and the investment of capital. If you are to function as the owner-manager, a proper salary for that type business should be determined. It may be less than your present salary, but don't ignore the many other fringe benefits to be derived from a small business ownership. The main point, however, is to establish what it would cost if you were to hire someone else to run and manage that business. Don't make the mistake of protecting your own present earnings by saddling the new business with a higher manager salary than is warranted.

To repeat the aspect of return on your investment capital: without operating any business, you can put your money to work by purchasing top-rated government bonds, corporate bonds, treasury notes, blue-chip stocks, or money funds. In the marketplace recently, you could get a fairly safe return that ranged from 7 to 10 percent. When economic conditions are more volatile, numerous other investments may offer even higher interest returns. Additionally, if your funds are correctly invested, the risk of losing your capital is far less than if it were invested in a small business enterprise.

From a buyer's viewpoint, then, how does a seller's asking price of $115,000 for a particular venture fit into this method of evaluation?

After all the preliminaries have been approved and the tangible assets appraised, the checkout procedure might assume the following:

A. Your qualified professionals have appraised and esti-
    mated the net worth (all tangible assets less all liabili-
    ties) as: $80,000

B. Your return on this same amount ($80,000), if invested
    elsewhere, would earn an arbitrary 10 percent annual
    interest rate: $ 8,000

C. A reasonable owner-operated salary for this type of
    operation is acknowledged as: $16,000

D. Your accountant's analysis of past average net earnings
    (before owner's salary) and projected earnings is ap-
    proximately: $34,000

E. The *excess* earnings (subtract D from B + C) average
    approximately: $10,000

F. For value of intangibles based on how well established
    the business is; a well-known name, location, number
    of years of profitability, and so on, multiply E, (excess
    earnings) by one to three times. This business seems
    somewhat established, so multiply by 1½.
    $10,000 × 1½: $15,000

In this procedural example, adding the value of net worth (A = $80,000) to the multiplied estimate for goodwill intangibles (F = $15,000) shows a total of $95,000 as a fair market price.

Perhaps the seller's asking price of $115,000 is too high—that certainly wouldn't be unusual. In any case, you will be able to start your negotiations with the lower amount, knowing that these evaluative steps have given you a flexible framework to determine earnings value. Changes can be incorporated all along the line, wherever reassessment is required.

For example, interest rates may very well be on the low side when you are contemplating purchase. Then the arbitrary figure of 10 percent should be changed to reflect this, which, in turn, will alter excess earnings and the goodwill formula. This may lead you to increase your offering purchase price.

You may also evaluate the intangibles of a super location and a very well-established standing in the marketing area as being worth *more* than what was reflected in the original calculations. Do these factors tend to make this business much stronger and less prone to failure?

During the give-and-take of negotiations between seller and buyer, other changes may be factored into this framework, and the dollar numbers can be easily reworked. Negatives may show up that cannot be reconciled into projecting a positive return of earnings, and the deal may be terminated or a new approach will have to be followed.

Suppose the calculations of excess earnings, E, showed up as a minus? Is the business unable to support a $16,000 annual owner-manager salary? Will it not provide as much earnings as you would be able to get from other less risky investments? If this were true, the business certainly would not be worth the asking price of $115,000. An estimate of $80,000 might be closer. In that case, no value would be allocated for the goodwill intangibles, and a great deal of extra effort may be required to improve the profitability factor.

If you have experience in this type of business, however, you and your accountant may be able to pinpoint the trouble areas that can be adjusted upward toward a better earnings picture. At that point, then, your negotiations will relate to a not overly successful established business—one that you are fairly positive you can turn around. Just be certain that those trouble areas you uncovered are not telegraphing a don't-buy signal instead.

Businesses for sale that are both successful and well-established are a rarity. Many require some sort of resuscitation to bring them to a peak, and many more have a variety of problems. In all cases, it pays to follow the street corner vendor's urgent invitation to "Check it out! Check it out!"

RETURN ON INVESTMENT (ROI)

Many consultants feel that return on investment (ROI) is the best way to determine the value of a business for the potential buyer.

As noted earlier, if you invest your capital into government bonds, notes, CDs, or insured municipals, you would get a return of interest of perhaps 7 percent, 8 percent, or even 10 percent with very little risk. At the same time you will be retaining your present job and salary. If you decide to invest that same capital in a business, the risk is much higher and you would therefore want to increase your return substantially. Small businesses are acknowledged to be high-risk investments, and that means both the original capital and the interest return are being jeopardized.

That, in itself, is why some authorities talk about doubling what you would get in interest from an investment to about a 20 percent or 25 percent ROI. That ROI figure simply relates to getting that amount of earnings from the generated profits. It does not include the owner-manager salary the business must pay you.

Refer again to the previous illustration of the checkout procedure for the $115,000 asking price. (See page 46.) It's easy to extract the ROI factor for further perusal. The average net earnings in D was $34,000. If you subtract the manager's salary, C, of $16,000, that leaves a net profit, before taxes, of $18,000.

A 20 percent return would mean multiplying that profit figure by five, to equal $90,000. Ergo, this could be the measure of a fair purchase price, and it would also indicate that you could retrieve your investment in four or five years, accordingly. When the purchase involves a down payment and terms, the ROI will change, but profits must increase to cover the notes.

Our previous illustration indicated that $95,000 might be a fair market price based on evaluating both the investment return and the personal involvement as owner-manager. Perhaps the $16,000 salary was too high, or too low. The arbitrary interest rate of 10 percent in item B might also be too high. Or maybe the goodwill should be trimmed.

That's exactly why formulas, earnings values, ROIs, rule-of-thumb, industry understandings, and other approximations are just that— guidelines. No one method can prevail, because each small business is different and composed of its own series of complexities.

The final checkout will still relate to a comprehensive analysis of the venture's past and present, and an estimate of its future. If you don't go through the whole procedure with a professional accountant, you could very well become another sad statistic—one of those who didn't make it because you didn't investigate thoroughly.

FINAL CONTRACT

By the time you reach the final contract stage, many a hurdle has been overcome and the prospects for clear sailing seem to indicate "full speed ahead." But, here again, it's time to make haste slowly. Make sure you know what you're buying—assets only, assets and liabilities, use of the name, patents, licenses, and so on.

It's important that the sales agreement or contract clearly spells out exactly what has been agreed upon, with a written listing of all assets being transferred and what if any liabilities are being assumed. To clarify the liability aspect, it may also be wise to list those that the buyer will not be responsible for.

No agreement or contract should be formulated and signed without a lawyer's assistance. Most experts also caution that the buyer should include a provision for operating covenants and inspection from the time of contract signing until the final settlement date. This will help protect you from any inventory depletion and prevent a lingering transition that could result in ill will between the parties.

At this stage, the purchase has been negotiated. The tax advantages that may relate to both buyer and seller should also have been reviewed and agreed upon. On that basis, the sales contract should list the most favorable tax-consequence breakdown of costs allocated to inventory, fixtures and equipment, real estate if any, goodwill, lease, noncompete agreement, consulting contract, and so on.

Will there be a specific method of payment? Is the seller accepting a down payment and then notes for the remainder, spread over a period of years? If so, what arrangements are being made for a default, for an accelerated payment, and so on? Will there be a chattel mortgage on the equipment? Whatever financial agreements apply, they must be spelled out in detail.

Within that purchase price, additions or subtractions will relate to prorating of insurance premiums, real estate and payroll taxes, rent, utility deposits, and inventory sales while the business is in escrow.

In the time period between the sales agreement and the final closing, will the buyer be assuming the present lease and the outstanding contracts? If so, these should be listed, along with the specific liabilities that are also being assumed. Because the buyer will be contract-bound, the when and what of the buyer's responsibility should be clearly defined.

In the meantime, of course, there's a lot for the seller to warrant. A clear title must be offered and the financial records that were represented during the sale must be true and correct. The buyer must also be protected in the agreement from any liens or liabilities that were not disclosed, or any potential negatives that would create title defects.

Pending transfer of ownership, the seller and buyer relationship should be agreed upon as to inventory sales, loss or destruction from fire and other casualty, access to premises, and any other aspects of the business that would be relevant to this in-between period. What if grounds for canceling the contract surfaced during this period? As noted earlier, the best method, if possible, may be to sign a contract and effect a closing at the same time.

Your attorney will stipulate an indemnification clause by the seller that will protect you, the buyer, from any costs or damages that arise as a result of misrepresentation or nonfulfillment of the terms of the agreement.

Part of the purchase price should be put into escrow for a specific period of time as security for such indemnities and the seller's fulfillment of what has been agreed upon. Your attorney will negotiate the time-table and escrow percentage in accordance with the degree of security required.

Have you and the seller agreed upon any training period, consultancy on the part of the seller, and, when applicable, a covenant not to compete for a given period of time within a specific regional restriction? If agreed upon, any and all these factors must be included in the sales contract.

Your attorney may wish to include other considerations for your protection, or specifics that are necessary because of the unusual nature of the business, and so on. In applicable states, both buyer and seller must comply with the provisions of the Bulk Sales Act.

This short review of most of the essential points in a buy-sell agreement will help you become *aware* of the mandatories involved. It also allows you to better understand your lawyer's professional jargon and the vital importance of his or her presence in this situation.

It's essential that the contract cover all requirements and that it be clearly understood by both buyer and seller.

5

How Others Did It

THE BUY-A-BUSINESS ENTREPRENEURS

As noted earlier, Dun & Bradstreet's statistics indicated that hundreds of thousands of firms are started every year, but even more transfer ownership or control.

No doubt when many of those who decided to buy a business are questioned, the why and how of their decisions will involve a multitude of reasons. But along with the differences in reasoning, there is a definite common thread that can help you make your own decision.

Despite all the drawbacks to small business that a flat economy and big competition bring, individual entrepreneurship is on the move and growing steadily stronger. Many people who want to gain some control of their lifestyles, skills, desires, and activities are making the move, taking the risks, and succeeding. Naturally there are obstacles and roadblocks along the way—even failures—but those problems exist in whatever direction you choose to go.

In this chapter we will be talking to owners of purchased ventures. Different businesses, from retail stores to service providers, will be our targets. The questions are basic. Why buy? How's it going? In retrospect, was it a good decision? The answers can highlight the benefits and the drawbacks of getting into a business of your own by means of a purchase.

The focus narrows down to this: if you intend to own and operate your own small business, is purchasing it the way to go? Let's hear about that kind of reasoning from some who did.

The Paper Patch is a card, gift, and special occasion store in a shopping complex of small boutiques.

Terri Caminker: My partner, Jan Nathanson, and I decided we wanted to have a business together. One Sunday I was looking through the business opportunity section of the newspaper and saw there was a card store for sale. That was exactly the type of thing we wanted to do, so we went ahead to check it out, to see what kind of margin the owner had, what the overhead was, and if any money was being made.

We never had any intention whatsoever about buying that business. We figured we could do the same thing ourselves, without paying for someone else's name and reputation. It was listed with a broker, so we met with her agent and went over the preliminary figures.

Well, it did look pretty good on paper—her sales, profit margin, and so on. The price seemed reasonable, too. Although we had no intention at all of buying *any* business, we decided to take all the paperwork to our accountant. He looked it over, sent for some other figures and backup material, and then said we'd be crazy not to buy it. So that was it!

The price was broken down into three categories. She figured the price for the fixtures, for the inventory, and then for her name—the goodwill, blue sky, or whatever you want to call it. We were willing to buy the business, but we both had other commitments and needed to postpone the closing for two months. Therefore, in the contract, we agreed to value the inventory at the date of closing and approved the price of fixtures and goodwill as originally stated.

At the closing, the inventory was valued at its cost—the wholesale price. Later, when we took over, we found that things were not as they appeared. Although numerous items were prepriced on the packages, the great majority were not. On the factory-priced products, you could figure the cost as half, but not on the others. When we started reordering we found what some of those items really cost and it took us a while to make up the difference. It was almost like buying an inventory at retail!

We were naive in not checking more thoroughly. Her records were right there and available to us. We could have looked in the catalogs and gotten the correct costs. Fortunately, this is the kind of business that has a fast turnover, so when we did get rid of that original inventory it was like starting over again—with the correct costs and returns. If this were a slow business and the items we practically paid retail for were still sitting there, then it could have done us in, that's for sure.

The basic shop was small and her inventory was mostly in cards, party favors, some gift items and calligraphy invitations she did herself. After we became familiar with the inventory, ordering, and selling, we decided to remodel. We made sure that all fixtures had storage space, but then we got so busy that even that wasn't enough. We then moved across the parking lot to this present location. It has three times the space and a vitally needed storeroom, which holds stock as well as a small office area.

The old store only had a small front window for display; this one has three for more show and greater visibility. It's brighter and cheerful and the customers love it. Our stock is much greater. We have cards of all kinds, invitations, helium balloons, T-shirts, booklets, gifts, custom calligraphy, gift wraps, special occasion paraphernalia, and lots more. Our new location was advertised in newspapers, magazines, direct-mail inserts, and because our location is on a corner, multiple signs. Everything is going great.

Originally, for the first six months, Jan and I worked full-time by alternating days or half days. Next step was a part-timer, and now there are two employees plus one part-time. However, one of us is always there with an employee.

We did make an equal partnership agreement with an attorney and we're now looking to arrange buyout insurance provisions for any future mishap contingencies. It's only been two years and our progress has been excellent—we are a lot smarter, too.

Previously I did have a very successful business in another area, one which I started from scratch—a needlepoint business. It began as a small stand in a women's clothing store, a concession. Later I was doing more sales than the store and I had to open my own retail outlet.

This was a business we didn't know anything about. We didn't know sources, buyer preferences, and so on, and I think it was much easier to buy this business than to start it. And it's just as rewarding to buy a business and build it up as it is to start one and succeed. We've done so much with this one and the rewards are certainly there!

Adventure in Travel, Inc. *is a travel agency that is located in a residence on a quiet street; the well-appointed offices are very professional but there's also a relaxed, casual air about the operation.*

Gail Norris: I've worked in the travel business for quite a while, so the choice of what type of business was an easy one. Additionally, my customers from a previous agency in a neighboring community had followed me here when I switched jobs, so there were a number of pluses when I bought this agency.

The previous owner was very sharing about the ins and outs of this agency and I was very aware of its structure and activity. She wanted to sell it for some time, and the moment came when I finally had some capital from the sale of a residence and we were able to negotiate a down payment and the rest on a contract, with provisions for noncompete agreements and all that.

The property is a major portion of this business, so the contract payments I have are paying for both the property and the business. Travel agencies, by themselves, are worth very little regardless of how much blue sky the previous owners may accord them. The value of this business is partly in its customers, partly in its long-time position in our small town (40,000 population), and partly because of the property.

This is the first and only travel agency in my town. I've lived here for twenty-five years and I've almost become accepted in the community now—I'm not just going to come and go. The continuity was very important, so was the location and the existing goodwill. Starting a new travel agency with another name wouldn't give me the same kind of credibility, even though it might have cost less money in some ways. Certainly the long-term obligations would have been much less, but I felt it wouldn't pay off, that it would have been an uphill struggle.

So far, the business is up to expectations, even exceeding them. It's just been a wonderful thing and I love it. We work real hard, we do whatever we need to do, and our goal was to make sure that the company was financially sound this first year and to see if we could turn a reasonable profit. We found, instead, that even in these very bad times, our business has grown 30 to 50 percent and our efficiency has increased the bottom line just more than I dreamed it could be.

My manager is a partner in the sense of managing the business operations; his blood, sweat, and tears have made it go. The stock is all in my name and the money that was put up for it was mine. We're both employees of the corporation, but we consider ourselves partners in a team operation. It's a good relationship.

A person with reasonable ambition has the feeling that they can make something go, the feeling of being in charge of making decisions and meeting the challenges. That's what's so exciting about a small business. My dad worked for a large corporation and I always thought his talents were being wasted. He was a tremendous organizer, not a particularly good people person, but good with bits of puzzle pieces and making things come out well. When he left the company, the only reward was a gold watch and a pat on the back. And I thought, Gee whiz, I saw some of those same skills in myself, but it would be a lot more fun to do it for myself. So when the opportunity came, I took it.

Frenchy's Pipe Shoppe & Tobacconist *is located in a large shopping cen-*
ter of retail stores. Across the parkway is an enclosed shopping mall with
luxury shops and two department stores.

Frenchy Lawrence: I'm a photographer by trade and have worked for
myself many times but never actually owned a shop before. Three years
ago I was looking around for a location to open a camera store. Starting
one from scratch in this particular field was not wise, so I looked for an
established business. After some investigation I decided that a camera
shop in this town was too competitive a venture.

I used to purchase my tobacco from this store and although I've been
a pipe smoker for over twenty years I certainly had no intention of
purchasing a tobacconist shop. The old man who owned it wanted to
retire and his son was not interested in carrying on. So, knowing I was
looking for a business, he proposed that I take over his shop—why not?
And once the seed was planted, I thought about it some more—and
started checking a bit.

There were only three *real* tobacco shops in this city of a half million
people. Even with the economy starting to go downhill, I felt that
smokers were going to continue to smoke. They might give up new
shoes and new cars, but they are going to need to smoke. I felt that I
was fairly safe as far as getting into something that would give me a
stable income. It might be more profitable than a camera shop, especially if the economy continued to go down.

But other than being a pipe smoker, I had no knowledge about this
business. So it was really an emotional decision backed up by some
logic. I learned very quickly and I got hold of all the books and things I
could lay my hands on, in some cases before I got into it. There was a
period of a couple of months before I actually decided to buy and
physically take over the shop.

Although it was an existing business, I started from scratch as far as
knowledge is concerned. He had been there for about fifteen years
and it was a long-established business, but he had let it run down
tremendously. I looked at his books and only later did I find they
weren't actual, they weren't real. He promised to give me help and
information about suppliers, but he didn't follow through. I didn't use
professional help—I did it all myself and in retrospect, I wouldn't advise others to do it that way.

I was very fortunate in this particular case because this is a very close-
knit business, and as soon as the word got out, a salesman came to me

and he contacted the others. As far as getting to know suppliers, that was now taken care of. They could very easily have stuck it to me in the beginning before I had built up any knowledge. But they're not that way. I've had salesmen say, "Don't buy this because it's not a mover." And, by the same token, they would contact competitors if they knew I needed something the others had. So, especially starting out the way I did, I was very fortunate it turned out that way.

As far as the books go, the business was much lower in volume than the former owner said it was. But I've built it up quite a bit since I first took it over. Because it was a long-established shop, anybody that smoked a pipe or cigars in this town knew the shop was there. It was just a matter of getting those customers back again, the ones who were no longer coming there. That identity was an advantage! I tried advertising, but it didn't work. The best advertisements were word-of-mouth recommendations.

Customers can now drop in and just chat, or have a cup of coffee while they're selecting a tobacco or brand of cigars. Everything is casual and relaxed. The aroma of many years of tobacco-blending is all around you and that's very pleasant for a smoker. There's a franchise tobacco shop, with lots of knickknacks, across the way in the mall—I don't believe you'll find it very relaxed or aged-aromatic; it's a lot more commerical, so to speak.

The first year was profitable. Nothing like his books would indicate, but there was a small profit. Since then, of course, it has been built up and the return is much better. Although the initial decision to buy this business was more emotional than logical, it did turn out to be more profitable and stable in a downhill economy than a camera shop might have been.

I must say, at this stage, that I am pleased with how everything worked out. In this case there was a definite element of luck involved. Here the owner was ready to retire, and even though he knew I was interested in other areas, he did make the offer to me. Fortunately I gave it some thought.

I guess there's a lesson to be learned here—don't be afraid to investigate every situation, no matter how far removed. It might just be the right opportunity after all.

The Fabric Manor *is a large corner store in a very active shopping center. It retails fabrics, notions, patterns, sewing machines, and all sewing incidentals. Vi Noble and Marge McKernan are partners.*

Vi Noble: Neither of us have been in business previously. I had been a loan officer in a local bank and Marge had worked for the city. Although we hadn't been thinking of a business, this opportunity came up kind of suddenly and we just decided to get it. We both like to sew and that enticed us.

Did we do our homework before buying? I guess the answer would be yes and no. Some of it really wasn't necessary because we lived here long enough to know the area and what's in the area. The location is one of the best because it's in a shopping center. We're situated next to the restaurant and our shop is right in the middle of the center.

Although this is a small community we draw from a number of other nearby communities. We even get people from farther away who come over and find merchandise that they can't get in their own town or bigger cities.

We knew this was a good shop, having frequented it ourselves, but we did get an accountant to go over the statements of the previous owner. We also checked with one of the salesmen who has been supplying most of the stock, and he thought it was a good price and a good business. The expectations in this past year and a half of our ownership has been satisfactory and I think we have actually been improving on it.

As far as starting from scratch goes, it takes a while to build a new business up and you may require more capital to do so. Personally, I would recommend buying an established business. I think an existing business has a much better chance of surviving in the present economy. Also if you start a new one and there's competition with others of the same type, you are fighting yourself. If you buy out one of the existing ones, you are better off.

New Dimensions Hair Stylists *is located in a shopping center of retail stores. There's just one long line of shops, with plenty of parking, bounded by two main thoroughfares.*

Tom Thomas: Before I bought this hair styling salon I was working in another shop—that was about six years ago. That shop was going to be closed and it was important for me to retain my customers. This could be done by transferring to another shop and, in effect, bringing the customers with me, or by opening my own business. In either case, the great majority of your clientele will follow you if the new location is within a reasonable distance.

The shop we are in now was a well-established one, with a fifteen-year record of operations in a very busy shopping center. It had been purchased from the original owners by a mother and daughter and things were starting to go downhill. They made a lot of wrong moves and they lost some key employees. And those employees can be your whole business, because when they go, they usually take their own customers with them.

I purchased the business because of the location, the ample parking, and the identity of a beauty salon being there for many, many years. One primary reason, I must admit, was that it is also only one mile from my house. No existing personnel were retained because I brought in my own. Two fellow employees from the shop that was closing and one additional girl from another established beauty salon, with their loyal clientele and my own, that was the start.

In addition, we passed out thousands of handbills throughout the neighborhood, advertising the fact that the shop was under new management and had much lower prices. You have to keep enlarging your original group of customers because eventually you will run out of them, due to illness or relocation to other regions.

If you buy a going business, you usually pay what that business is grossing or netting, and this can sometimes be more than starting from scratch. In this business, however, you have to be aware that you are not always buying existing customers. Maybe in a small town, yes, but even there, the employees may take their following to another beauty salon in town. Just be sure to check what you're paying for and what you're getting.

In this salon, I could not have set this operation up from scratch. The costs of equipment and installation would have been too high. The sinks alone are $200 each, the hair dryers $300 each, and those darn mirrors cost over $100 each. You can just about figure $2,000 per station for this setup, and that factor alone would have involved $24,000.

From my viewpoint, at that time, it was definitely better to buy an established business. I wouldn't have been able to start otherwise. And now it's six years later, so I guess you can mark it down as having been a successful move.

Ford Restaurant Supply *wholesales equipment and supplies to restaurants. Offices and a very extensive inventory are housed in a large leased facility on the main commercial boulevard.*

Jack Mervis: I graduated college with a business degree and transportation was my major. I went to work for a management consulting firm dealing mostly with mass transit and stayed with them for a total of seven and a half years. During the last year and a half, we looked to get back here—my wife's hometown. My goal, all my life, was to own my own business—my family is oriented in that direction. I knew I would work for someone else up front first, but after that, I wanted to get into a venture that belonged to us.

During that year and a half we looked at a lot of businesses, franchises included. Just a lot of things, looking through the paper mostly and by word-of-mouth also. This particular business was listed in the paper through a broker. My father-in-law began the initial investigation because he was living here and we kept in touch by phone.

I probably had no idea of starting anything from scratch, not from a very beginning. Our intention was to look very strongly at franchises and/or an existing business. Basically, I knew we would be getting into something I would know nothing about. Since the overwhelming reason for failure is the factor of inexperience or incompetence, I had to look to areas where this could be overcome. Franchises are a way to get some support, some training, something that would enable you—even if you don't know the business—to become successful.

If you buy an existing operation, you have a couple of things going for you, possibly. One would be the people in the organization, at various levels, who would hopefully continue their functions in the business. In the meantime, you are in more of an administrative position—if it's of any size. Even if it's not, you would still have those people to lean on. Also, if it's a winner, you have some positive cash flow. You have some things going for you where you can always go out and hire the people you need, people who have the experience in the business. That'll carry you over until you get a chance to get your own feet wet—after all there are a lot of things already laid out for you. The customers are there, the competition is known, the level of business is there, many things are *visible* and you don't have to learn them from the beginning.

Even the small things are established, things that may not seem like they could make the difference, one way or another. In fact, if you add all those things together, if you had to start from scratch to do all of them; it's almost impossible for any one or two people to get all that organized. At least not when you're struggling to master the basic fundamentals of a new business at the same time.

When I first looked at this business, the restaurant supply one, I said, "It's very practical, it's equipment that's needed, it's really retail in the respect that you're selling to the end user. I think it's something that I can learn, because I would certainly put a lot into it and I do learn quickly."

Once I got into it, however, I was overwhelmed by the technical end. There's so much to learn about new restaurant installations and remodeling. In addition, there's six thousand items in this store and neither we, nor anyone else, carries everything there is on the market. The technical aspect of the varied refrigeration units and ovens were pretty complex, nothing you could pick up in a day or two.

Part of our purchase agreement was that the previous owner would stay for sixty days, which he did. In retrospect, I don't know what I expected to learn in sixty days. Just the things that we had to do pertaining to taking over the business, all the legal stuff that carried over during those sixty days—there wasn't that much time to learn much of anything.

We used all the professional assistance we could get. We also used five teams to take physical inventory, with one person representing the previous owner and one for us. Everything was extended out to the most recent purchase price and we also adjusted values for older stock, discounting for inventory that was in the building for nine months, eighteen months, and so on. We looked at the market, our competition, and since we had one of the largest inventories in the state, there wasn't any *identity* problem. The books showed a successful operation—he did well, very well. And everyone looks for the most secure operation, so we figured the worst, where we might lose X percentage of the business the first year because of old owner–new owner type of thing. Fortunately, this didn't happen.

His staff—well, he had a lot of turnover in the floor salespeople, there was only one real salesperson who was an oldtimer, a walking encyclopedia in this business. The others were really sales clerks. One of our first activities has been sales training and we have a sales meeting every single morning. We don't miss one morning. We also added field salespeople, something he didn't have; he concentrated more on walk-in customers. I've hired a new sales manager and he's been in this business elsewhere for twenty-some years. He's just been a godsend to me, much more than an employee—a real friend, an adviser. I don't think I could have done most of this without him.

My wife, Donna, has degrees in sociology and counseling and she also didn't have any previous small business experience. We had some turnover in the accounting area and there were many things that had to be done to get things in order. There were many nitty-gritty kinds of activities that had to be changed or implemented, stuff that's got to be done even though you hate to do it. And that's where Donna was planted, in the accounting area. But that's not where she'll stay. If she's going to continue to work here, it will be in the sales area—that's where she'll be stimulated and be valuable.

We are a corporation, and the stockholders are Donna's father, Donna, and myself. We're all very satisfied with the way things are going, but there's much more to be done. It's very exciting!

IN SUMMATION

Most of the interviews highlight the advantages of buying an established business—especially when the buyers had no previous entrepreneurial experience. Of course, the cautions still exist and the warning for the buyer to beware is absolutely valid in these circumstances.

That's one of the problem areas that show up with these new owners. There's a lack of check and double check with regard to the seller's claims, records, and general past performance. Most did not concentrate on the necessity for full professional assistance—they acknowledged the need, but didn't always follow through. Only one or two related to a study of their market and the desirability of understanding the area, customer profiles, competitive circumstances, and so on.

Admittedly, these were mini-interviews and their main purpose was to probe the why of the decision to buy an existing venture. But enough discussion ensued to establish a lack of follow-through on the part of some of these entrepreneurs in the areas of preparation and investigation.

The one dominant benefit of buying an operating business is that it exists and many aspects can be seen rather than conjectured. The interviewees discovered some problem areas, but none, apparently that couldn't be overcome by commitment and on-the-job learning. Of course, that's the heart of it all. It is usually easier to acquire that training within an established venture than in one started from scratch.

Certain things are more predictable, especially the level of income being generated. Many other areas are already structured, thus freeing the new owner to study and absorb the operation more quickly. In a new start-up, everything is going and being created all at once, which can be traumatic to someone who lacks previous experience.

Although this small number of buy-a-business entrepreneurs did a lot of their decision making through gut feeling, the admonition remains the same: check out everything you can before buying. Use professional assistance, where necessary, to back up your own experience and knowledge. Paying too much and purchasing a lot of blue sky is quite prevalent when you don't know the field.

If possible, enter a field you already know, or work for someone else in that industry, even for a short time. This can give you more time to learn and to concentrate on those entrepreneurial areas that are new to you. The facts of the business you contemplate purchasing may be fairly evident, but give a great deal of thought to the potential that you may bring to the venture. It may make a meaningful difference, as expressed by some of those who were interviewed.

Many of the new owners have only been in their ventures a short time. Even if a profit is evident thus far, they cannot be considered successful until a few years have elapsed. The change in ownership, the fresh enthusiasm, the influx of new energy and ideas, may be responsible for that initial glow of health. Let's hope they continue and grow in both the experience and knowledge that will help ensure their future success.

Although these interviews are not meant to be lessons, you should be aware of some of the problems or benefits they expose.

The Fabric Manor benefited from its location—a very active shopping center in an area without major towns or shopping malls. Checking with the salesman who serviced the store was a definite benefit. He was a good gauge of previous activity and of The Fabric Manor's comparable worth in relation to the other stores he handled.

The owner of Frenchy's Pipe Shoppe did it himself and found out later how bad the books were, along with other negatives. He wouldn't advise others to do it alone. Get some professional assistance.

The owner of New Dimensions Hair Stylists knew his business, and that was a tremendous asset. Another was his inexpensive and very effective advertising/promotion campaign, using thousands of handbills.

Lessons can be gleaned in every interview—not only with this group, but also the others that will follow in the new start-ups and franchising sections.

Start a Business

Is this a good time to start a business?

1981 was a time of galloping inflation and high interest rates. Nevertheless, a record 587,000 businesses were started.

In 1982, more unemployment and bankruptcies occured than at any time since the thirties. But by the end of that year, business startups set another record.

During the following years, the nation's financial health improved and new startups kept increasing.

Perhaps, then, now or anytime is a good time—especially if you prepare for it.

6

The New Business Option

STARTING FROM THE GROUND UP

In starting a business from ground zero the approach is often different than when you buy a business.

Existing skills and experience or likes and dislikes, for example, may often be the determining factors in what type of established business to purchase. These specific aspects may also affect a beginner's decision concerning the type of venture he or she starts.

In many cases, it's a sudden idea that sparks a beginner's entrepreneurial urge. In other instances, an idea has been nurtured over a long period of time and finally it blossoms.

That idea may involve a product or a service, and its implementation may be retail, wholesale, mail order, or manufacturing. It may be completely new, or it may be an addition to an existing entity that creates a new twist, a combination form, a different approach or offers radical consumer savings, production costs-effectiveness, energy conservation, and so on.

This embryonic stage is the real beginning of small business ownership. Before momentum can carry you away, stop and reflect for a moment. Remember the Dun & Bradstreet statement in the opening chapter:

"Every year, hundreds of thousands of firms are started, almost an equal number discontinued . . ."

Yes, the failure rate within that discontinued group is high, especially among those who start on the bottom rung, from scratch. The main reasons for failure center around incompetence, lack of experience in the chosen field, poor location, faulty selections of product line, insufficient capital, and so on—factors that can be grouped under *poor management* cause over 90 percent of the failures.

The judgment or lack of it involved in the above reasons can all be traced to the absence of managerial competence. That's why, at this point, the caution flag is raised so that I may reinforce and reiterate some of the statements made in the introductory chapter.

1. If you have no knowledge of business management basics, prepare yourself by attending small business education courses, seminars, and SBA-sponsored sessions on management practices.

2. Read small business publications, trade journals, and the many government booklets that cover every aspect of starting and operating your own business.

3. Talk to owners of small businesses. Discuss problem areas, solutions, and successes. Attend open Chamber of Commerce meetings where guest speakers are featured.

4. Work in the field you contemplate entering if you have no previous experience or skills in that area. If you are in that field at present, try to become more involved with managerial procedures—pricing, purchasing, marketing, finance, and so on.

If the above cautions seem to verge on the grim side, so be it. Entrepreneurship isn't a casual game. If you sink all your efforts, energy, and capital into a venture and fail, the results can be disastrous.

That brings us back to the assumptions made earlier. By this time, you should have appraised your personal characteristics as a potential entrepreneur and classified your creativity and leadership traits. Additionally you also have come to grips with and accept the necessity for hard work, enthusiasm, and the consequences of taking risks. Your score in the above categories has hopefully been a positive one!

As noted previously, recognizing the green light for going into business is what this book is all about. Since you have definitely decided to investigate and evaluate entrepreneurship, the question is still which entrance category holds the best hope of success for you. Let's explore the second option, starting a business from scratch.

HOW SMALL A START-UP?

Small business is a relative term and different images of such can be sketched out, depending upon the viewer. To the Small Business Administration, sales volume of just under $1 million, or fewer than 250 employees, are small businesses.

Many business owners and aspiring entrepreneurs apply the following generalities to small businesses:

1. The business is *owner-managed*, with a few employees or none at all.
2. The business is *local* in operation, or, at best, not beyond the scope of neighboring regions.
3. The *initial* financial investment is not much above the mid-five-figure mark.

With present-day inflation, of course, the monetary investment can move somewhat higher. This will also happen in relation to the type of business selected and the resultant equipment or inventory needs. Generally speaking, however, small business to most beginner owner-managers means just that—not very big!

Whether it's service or manufacturing, for example, a great number of start-ups have originated in the garage, basement, or even the kitchen table. Mail order has to be counted in that group also, and in some spectacular success cases, this form of merchandising has then taken over the whole house, or required the owner to lease a warehouse to keep up with the demand.

On the other side are the more financially demanding businesses, such as retail stores with their need for furniture and fixtures, inventory, and advertising. Restaurants and coffee shops can also involve expensive equipment, varied personnel, and perilous food-management problems.

Manufacturing and wholesaling ventures that require large premises and/or heavy equipment, transportation costs, and delivery vehicles are in the upper-bracket financial-need category. Keep in mind that modest start-up capital expenditure refers to the initial outlay only.

That doesn't negate the use of large expensive machinery when it's been obtained on a lease basis or the manufacturer's own generous time-payments schedule. In other types of start-ups your suppliers of inventory and fixtures may extend some longer-term credits in the initial stage.

Starting your own business from the ground up is a wide-open situation. It can involve a total financial outlay of a few thousand dollars, or a few hundred thousand. Many considerations and parameters will eventually determine what your takeoff point will be. The subsequent chapters will explore these areas and help target your beginning needs.

BACK-TO-BASIC BASICS

Some of the preliminary factors that apply to purchasing a business are also applicable in considering a brand-new venture. Their resolution will have a bearing on just how big that small business will be. The very nature of the proposed operations and any limitations of your finances or capabilities will obviously create some constraints. All in all, however, these are some of the questions to answer in the earliest stages:

> Is your product or service new or established?
>
> Do you have skills or experience that relate?
>
> What size business can you handle?
>
> Do you intend to go it alone? With employees?
>
> Is there a preferred or mandatory location?
>
> How much of your own capital is available?
>
> How much additional capital can you raise?
>
> Are partners being considered? For capital? For complementary skills?

As the entrepreneurial urge starts to take over, you naturally will have thought about and explored some of the above questions. Maybe you have even quickly evaluated the idea of looking at an operation that already exists, something along the lines of whatever sparked your initial interest. It's this kind of mental probing and testing that should then spark some more extensive research into the success potential of starting your own small business.

To continue the process, this "what if I started my own?" preliminary thinking, now calls for some additional focus. A bit more cerebral crystallization of the original idea and a surface review of what the idea really means in terms of can-it-fly-as-a-business seem to be the next steps.

INC AND MORE

INC doesn't stand for "incorporated" at this stage. It's merely a memory device to question and review that product or service that will make you an active entrepreneur.

Idea: Many new start-ups begin with an idea. Whether the idea is based on some existing business or is brand-new, it must be defined.

If your idea involves a product, will you manufacture, subcontract, assemble, or buy it? Will it be more suitable for retail or mail order? Does it require a sales staff or distributors? If it's a new product, will you need a model, a patent, or a copyright? If it's an existing product, what makes your product better than the others?

If your idea is for a service, can it be handled by you, or will it require other personnel? Are special skills and/or equipment required? If you don't have the skills, are they available through employees? Can the service be organized and marketed? Is it a new service, or an improvement of an existing service?

If your idea is for a retail establishment, will it be something new or competitive? Will location be its primary asset? What will set it apart from other retailers? Will the adjacent stores create the type traffic you desire?

Need: Is there a real need for what you have to offer? Does a market exist, and is it reasonably *large enough* for you to enter? Will there be opportunity for future growth?

Where are the buyers who need your product or service—in industry or in the consumer marketplace? Are there any other restrictions to your market relative to age, affluence, geography, or season? Will you have to create a market?

Competition: Whether the product or service is new or existing, who or what are the competitors? Are they direct competition? Are they large and able to withstand your efforts? Where are the competitor's marketing areas?

If direct competition exists, how does your offering stack up in quality, price, benefits? If it's a new product, is it easy to duplicate? Will it be protectable?

These questions, and many more you can add in the categories of Idea, Need, and Competition (INC) are a simple prerequisite to the task of making a comprehensive plan to convert your entrepreneurial thoughts into a successful reality.

That's what planning is all about. It's an effort to ensure success before you get started. Going through the preliminaries is highly meaningful. The sobering fact is that you and your capabilities *are* the business. Initially it will be your strengths that transform the ideas into the business actualities.

Don't be misled. The stories of a few start-ups that turned into overnight riches are overwhelmed by the thousands of corresponding failures. Cut down those high odds against you by incorporating some of the survivor steps mentioned earlier—self-appraisal charts, education courses, and reading, talking, and working in the field you have chosen for your ownership venture.

CHAPTER

7

The Initial Once-Over

ADVANTAGES OF STARTING FROM SCRATCH

Since practically everything about the launch of a brand-new venture is up to the individual who starts it, that very factor may be the total sum and substance of the advantages for this type entry into the small business world.

You are your own boss, and that involvement enables you to do the following:

1. Select the type of business you will operate.
2. Determine the size of the operation.
3. Determine the business's legal format.
4. Decide to operate the business alone or choose partners.
5. Select location and facilities.
6. Set policies and direction.
7. Determine initial promotion.

These prerequisites and others are in your hands. The opportunity to use your ideas, your creative input, and your own brand of follow-through now exists. Depending on available finances, you can start out as small or as large as your energy allows. You don't have to settle for an existing location or facilities—they can be tailored to what you believe necessary for success.

The time element of when to begin is another factor that you control. You can evaluate the advantages and disadvantages as to season and your personal timetable. If subcontractors and suppliers are a part of your venture, they will be of your own choosing. The same will hold true for associates and/or personnel—people you will select to complement your own experience and energy output.

If the entrepreneurial urge stemmed from the need for independence and the opportunity for doing things your way, those factors certainly show the advantages of an up-from-the-bottom venture.

DISADVANTAGES

Many of the negatives attributed to starting from scratch are a direct offshoot of not being previously established. You are now part of an on-line learning experience. Mistakes from pure inexperience are bound to happen, and their effect may prove very costly. Other disadvantages include the following:

1. Borrowing capital is more difficult.
2. True start-up costs are not easily determined.
3. Initially a salary or draw may not be possible.
4. No track record exists for guidance.
5. A good deal of time is required to build customers, to fit into the correct market, to establish a reputation, and to become profitable.

True, there are occasional stories of overnight successes, but historically it takes two or three years to establish a new venture. Most of that time is spent in continuing your own small business education with on-the-job training. Excess capital, if any, is usually plowed back into the business to strengthen cash flow, increase inventory, ease expansion, or buy the things you couldn't afford before.

If you are so anxious to start your new venture that you don't take the time to prepare and neglect to do some market research, that will become the nucleus of another series of potential horrors:

- wrong location
- insufficient market
- competition too strong
- costs miscalculated
- wrong inventory
- bad suppliers
- insufficient capital
- product or service advantages overestimated.

These problem areas, if allowed to happen, are a direct responsibility of the individual who starts the business. Before starting out, you must maximize whatever strengths exist and overcome the areas of inexperience and weakness, either through developing your own expertise or bringing in the help you need. Otherwise that great bugaboo of new business, managerial incompetence, will create problems.

The list of possible disadvantages only serves to reinforce the fact that starting from scratch is logically acknowledged to be the most perilous way of getting into business. The risk of failure is greater than if you buy an established business or operate a franchise unit, but the advantage of being able to start small, full-time or part-time, has lured many a pioneer to opt for the brand-new format.

WHAT KIND OF BUSINESS?

Small business is the business of the United States. Numerically, well over 90 percent of the nation's businesses are in the small category. This total encompasses manufacturing, wholesaling, retailing, and service operations.

The largest group, almost half, represents retailers. Growing very rapidly in the past ten years are the service businesses that cater to the general public and numerous industries. They now number almost 30 percent of the nation's small businesses. Manufacturing, wholesaling, and the various financial ventures account for another 15 percent, and the remainder consists of various combinations of the above, plus a miscellaneous and nontraditional category.

A perusal of a large metropolitan area's classified phone book will give you a good representation of the business types in the various categories. Also helpful are the *Census of Business* listings from the U.S. Department of Commerce and Dun & Bradstreet's *Key Business Ratios*. These sources may stimulate you to consider some options that may not have come up in your original thought sessions.

Selecting the right business is one of the basic keys to achieving success. Remember that the success factor is not solely measured by financial returns. The venture must enable you to achieve a desired lifestyle and also offer the opportunity for a great deal of personal satisfaction.

Retail Ventures

The largest category of entrepreneurship, retailing, is also the most familiar, since we are all consumers. When it comes to evaluating retail ventures, however, the variety available in this category will boggle your mind. Just perusing a simple listing will confirm this, but at the same time it may energize you to further analyze your hobbies, likes and dislikes, and past experience to see if they might fit areas you hadn't seriously considered:

Antique shop	Gourmet foods
Appliances	Groceries
Art gallery	Hardware
Art supplies	Hat shop
Auto supply	Health foods
Backpacking and camping	Hobby shop
Bakery	Homemade candies
Bar/lounge	Household appliances
Beauty parlor	Ice cream shop
Beverage stand	Infant wear
Bicycle shop	Jewelry
Bookstore	Kitchenware
Burglar and smoke alarms	Leased department
Butcher shop	Liquor store
Card and novelty shop	Locksmith
Cheese shop	Luggage store
Children's wear	Medical supplies
Coffee shop	Men's furnishings
Computer store (software)	Music
Cookie emporium	Paint and wallpaper
Crafts gallery	Paperback books
Dairy	Pet shop
Discount store	Phone store
Donut shop	Photography shop
Drugstore	Pipe and tobacco
Electronics	Plant store (nursery)
Fabric shop	Printing
Fast foods	Radio and TV
Floor coverings	Restaurant
Florist	Salad bar
Food stand	Shoe store
Fruits and vegetables	Solar products
Fur shop	Specialty foods
Furniture	Sports store
Garden supplies	Stationery
Gas station	Teas and herbs
Gift shop	Tire center

Toy store	Women's boutique
Used books	Woodstoves
Variety store	Yogurt bar
Video cassette shop (rentals)	

That's a pretty good list, but it's still not complete. You, with your new idea, can be an addition. And various specialty factors may also be added to those already listed: soup bars, muffler shops, learning centers, energy-saving devices, hosiery, jeans only, western wear, and so on.

In fact, there are some who advise that specializing can create a positive competitive stance in a new business start-up. It establishes an immediate identity for your venture and offers a specific focus for the consumer's needs. There are many of these successes in the above list: paperback bookstores, used books, fabric shops, salad bars, cheese shops, health foods, tire centers, woodstoves, and so on.

Don't forget one of the giants of retailing—mail order. It isn't on the list because it is one area of merchandising that can take in the majority of items already listed, and more. Instead of vanishing under the plethora of new marketing strategies, it has thrived and grown. Many of the largest corporations have started their own or purchased existing mail-order ventures. Increased postal and printing costs have made it more difficult for new start-ups, but there have been some spectacular recent winners, and that fact helps fan the interest of many a beginning entrepreneur.

Service Ventures

The services area is the growth industry of the nation. As consumers in both our personal and business activities, we shouldn't be surprised by the proliferation within this category, for we are the ones who've created the need.

Many of the service businesses require skills and experience— locksmiths, beauticians, computer programmers, printers, and so on. Others, however, can function fairly well if the new owner-manager has a quick mind and nimble fingers—phone answering, delivery/messenger, maintenance, personnel agency, equipment rentals, and so on.

The latter aspect is especially true of those ventures that require minimal equipment and inventory or none at all. Within that format, many have been practically started on a shoestring. All service ventures, however, will need a certain degree of the same basic ingredients— personal energy, a correct and viable market, sufficient capital, effective management, and competent personnel.

Because of those requirements, the franchise industry has also been able to expand very successfully in that direction. The following listing of services or service-oriented businesses, although extensive, cannot be considered complete; new areas are opening every day.

Automotive services:	repair shops (all components), car washes, parking lots, auto leasing, simonizing, tuneups, lube centers, steam-cleaning of motors, diagnostic testing.
Amusement and recreation:	theaters, movies, golf, miniature golf, bowling, amusement arcades, film distribution, orchestras and entertainers, swimming clubs, discos and ballrooms, tennis clubs.
Business services:	cleaning and maintenance, advertising, public relations, consulting, accounting, legal, financial, collections, transportation, equipment rental and leasing, telephone answering, computer, insurance, security and protection, test marketing, personnel agencies, warehousing, landscaping, printing and artwork, delivery, taxi and limousine service, trucking, transcriptions.
Personal and family services:	laundries, dry cleaning, shoe shines, barbers, beauty parlors, medical, legal, personal shoppers, suntanning parlors, saunas, photo studios, day care, baby-sitting, interior decorating, party rentals, pet care, travel and real estate agencies, photocopying services, instruction (driving, dance, weight control, and so on) tax preparation, brokerage and investment.
Repair and maintenance services:	jewelry, appliances, furniture, reupholstery, shoes, clothing alterations, equipment repairs, electrical, business machines, glaziers, heating and air conditioning, painting and decorating, remodeling, roofing and insulation, gardening, housecleaning.

Other services: hotels and motels, engineering, surveys
                                     (varied), design, architectural, contract-
                                     ing, communications.

Manufacturing, Wholesaling, Distribution

When we think of manufacturing, the image of extensive plant areas and heavy equipment comes to mind. But that wouldn't quite fit our view of small businesses.

Let's keep the focus where it belongs, then, on such manufacturing processes as bakeries, clothing ventures, craftworks, displays, printers, and many a machine shop operating in a small loft or garage.

Not to be neglected in this more modest category are the idea people and inventors who are physically creating their products from raw materials or an assembly of subcontracted parts. Similarly, many smaller entrepreneurs are engaged in some form of fabrication where, by machine or hand, they are reprocessing or converting elements.

Assembly of parts or electronic elements to form a specific unit or a final end product are fairly common forms of manufacturing. Dolls, apparel, toys and games, food products, small appliances, computer components, novelties, jewelry, sporting goods, and printing materials have also successfully emerged from these small business "factories."

Who are the customers? They will range from the individual consumer to the industrial purchasing agent, from the retailer to the wholesaler, from mail-order firms to government agencies—it really depends on the nature of the product.

This is also the stage where wholesalers can enter the picture, for they are the middlemen, in between the manufacturer and the retailer, or the manufacturer and various other types of buyers. Distributors or jobbers also have functions relative to the wholesaler.

Where the manufacturer does not sell directly to the customer and has no sales staff or company representatives, the distribution of the merchandise or materials is normally handled by a wholesaler. Often that wholesaler buys and stocks large inventories of the manufacturer's products and then distributes smaller quantities to the various buyers. It's the wholesaler's sales staff that finally moves the goods off the shelf and into the marketplace.

The types of goods involved in wholesaling seem to be unlimited. Wholesale operations have encompassed automotive supplies, chemical and maintenance products, beauty and barber supplies, confectionery, stationery, electrical supplies, flowers, fruits and vegetables, groceries, paper products, toys and novelties, jewelry, hardware, small appliances, kitchenware, and much more.

For the new start-up entrepreneur, however, the wholesaler requirements of a sales staff, large inventories, warehousing, and transportation are realistically out of reach. But there are definite potentials for an initial modest beginning in this field. Guidance for such a venture can be garnered from the trade magazines and trade associations that often report when less-established manufacturers are looking for distribution channels to get their goods into the marketplace.

Attempting to distribute or wholesale one of these offerings would be a valuable learning experience. It could be handled part-time and give you an opportunity to actively participate in the steps required to create an operational reality.

The simple act of investigating one of the many offerings, one that may strike your entrepreneurial ardor as being a good potential, can be both stimulating and instructive. A preretirement acquaintance of mine did just that and profited greatly from the lesson. First he sent for a sample. Then, because of a natural apprehension, he asked friends, acquaintances, and even strangers what they thought of the product and if they would pay the suggested price.

Their responses made him try to evaluate what the market might be and the degree of need that might exist. Next his thoughts turned to how he might promote the product to establish his dealership identity, create product exposure, and stimulate demand. The practicalities and costs for advertising, public relations, local interviews (if some unique aspect could be developed), coupon flyers, contests, and so on, all filtered through his thoughts, with "possible," "probable," and "no way" evaluations.

He then queried the manufacturer as to mandatory quotas, area of distribution, guarantee of territory, backup promotion, existing printed materials that might be used, applicable government regulations, and a few other questions that cropped up as he continued his probing.

What was the result of all this investigation and preliminary thinking? He decided *not* to go ahead! But look at all he was forced to consider and the active steps he took to evaluate. He didn't know all this beforehand. He discussed it with others who had more experience and was able to follow through with their advice and his own common sense.

He is now a firm advocate of investigating before finalizing anything. In his mind it was well worth the cost of one product sample and a good deal of personal energy expended in preliminary research. Of additional importance, the investigation finally released him from the fantasy aspect of small business—that dreamland of "someday I'd like to start my own venture."

In fact, that new realism has resulted in his present focus on a small business that will make use of his present skills and experience. Initially, it will start as a sideline, a moonlighting situation, but he hopes to see it develop within a short time as an early retirement, full-time venture. He recently dropped his new business card on my desk.

Home-Based Businesses

For a change of pace, we should also consider those ventures that are started in the home and often remain there. Somewhat like mail order, this is a field that can consist of almost every type of business in all the categories previously discussed.

Interestingly enough, completely new operations are constantly being started, because this field continually reflects the current needs or fads of the day. Whether it involves videotaping sports events or marriages, or using a word processor for typing services, this category of business keeps up-to-date. One of the very latest trends, for example, is working on your present job at home via a home computer hooked up to the company's main terminal. Press a transmission switch and all the calculations or research copy you worked on is fed into the central records.

But that's getting ahead of the game. Home-based self-employment has been around for a long time. Usually it has involved skills of one type or another. In recent years, however, many ventures have been originated by those who were able to spot unfulfilled needs resulting from social or marketing changes. Additionally, some came up with bright, innovative ideas. Making these a reality can involve starting on a small scale while still working, or starting out full-time with an adequate investment of time and capital.

As it succeeds, you may wish to keep it a home business, or it may grow into a full-fledged retail, service, mail-order, or manufacturing operation. Even without that end goal, don't be lulled into believing that a home business is a much simpler way to start a business and be your own boss. The basic principles still apply. To be successful, there must be a need for your product or service, and there must be sufficient numbers of customers to make it profitable.

In addition, you must have or quickly begin to acquire a working knowledge of marketing, advertising, management, and correct pricing. Operating a business from home doesn't make you any less an entrepreneur than if you had an outside establishment. It may, however, give you a better opportunity for on-the-job training at a slower and less costly pace.

8

Locating the Business to Target

WHICH CATEGORY TO CHOOSE?

As an initial exploratory thought, let's consider another one of those beliefs that has been bandied about regarding the meaning of the word "entrepreneur." Here again, some authorities have maintained that the true entrepreneur is not at all concerned with the kind of business he or she will run. True entrepreneurs, they claim, are concerned only with the bottom line. Will this business be a profitable one? Is there a potential for an excellent growth rate? How long will it take to return original investment? And, so on, and so on.

If this is your cup of tea, terrific! But if you want to attain some nonmonetary satisfaction as you deal with all the potential perils, then my strong recommendation is to, at the very least, not dislike or be bored with the business you finally choose.

As far as choice goes, there are many aspects that will have to be factored in, just as there were in the purchase of an existing business. Of course it's much easier to choose a category of business when you can see and feel the physical venture, watch the action for a few days, and study the past history of a total operation. It's the very sharp difference between what has already happened and what may happen.

As far as the category of business is concerned, these are the approximate percentage choices of other entrepreneurs within the major areas.

- retailing   50 percent
- services   30 percent
- manufacturing   5 percent
- wholesaling   5 percent

Your decision will depend, to a large extent, upon the following:

- past experience
- skills and knowledge
- personal likes and dislikes
- work objectives
- personality and stamina.

RETAILING

It's easy to be positive about the most popular category of all, retailing, if your past work experience involved retail selling and your personality is suited to favorably interacting with consumers. Perhaps, because of past work routine, you have already adjusted to a six-day work week, plus one or two evenings a week.

What about the beginning entrepreneurs who are contemplating their first retail venture? Will long hours, dealing with the general public, and being "always wrong" strike them as insurmountable negatives?

What about the type of retailing? Will small sales, heavy inventories, numerous styles and/or colors, fragile items, perishable products, and so on be an irritant or an accepted part of the game plan? Can you cope with days of hardly any customers and only $5 in sales, and, conversely, days when sales are so fast and furious that you're on your feet all day and have to work late to put things in order?

MAIL ORDER

If dealing with the general public is not one of your likes and doesn't fit with your work objectives or your personality, maybe the category of mail-order retailing will be appropriate for you. There's no direct contact with customers, payments usually accompany orders, starting inventories can be small (or nonexistent, if you are using a drop-ship supplier), hours of work are set to your own convenience, and a part-time start-up will only require a small initial investment. Creative advertising and effective product selection for this field are definite assets that can assure success and growth.

SERVICES

The same kind of thinking and analysis that apply to retailing also apply to the other business categories of services, manufacturing, and wholesaling. In some instances, your skills and work experience will automatically point you to one of the service ventures—the second largest field among small businesses.

Whether it's accounting, automotive servicing, music, photography, interior decorating, or whatever, this category may be the most logical avenue to satisfy personal interest, to maximize existing knowledge, and to probably ensure the potential for a successful operation.

In fact, in interviews many owners who started their businesses from scratch have definitively targeted previous knowledge or experience as the prime ingredient in their survival and success. This does not rule out the "new idea" or "never did it before" types of start-ups. They will simply require more effort and more on-the-job training, as well as a strong penchant for effective management practices and problem-solving techniques.

MANUFACTURING

When you first contemplate manufacturing, fabricating, or assembly, the skills/experience aspect may not come into immediate focus. But it does apply just as strongly here as in the other categories.

An accomplished wordsmith might decide to write a series of booklets on diets, low-calorie cooking, herbs, or gambling techniques, and then "manufacture" them for direct-mail sales or distribution to retail stores.

A crafts person might be involved with manufacturing art objects, jewelry, do-it-yourself kits, or "how to" pamphlets. Sales outlets would include gift boutiques, department stores, galleries, or hobby shops.

A top sales representative might devise some meaningful improvements or additions to one of his or her present products. Fortified by an in-depth knowledge of the field and direct contacts with all of those involved, the sales rep might manufacture or subcontract this improved product through a new small business venture.

In cases where large corporations have turned down multi-thousand unit orders because the amounts were too small, a few employees have formed small, independent businesses that then subcontracted those orders from the corporation. All factions benefited—the buyer, the corporation, and the new entrepreneurs. In some instances, initial financing was partially obtainable from the corporations.

WHOLESALING

Wholesaling is one of the main conduits of distribution, the moving of goods from the manufacturer to the wholesaler and then on to the retailer. The retailer, in turn, sells to the end-user—the consumer.

In the case of industrial products, the movement may be from the manufacturer to a wholesaler, to a dealer and then on to the company or institutional users. Institutional users are actual consumers and they include schools, hospitals, and government and private agencies, as well as large and small industries of all types.

Wholesalers are the middlemen of the distribution chain. They usually buy in large quantities and maintain extensive inventories in their own warehouses. Smaller quantities are then sold to their customers— the retailers and dealers. In terms of small business, this type of heavy investment necessary for large quantity buying, warehousing, transportation, and sales staffs seems to negate a starting-from-scratch venture.

However, you might consider certain variations of the distribution setup, where much more modest applications can and do occur. The term "middleman," for example, has blurred sufficiently to include agents, brokers, dealers, distributors, manufacturer's reps, and independent salespersons.

Almost all are actually in business for themselves; they may represent one or more manufacturers without being on their payroll. The products they handle may be nationally sold or regional in nature. As independents, their home bases can be as varied as the almost unlimited nature of the products being sold.

Some operate from their homes or cars, others from their briefcases and phone answering services. Still others will have one or more offices with secretaries and staff. Most of them started their operations in a very simple setup and are now handling a variety of products from different manufacturers.

If this method of entry into the wholesaling category appeals to you, there is a way to go for some initial research. Many new products are featured in small business opportunity magazines and newsletters, with offers of dealerships and regional distributorships. You will have to evaluate the sales potential and market acceptance of these products, as well as many other factors involved before you make a decision.

A great number of these offerings would be considered speculative, for many reasons. They may be very new and only partially tested, very regional in exposure, of limited need or insufficient market demographics, inferior or not favorably competitive with other similiar products, and so on.

At the same time, however, taking a chance with one of these products may provide some terrific on-the-job training. Your involvement might be on a part-time basis without any great expenditure of capital or need for facilities and equipment.

EXISTING CATEGORIES

To some of you, the choice of a business category may not be an important first step. If you have already given thought to a specific venture, it automatically falls into its own category. Based on your previous work experience, you may have expressed a variation of one of the following statements:

"I'd rather manufacture something and leave the final sales transaction to someone else."

"The consumer is a real pain; it's a lot better to deal with people in industry."

"I couldn't take working in a store—the hours are murder and it's too confining."

"I'd like a business where it's cash before delivery, you don't see any customers, you can live anywhere."

This kind of thinking can immediately pinpoint a category, and it's the same kind of review that we'll be doing later to select a type of venture that will satisfy your needs. If you do feel strongly about a specific business category, negatively or positively, it pays to heed that feeling and let it guide you toward the area that satisfies you most.

Many companies, especially small ventures, have been formed as offshoots of present occupations or existing businesses. If you discover this kind of opportunity, your selection of a category becomes easy.

This doesn't mean setting yourself up in direct competition with your former employer—that may result in more problems than you can handle. But there are opportunities in going from your regular job to an allied field, for example.

A salesperson often hears of customer problems in another field that doesn't conflict with his or her firm's products. Maybe it's a common problem concerning a customer's need for a source that can deliver small runs of a subassembly part. The opportunity might be too small for the big firms, but big enough to get a small company started—*your* company.

One typist had been taking in special-order, high-quality jobs at home, after her regular office stint. She developed so many clients that she finally formed a transcription service with a half dozen employees. Transcribing interview tapes and typing manuscripts and instruction brochures are now among her specialties.

In other words, creatively look around your own bailiwick. You may already have an existing category selection that's a fertile area for a start-up.

BEGINNING THE SELECTION

Within the various categories of businesses examined earlier, there are many types of operations to choose from. If you can select the right opportunity, the chances for personal satisfaction and financial success are greatly enhanced.

Now is the time to discard the roulette wheel, the dart-board and the pin-sticking methods of selection. Dispense with shallow thinking, spur-of-the-moment unbridled enthusiasm, and the knee-jerk reaction to entrepreneurship as salvation from an unhappy job situation.

Choosing the type of small business that will completely absorb all your time for the next three, five, or ten years is not something that should be left to chance or whimsical thought. Unlike an erroneous choice of a stereo, a car, or a job, the wrong business is not so easy to discard or change. It's also much more costly in terms of self-esteem and both current and future lifestyles.

When you buy a business or join a franchise, that final choice is subject to a good deal of research and analysis. In the case of a brand new start-up, however, the analysis emphasis will be focused on *you*, the potential owner-manager. Your future operation has no past accounting records to peruse or franchisor qualifications to check out.

Since the business will be you, that's our starting point in determining the type of opportunity that will fit you and your aspirations. All the preliminary thinking and surface evaluations that were touched on previously will still be valid, except that they will now be examined in greater depth.

What you expect from an entrepreneurship and what you can bring to it are the two most important factors to be examined. In a sense, it's a study of your lifestyle and your résumé of previous jobs and related experiences. One involves your desires and the other your varied capabilities. For a proper evaluation, it's essential to be as honest as you can in your appraisals.

Before any business venture, your self-evaluation must show the proper entrepreneurial traits. Because a fresh start-up is so dependent upon the "you" factor, it may be appropriate to give a quick overview to one of the SBA's rating scales for potential proprietors:

Are you a self-starter?

How do you feel about other people?

Can you lead others?

Can you take responsibility?

How good an organizer are you?

How good a worker are you?

Can you make decisions?

Can people trust what you say?

Can you stick with it?

How good is your health?

The rating scale is not really based on yes or no answers, but on degree. Although there are no percentage scores, your answers will help you understand the importance of your personal traits with relation to becoming a small business owner-manager. You may even be encouraged and stimulated to think up a few other questions about yourself that would pertain to running your own venture.

When you are an employee, there is always someone to turn to above or below you for physical help, advice, guidance and/or orders. As an entrepreneur, you have to self-start, get the jobs done, be responsible, and make all the decisions. That's the vital ingredient of independence, a must in small business operations.

Risk-taking is another important quality. If you're the type who has always played it safe and been somewhat conservative in decision-making, the odds may not favor your entry into the small business field, where risks are often a daily occurrence. Keep in mind, however, that risk doesn't mean rashness or gambling. Instead, business risks are calculated risks, risks that are well thought out and have good probabilities for success.

Initially, in the start-up stage, risk-taking reflects the willingness to leave the security of a weekly paycheck—but only after you've done your homework and the necessary preparation for entrepreneurship. In the actual business operation, it means being aware of and following up on opportunities that offer positive potentials—but no specific guarantees.

SELECTING THE RIGHT OPPORTUNITY

Skills or past experience may lead to a quick decision for some. The accounting employee wants to start a bookeeping and accounting service. The mechanic and locksmith will open their own repair services. The woman's wear sales clerk is now ready to run her own boutique. Employees in all sorts of companies—department stores, publishers, wholesalers, manufacturer's sales staffs, advertising—all may be willing to confront the risks of entrepreneurship in their own work areas.

They stay in their present fields because they still derive satisfaction from their current type of work, or simply because the skill and experience they have developed will give them their best financial returns. Their odds for success also increase a great deal, because their new ventures won't require complete on-the-job training. They already know their profession—the additional learning will concern management practices and administration in the areas their jobs did not encompass.

But other would-be entrepreneurs may not wish to continue with their present job skills because they are not using their total capabilities. Or they may wish to be involved in a new growth field, or to develop a hobby, a long-held interest, or avocation into a new career. What standards should they use in making an evaluation?

Again, people in this situation should review their lifestyles and capabilities. When analyzing a specific business opportunity with relation to these factors, you will spotlight one or more deficiencies. If these deficiencies are of serious consequence to your desired lifestyle or the capabilities you possess, then this may suggest that you ought to consider another type of venture.

This kind of review will also be important in buying a business and joining a franchise, but it's *more* vital in the case of a fresh start-up. Remember, there is a much greater percentage of failures in the start-from-scratch gateway to small business ownership.

LIFESTYLE

How can lifestyle affect your business choice? Here are some check-lists that can help crystallize your thinking.

Why do you want a business of your own?

_____ dissatisfaction with present job

_____ don't get along with employer

_____ other employees a problem

_____ too much pressure and responsibility

_____ don't like working for someone else

_____ to achieve recognition

_____ for personal enjoyment

_____ as a challenge to succeed

_____ to make use of all capabilities

_____ to increase future earnings

_____ to be independent and make all decisions

_____ to build something for my family

You will note that there are definite negative and positive reasons to be checked off. Certainly it's not unusual to look for escape where dissatisfaction exists. But, if that's your predominant reason, watch out!

In your own business, the work will be harder, the hours longer, the "bosses" more numerous, the responsibilities greater, and the initial returns much less. The escape syndrome, if it's the major reason for your decision of entrepreneurship, will greatly influence and *decrease* your chances for success. Positive reasons, on the other hand, tend to increase motivation and enthusiasm—two necessary ingredients to help get you into the winner's circle.

What do you hope to achieve financially?

_____ $15,000–$25,000 annual income

_____ $25,000–$40,000 annual income

_____ $40,000–$50,000 annual income

_____ over $50,000 annual income

_____ pension–profit-sharing plan

_____ medical and insurance plans

_____ other fringe benefits

Keep in mind that the annual income expectations are targets for after the business has been established. Occasionally a new venture takes off immediately, but normally it may take a few years before everything clicks—ample customers, correct inventories, positive reputation, good suppliers, and experienced personnel.

Additionally, can the business you are contemplating earn the income you desire in the early stages? What about five or ten years from now? A residential locksmith working alone is income-limited—but he or she could add a line of burglar alarms, commercial protection installations, and extra personnel to increase sales three- or fourfold. Estimating your goals before you start can help determine the type of business, as well as the required size of the operation. If a specific income is desired, it can also negate a venture that is incapable of achieving that goal.

What business characteristics do you want?

_____ mostly indoors	_____ mostly outdoors
_____ working alone	_____ working with people
_____ owner oriented	_____ personnel oriented
_____ sales emphasis	_____ production emphasis
_____ heavy inventory	_____ selective inventory
_____ minimum paperwork	_____ paperwork O.K.
_____ creative	_____ structured
_____ high-cost units	_____ low-cost units
_____ extensive customer contact	_____ minimal customer contact
_____ heavy travel	_____ restricted travel
_____ full-time involvement	_____ part-time involvement
_____ five-day week, regular hours	_____ as-necessary hours
_____ always as owner-manager	_____ eventual supervision only
_____ high-growth situation	_____ modest size/stable
_____ city location	_____ rural or suburban location
_____ eventual absentee ownership	_____ no absentee

As noted, the business characteristics are a combination of personal likes and dislikes, and perhaps a reflection of past work experiences, as well as other individual needs. From your own standpoint, many other characteristics could be added to establish more personal all-encompassing criteria.

We are all familiar with business acquaintances or fellow employees who are avid sports buffs, dedicated family men or women, supercreative individuals, and even workaholics, to name a few. Each has his or her own set of requirements: mandatory sports time, no extensive travel away from home, stimulation via manual design or cerebral effort, and the "my work is my salvation" syndrome. If they are requirements that *must* be satisfied, then it would be somewhat questionable to select a business whose characteristics cannot accommodate these specific needs.

RÉSUMÉ

Let's take a look at your résumé, the usual job information summaries that list your previous work experience, education, hobbies, and personal statistics. As in a job interview, our interest will focus on capabilities that apply to the small business arena.

As an employee, did your work include any of these aspects to any appreciable degree?

_____ administration

_____ sales

_____ production

_____ design

_____ bugeting/forecasting

_____ clerical/secretarial

_____ bookkeeping/accounting

_____ marketing/advertising

_____ purchasing and supplier contact

_____ customer contact

_____ personnel supervision

_____ personnel hiring/training

_____ interacting with others

_____ mechanical/technical skills

In which areas was this experience?

_____ retail

_____ wholesale

_____ manufacturing

_____ distribution

Don't sell yourself short. Invariably, even though you were assigned to a specific job function, you had ample opportunity to relate to more than one area. Most jobs involve dealing with people—other employees, supervisors, sales personnel, customers, management, suppliers, and so on.

In smaller companies, job functions overlap considerably and most likely you were exposed to almost every area of the business. The smaller the company, the more varied the job duties—an invaluable experience.

Many of the functions you engaged in as an employee will relate to some area of operations in your own small business. Even if you only absorbed some aspects of business by osmosis, they will be valuable—for example, noting your company's advertising, the method of handling inventory, how much stock was kept on hand, customer follow-ups, employee relations and training, and the always-present wastefulness.

These factors apply whether you were on the production line or in the office, on the retail selling floor or at the mail-order fulfillment desk.

If your previous jobs relate directly to the business you are starting, that will be an enormous plus. But there will also be much more to learn. No matter how much experience you already have and how intensively you study, the greatest knowledge for the new entrepreneur will come from the everyday on-the-job activities.

At this point, though, take a more intensive look at your job résumé and try to honestly determine what capabilities from your previous work experiences can be applied to your own business start-up. Where you have checked the listed categories, expand them to include all the peripheral elements that will be meaningful to you as an owner-manager of a small business.

In continuing a consideration of your résumé, let's examine the category of hobbies and other activities.

Which of the following are you *actively* involved with?

_____ sports

_____ hobbies

_____ professional organizations

_____ union activities

_____ community organizations

_____ school committees

_____ fraternal organizations

_____ political organizations

_____ charitable organizations

_____ cultural activities

Will these types of activity be of some meaning to your plans for the operation of a small business? Of course, and it's easy to see why. Real involvement in these nonwork activities necessitates a good deal of commitment, discipline, and follow-through. Often there's plenty of interaction with others, negotiations, and planning ahead. Add motivation and enthusiasm, and you've run through a list of attributes necessary to be an entrepreneur.

A neighbor of mine in air conditioning repairs and maintenance is a perfect showcase of capabilities that were developed by involvement with a fraternal organization. He ran the gamut from raw recruit to grand master, from committee participant to head organizer, and all that went on in between. He has been responsible for arranging dances and picnics, including the entertainment, supplies, promotion, contracts, and financing. He had also attended and spoken at regional meetings and participated in national programs. As a result, he has had a very thorough indoctrination in many diverse areas that were completely different from his normal work environment.

You can gain such diverse experience in all types of nonwork activities. Of course, if you just play golf, for example, your involvement will only relate to a few business-related factors. But if you were responsible for the club's golf tournament, then many other abilities would come into play.

Hobbies often require buying and selling, negotiations, attending shows and seminars, and intense study of relevant information. Political activity and school committees can attune you to compromise, character evaluation, and public speaking.

Don't just check off the activities on the list. Instead, extract those facets of the involvements that will prove useful to your business start-up.

There's an additional bonus to this review of hobbies and other activities. It's a great reminder to explore and consider whether one of these activities might be the basis of a new business opportunity, one you hadn't thought of before.

Potentially, there may be a big plus to getting involved with something you presently enjoy and already have some knowledge and hands-on experience with. There have been many instances of individuals who have derived great satisfaction from their volunteer efforts and later decided to continue them full-time and professionally.

Some instances of businesses that may be formed this way are promotion and public relations, newsletters, catering, fund raising, preschool care, personnel services supplying nursing care and companions, and planning and running events for various organizations.

Businesses can also grow out of the sports and hobby fields. Examples include sole proprietorships and companies that relate to sports supplies, charter boating and fishing trips, tennis and golf clinics, miniature golf, and instruction books, records, and cassette tapes.

We are all aware of those who have gone from dedicated hobbyist to professional. Most antique shops, for example, started from a genuine love of that fascinating field. Hobbyists may become producers of hobby conventions, proprietors of comic book stores, swap meet organizers, or philatelist dealers. Or their businesses may involve classic car parts catalogs, mail order of unusual tools, retail coin and stamp operations, magic shops, and so on.

If you use your thinking cap and survey the nonwork activities on your résumé, you may discover a whole new world of business opportunities. At the very least, you can compare their potential with any other ventures you are now contemplating.

Usually the normal résumé includes a short reference to education, age, and health status. These items also have some application to entrepreneurship capabilities.

Although the degree of education can range from high school to graduate courses, it's what you've learned rather than how much time you've spent in classrooms that counts. Whether you are a dropout, or a Phi Beta Kappa does not necessarily relate to the degree of success in your own venture as it certainly does in a job situation, where hiring and promotion are definitely linked to your formal education.

In your own business, it's the courses in bookkeeping, shopwork, drafting, sales and marketing, science, typing, management, and so on that can add to your business-running capabilities. Today fluency in foreign languages is more meaningful in business than ever before. Depending on the type of operation you finally choose, it will be easy to identify the courses that will have applicability. Don't be bashful about taking some management courses now, while you're still tackling these preliminary steps.

Age and health must also be considered. For the young and healthy there may only be the problems of long hours, frustration, and stamina. But for older persons or persons with physical handicaps, the type of business being contemplated should reflect and avoid adverse inherent characteristics. Potential proprietors with weak feet shouldn't select ventures that require standing ten or twelve hours a day. If physical strength is in question, avoid operations that call for lifting heavy cartons or equipment.

Where physical handicaps exist, make sure that the positive powers are employed and the negative activities minimized. Of course, many of the areas in question can be overcome by the use of other personnel, under your supervision. This factor should be a part of your considerations.

Age is mental and emotional, not just physical. Judge yourself accordingly, for long hours don't only reflect physical fatigue. If kids irritate you, forget the ice cream store—no matter how profitable! If you find consumer complaints and servicing annoying, they shouldn't be the main factors in your business. On the other end, aggressive and/or always-late suppliers can send the blood pressure skyrocketing.

Don't forget to review all the aspects and quirks of age and general health—they are a definite part of your capabilities and will affect the progress of your business.

Perhaps this stage of evaluation with respect to starting a business from scratch has already helped you decide which category and type of venture appeals to you. Or maybe you are still trying to choose among two or three possibilities that seem to promising.

In all cases, however, take the time to check how your selections will satisfy the elements of your lifestyle and your capabilities. One more important detail: make sure you will enjoy the type of business you finally choose. That factor alone can greatly enhance your odds for success. A positive rating on all these aspects will definitely get you closer to the bull's-eye for selecting the best opportunity.

The next chapter or two will continue the evaluation of starting a new business by examining the other vital factors of type of organization, competition, marketing, capital, and business plans.

9

Going for the Bull's-eye— What Do You Need for Start-up?

GETTING STARTED

At this stage, you've been through a number of preliminary steps of starting from scratch:

- initial thoughts about your own venture
- appraisal of your personal characteristics
- review of categories of small businesses
- consideration of types within categories
- advantages of starting new
- disadvantages of starting new
- lifestyle needs
- résumé of capabilities and experience
- application of all the above to help select the best opportunity.

That's a fairly good starter list, but it's truly only the beginning. The process of transposing these preliminaries into a commercial reality means addressing a whole slew of additional real-life entrepreneurial factors. This is where you get involved in a completely new series of steps.

Now the specific business you're considering should be subjected to a much more relevant and in-depth analysis, one that requires the kind of information and research that will establish its practicability and on-going potential.

A BUSINESS PLAN

Do you need a business plan? The simple answer is yes. For bank loans, venture capitalists, SBA participations and independent investors, nothing can be done without a business plan. Their needs call for a comprehensive document that encompasses just about everything you can think of concerning the character, formation, purpose, and sales projections for the business, plus in-depth financial data and supporting documentation.

That's all well and good for their purposes, but at this point in time it's what *you* need that counts. Rather than an extensive structured business plan (examples run from two to ten pages), our interest should be targeted toward simply answering a number of questions that you should be researching at this stage and will have no trouble in handling *before* starting. If you do, then you're *not* ready to begin your venture!

What type business have you decided to start?

How much start-up capital will be required?

What is the form of business organization?

Who are your customers?

How big is your market?

Where is your market area?

Who are your competitors?

How strong is your competition?

Why are you better than the competition?

How will you sell your product/service?

How will you manufacture or buy?

Who are your suppliers?

Do you need personnel? What kind?

What kind and amount of space do you need?

Where will you locate and why?

Are licenses or permits required?

What kinds of insurance will you need?

Will your business be cash or credit?

Can you estimate sales/expenses for six months?

Is this a growth business?

Have you thought about initial promotion?

Within each of these questions, there are a half dozen or more other observations that have to be made. Although you won't have all the answers at your fingertips, that's what your ongoing research and this awareness book is all about.

Some information can be acquired by simply putting on your thinking cap and applying your common sense and past experiences. Most of the information, as indicated earlier, will be gleaned from other similar business owners, suppliers, competitors, specific trade associations, and the local business community. Add to those all the pertinent and applicable publications, and you have a wealth of source material.

If you answer all the questions with the knowledge gained from this applied research, then you have in effect established a business plan. Perhaps it is not the structured plan so often recommended, but it is a less intimidating plan that tells you whether *what* you intend to do and *how* you intend to do it, make sense.

With the help of an accountant, you may also be able to project sales, costs, and profits for one or two years. All this serves to accomplish a few other extremely important elements: it indicates the "go–no go" potential of your proposed venture and it improves the necessary management skills you will require.

WHAT ABOUT STARTING COSTS?

Whatever the type of business, the principle of figuring costs is not much different from working out your personal budgetary needs. What will you be doing? What will you need? How much will it cost?

In business start-ups, whether retail, service, manufacture, or wholesaling, there are always the expenditures of rent, equipment, supplies, inventory, salaries, insurance, and a half dozen more. Some of these are the initial one time, start-up costs; others are the ongoing expenditures of business operations.

It's not unusual to detail the costs for furniture and fixtures, for example, and completely forget the charge for installation.

If you never experienced the deposits necessary for public utilities, your estimating pencil will slip right by those charges. Maintenance and contingencies are another pair of business areas that shouldn't be over-looked.

In estimating owner salaries, will you be taking a regular weekly wage or do you intend to take a nominal salary plus additional sums from net profits during the year and at the end of the year? When a partnership I was involved with began operations, each of us put up starting capital and in addition deferred all salaries for the first three months. By year's end, we were able to pay the total deferral out of profits.

With a retail venture, fixtures, decorating, and starting inventory may be the costly highlights. In the manufacturing and service areas, the greater expenditures may be in the machinery, equipment, and wages categories. Delivery costs may relate to all of them—in some cases requiring the company's own delivery equipment, in others using an outside service.

As you can see, just getting through some of the basic fundamentals requires great attention to every relevant detail and a backup of fairly accurate information. There's much that can be easily overlooked. To avoid that you must research the correct sources and check everything that will pertain to helping you start and run your own business.

ESTIMATING STARTING COSTS

The Small Business Administration publishes many free and low-cost materials to help you estimate initial costs. Their free pamphlet, "Check-list for Going into Business" (Small Marketers Aid-SMA #71) lists many of the questions to be answered. It also has a worksheet to estimate starting costs, which will help ensure that you don't overlook some vital category. Although the emphasis is on retailing, the listings are applicable to most operations:

Monthly expenses

Owner-manager salary

All other salaries

Rent

Telephone and telegraph

Other utilities

Delivery expenses

Supplies

Legal and accounting

Taxes and Social Security

Insurance

Interest

Maintenance

Advertising

Miscellaneous

It is best to multiply the above monthly costs by three, six, or eight months, in order to have enough capital available to carry the business until it becomes self-supporting. The size of the multiple depends upon the type of operation and how long you think it will take to get it rolling along under its own steam.

Remember, you have no business until you have customers—people willing to pay for your products or services. And it often takes time to build a clientele.

Another factor that will influence capital requirements is the cash-flow character of the business. Will it be all cash, or mostly credit? Will charge accounts be a major part of the operation? If so, you will require more operating capital, more cash to keep going until your charge accounts pay for their purchases.

Starting costs you only have to pay once

Fixtures and equipment

Installation of fixtures and equipment

Decorating and remodeling

Starting inventory

Deposits with public utilities

Start-up legal and other professional fees

Licenses and permits

Truck or delivery vehicle

Advertising and promotion for opening

Accounts receivable (what you need to buy more stock until credit customers pay)

Cash (for unexpected expenses or losses, special purchases, and so on)

Other

Add the monthly expenses (multiplied three, six, or eight times) to the one-time starting costs and you will have a pretty good idea of how much money you will need to start your business.

It sounds simple, doesn't it? But at this point you may be asking:

"How much rent should I allow?"

"How do you figure advertising costs?"

"What's the best starting inventory?"

"What do I allow for equipment?"

"How can I predict delivery expenses?"

Admittedly, unless you have a very good background in the business you are starting, some of these answers will just be guesses. If you over- or under-guess too much it will certainly adversely affect your total of estimated costs. So the best course is to start at the beginning. Try to honestly determine, as accurately as possible, what your *total sales* might be for the first year.

If your own knowledge does not enable you to estimate this sales volume, then you will require some input from your industry's trade association, the wholesalers or suppliers, and perhaps your banker and other entrepreneurs in the same field.

OPERATING RATIOS

Once you have set a figure for that first year's sales volume, the next step is to obtain typical operating ratios for your specific type of business. They are usually denoted by percentages—the average ratio for each category of expense, multiplied by the anticipated sales volume.

Two booklets that are very valuable for understanding ratios are "Expenses in Retail Businesses," published by the NCR Corporation, and the "Barometer of Small Businesses," published by the Accounting Corporation of America. Various trade sources, such as industry magazines and their respective trade associations, are the usual basis for the ratios that are printed in these booklets.

That's just one example of the vital knowledge you may be able to obtain from trade associations. It's to your advantage to make maximum use of their research, knowledge, advice, and statistics when you are floundering around in the "I don't know" areas of starting a small business from scratch.

If, for example, you are starting a small hardware store, the average operating figures from the National Retail Hardware Association will offer some interesting guidelines. Based on the category of $100,000 to $200,000 in gross sales, let's extract those costs that might be useful in approximating the estimated *start-up costs* of your new venture:

Number of stores reporting	174
Net sales volume	$160,000
Net sales	100%
Cost of goods sold	64.04
Margin	34.96

Operating expenses

Salaries—owners, managers	7.67%
Salaries—other employees	8.78
Payroll taxes	.93
Group insurance	.41
Benefit plans	.16
Heat, power, light, water	1.26
Repairs to building	.34
Rent (or real estate taxes, insurance, mortgage interest)	2.86
Advertising	1.90
Depreciation (except real estate)	.85
Insurance (except real estate or group)	1.11
Taxes (except real estate or payroll)	.46
All other expenses	4.84

By multiplying the net sales volume ($160,000) by each percentage of expense, you can calculate the approximate dollar costs involved.

In the ratios listed above, rent or ownership expense averaged out to 2.86 percent of net sales, or $4,576 per year. Similarly, advertising, for this type of business, was noted as 1.90 percent of net sales, or $3,040 per year. Because these are composite averages, some stores will have reported much higher costs than others.

Although not perfect, this type of information from industry operating ratios can help guide you in what to allow for your start-up costs in rent, payroll, utilities, insurance, and so on. Your research in other areas will help to indicate the average costs for fixtures and equipment, starting inventory, professional fees, and so on.

Put all the information together and suddenly the estimated costs to start will take shape. You will now have a fairly good idea of your own venture's starting capital requirements, and it won't all based on pure and simple guesswork.

SCORE

If you've done your preliminary homework, the Service Corps of Retired Executives (SCORE) should be familiar. Basically, it's an organization sponsored by the SBA, and it offers free counseling service to those who are contemplating starting a small business.

This counseling is also available for small businesses that are having problems in any of the numerous management areas that can affect their survival and profitability. The counselor roster consists of highly skilled retired executives with expertise in the fields of retailing, manufacturing, and wholesale or service-oriented organizations.

Counseling is available on a long- or short-term basis and every effort is made to match their skills with your needs. If necessary, additional expertise will be obtained from ACE, the Active Corps of Executives, whose members are engaged in the everyday ongoing management problems of small business.

There are over three hundred SCORE/ACE offices throughout the fifty states. They are a great source for checking out your start-up plans and getting additional guidance in areas in which you lack previous experience. Check the phone book to see if an office is located in your vicinity and call for an appointment.

I dropped into the very active and helpful SCORE office recently for a follow-up on their upcoming *seminars* relating to taxes, record keeping, management problems, and finance. A great deal of informational material was available on their reception table.

One piece, in particular, related some preliminary points that would be useful to all, no matter what the type of business or its location. Let me extract some highlights:

1. Know the executive officer of your Chamber of Commerce. He or she has much small business knowledge and printed material about the area.

2. Know your banker, and be sure he or she knows you! The banker will know your area, the average income, competitive situation, real estate, and rental values. A local banker can and will be of great help—if you ask.

3. Visit your trade association offices and the manager. These organizations have a wealth of material you can study.

4. Visit your local library; the librarian will happily place in your hands most of the reading material you specifically need. Hours spent here can result in many dollars saved because you can

acquire adequate information upon which to base sound decisions.

5. Before your business can earn money, you will have to make an initial investment in start-up costs, and then continuing expenditures for operating the business.

6. Make a capital needs study and forecast, a profit forecast, and/or monthly cash flow estimate. Your accountant can assist you in the preparation of this study. In other words, know where you are going financially.

SCORE offers a good deal of excellent advice, so when you need sources of assistance, don't forget to visit the offices in your area.

FORMS OF BUSINESS ORGANIZATION

You have so many things to think about in starting a new venture that there's often a tendency to put this category on the back burner. Don't! In fact, it's an area that's right up there with all the other preliminary stages. It may even jump out into first place, especially if you have partners, or investors at the very outset.

There are three basic forms of organization that apply to all ventures whether you buy a business, start one from scratch, or join one of the many franchises. Each form of organization has its good and bad points, ranging from the simplest and cheapest to the most complicated and expensive. The form you choose will be a result of what you need and what you have to offer. This relates to your past experience and skills, your capital requirements, and your lifestyle.

Sole Proprietorships

Most small businesses start out as sole proprietorships and the great majority—about 70 percent—of all small ventures operate in this mode. Keep in mind that it's an initial choice. If business needs and conditions change, there's no problem in converting the organization to a partnership or corporation.

It's the easiest form of organization and the least expensive. A certificate of doing business or a fictitious name statement may be the only requirement to get started. This is usually filed with the county clerk's office, and its purpose is to indicate the true ownership of the business, for both your debtors and your creditors. The fee is nominal. Check whether your specific business requires any special permits or license.

Such a setup can be great for your ego. You will have complete control over the business. It will be a terrific success or a miserable failure—and it's all your doing! Usually, too, the starting capital is all your own money, or borrowed money. Organizing a business in this way may not only be a matter of pure ego, of course, but more the desire to meet the challenges on your own terms, to see if you can make a go of the business with your ideas, skills, enthusiasm, and confidence.

Federal taxes are simplified for a sole proprietorship. There are no extra IRS forms to fill out monthly; you just show the profits or losses from the business on your individual tax return, using Form 1040, Schedule C. Your Social Security contribution is covered by the payment of a self-employment tax.

Of course, there are a few disadvantages too. As a sole proprietor, you have total personal liability for any claims, debts, or lawsuits that may arise in the operation of your business. Additionally, if you, as the owner, are incapacitated or die, the venture must cease and all aspects of the business are terminated.

Partnerships

A partnership is a business marriage, but it need not be restricted to two people. Partnerships can and do involve two or more individuals contributing to the business.

As in marriage, there can be plenty of disagreements, both personally and professionally. Pulling together is the order of the day, and an insistence on doing things your own way may truly be the end-all, rather than the takeoff of the partnership. That's why it's imperative that a written agreement between partners be set up with an attorney.

It's advisable to spell out all the details—number of shares, remuneration, duties, responsibilities, capital investment, buy-sell terms, and termination procedures. Although such details are not required by law, it would be foolish for any of the partners to think they can operate the business without spelling everything out in a legal agreement.

There are two forms of partnerships, general and limited. In the general type, all partners are equally liable for any claims or debts relating to the business. This is an unlimited liability and involves each partner's personal assets. Any one partner can involve all the others in a responsibility for claims or contract terms. Usually, the general partners will share equally in both their contributions and distribution of profits and losses.

In the limited partnership, investors can become partners without incurring unlimited liability. They are usually responsible only for the amount of their original investment. Most of the time, the limited partners have contributed capital to the business but are not involved with the physical operation of the venture. To use this limited form, however, there must be at least one general partner, and this arrangement should be indicated by signing a contract agreement and by filing a special certificate.

IRS paperwork is a bit more complicated than for the sole proprietorship. The partnership must file a Form 1065 with the Internal Revenue Service, along with a Schedule K-1 that shows the shares given out. A copy of that Schedule K-1 is received and filed by each partner, and attached to his or her own Form 1040, where the partnership income or loss is added to other personal income.

Some definite advantages accrue to the partnership form of organization. Most partnerships are in the general format and usually start because of the need for a combination of skills or additional capital. They're not difficult to set up—usually that can be accomplished with the registration of an assumed-name certificate and any licenses or permits required by that type of business. Because of the legal costs of the agreement between partners—not required by law, but mandatory for avoiding many partnership disputes—the partnership form of organization is more expensive to initiate than a sole proprietorship.

The best advantage is the partners' mutual needs. After estimating start-up costs for your venture, you may find that the capital required is beyond your own resources or borrowing capacity. Similarly, research and review of your proposed venture may indicate management or skill areas where you cannot function well because of a lack of experience in one or more areas. Or suppose you incur a temporary disability and can't run the business for a while—that's where a partner can be a lifesaver.

Such considerations may indicate the necessity to join forces with one or more partners for your venture's success. Possibly hiring an employee who can provide the necessary skills may be one way to handle this area, but would it be more productive and meaningful to have a partner with this capability? That's the kind of thinking and evaluation that may result in the final choice for this form of business organization.

Corporations

Ah, this is the biggie, yes? Not necessarily. Small and even one-person firms have chosen this format as the best way to fit their needs. My own last corporation consisted of just one employee—me! True, I was the president, but I was also an employee. The more common setup involves a number of individuals with varied skills and/or capital.

A corporation is an artificial being with its own identity as a legal "person." The owners of this form of business become shareholders and employees of the corporation. It is the most expensive form to set up, requires the most paperwork, comes under the most regulations, and is most costly to run.

The record keeping is more extensive and there are more taxes to pay. As the sole employee of my corporation, for example, both the corporation and myself—employer and employee—each contributed to the Social Security tax. Additionally, there were federal and state unemployment taxes, workmen's compensation insurance, and double taxation on profits—taxes on corporate profits, then taxes again on dividends, *if any*. To keep up with all this reporting and regulations, there are continuing accounting costs, and sometimes additional legal expenses as well. Specific corporate returns are necessary for federal, state, and local taxes.

From the time of filing articles of incorporation with the state to the final dissolution of the business, there is more paperwork, regulations, and monies expended than with any of the other forms of business organization. At this writing, costs of forming the corporation range from $300 to $1,000, including legal counsel. Although it is possible to do it yourself, it would be most advisable to have an attorney initiate this complex form of organization.

Somewhere along the line, of course, there must be advantages. Yes, there are and, with professional guidance, you will have to determine whether they're worth it. For the large venture, the choice may be obvious. But at this stage, it's the beginner owner-manager with the start-from-scratch operation that's on the drawing board. That, and the nature of your venture, are the ingredients that should be considered in evaluating the tax and nontax advantages of the corporate form.

With the corporate form owners avoid the problem of unlimited liability in the other entities. Where special circumstances do indicate personal liability, it is limited to the amount of their original investment.

Shares can be sold to raise capital. This may involve a few investors or, if your plans are formulated toward a large operation, an extensive stock offering to the general public.

In the event of the death of one or more of its originators, the corporation continues because it is a legal entity unto itself. Transfer of ownership is also facilitated by simply selling the stock whenever you wish to call it quits or retire.

In the corporate form of organization, fringe benefits involving medical reimbursements, specific life insurance plans, profit-sharing programs, and other expenses are easily structured. Personal tax benefits may be possible depending upon salary/income distribution and the new tax bill limitations.

The Subchapter S corporation is a version that combines some of the advantages of a partnership and a corporation with relation to the tax situation. Legally it is a corporation, but corporate tax forms need not be filed. Instead, a Subchapter S corporation files an information return and the owners pay the taxes as personal income, or deduct the losses accordingly. Other technical aspects are involved in this setup; an accountant and attorney can help clarify and advise you as to the advantages for your specific venture.

Choosing the One

Because it's important to start out with the best of everything on your side, don't slough off consulting the professionals when choosing the type of organization for your business. It's still your decision, but it's a better choice when you know all the ins and outs and can then match them up with your specific needs and objectives.

One retailer I interviewed rejected his attorney's sole proprietorship advice and insisted on the corporate form simply because it made him feel better, more secure. He wanted an absolute wall between his business and his personal holdings and family lifestyle. His venture was a modest one. The paperwork and regulations involved drove him up the wall many times, but he stuck to his guns about retaining the corporate organization.

Sole proprietorships may seem to be most appealing, and you are the boss. But don't have any accidents or become seriously ill so that you can't run the business. Don't think about the joys of a long vacation either, not when you and your skills are the heart of the business. If you do have employees, you will have to train one to take over for a while in an emergency—otherwise the whole business may go down the drain!

So, partnership sounds like the answer. Right? Not always—not if you've seen some of the hassles partnerships may get involved in. Too often, in checking on each other, partners' preliminary thoughts and investigations concern the experience, skills, and background each could bring to the partnership. That's vital, but you must also seriously consider a few other attributes, such as personalities, temperament, and the ability to get along with others.

Those are the areas that cause minor disagreements to fester until the simplest problem is magnified into an insurmountable obstacle serious enough to fatally damage the "marriage" and call back the attorney for implementation of the buy-sell clause in their partnership agreement. Nevertheless, this form of organization is a popular one because of the many advantages it offers.

Some experts think the pluses of a corporation are truly meaningful. Maybe so. But just because the corporate form allows you to sell stock to raise capital doesn't mean you'll get the money you need. The corporate papers are not what convince a banker, for example, to lend you money. To the bank, your venture is still a start-up situation, and it's still the riskiest gamble in the entire business world. Investors are not blinded by the "Inc." or "Corp." after the name. They want to know who you are, how much capital you're investing, and what kind of speculative odds they will be facing.

Nevertheless, there are some very strong advocates for a corporation structure. In their thinking, there is no choice at all—a corporation is simply the best way to keep your personal liability as low as possible. Also, double taxation is not that onerous, since the tax structures do favor a corporation in many ways.

Most from-scratch ventures take a few years before any meaningful returns show up. In the other organizational forms, those initial losses can be deducted on your personal income tax. Not so with corporations—that's why the Subchapter S version of the corporate form may make more sense to some new ventures.

As the venture progresses and changes do occur, your chosen organization form may be able to accommodate these growth aspects. If not, there is no great difficulty to restructuring the form. Many new entrepreneurs start out as sole proprietorships, and when positive expansion demands additional resources or capital, they move on toward partnerships or a corporation. Similarly, after much on-line experience, some of those who may have been involved with partners become convinced that being the sole boss is the only way to go.

Are you starting to get confused about which form to choose? Don't. The whole purpose of these pro and con, ping-and-pong routines, is to have you think out the options. Talk to the professionals, examine your objectives and the character of your proposed business, review your personal goals and feelings, then make the decision. Advantages, not emotions, should be the basis for your choice.

10

The Final Approach—
Understanding
the Marketplace

THE MARKETPLACE

Getting the answers to start-up costs and the type of business organization best suited for your needs are positive jumps over some pretty high hurdles. Of course, it's no surprise that there are a lot more hurdles to go—some even more important than the one you just sailed over.

For example, do you *really* know your market and what the customer's needs will be? Or is it your own unbridled enthusiasm that stamps the product or service you intend to offer as so superior that customers will surely beat a path to your door.

Is the market you intend to reach large enough to warrant the percentage of sales that will result in a potential of profitability? Will the location you choose be the best one to ensure reaching those who will want to make use of your product or services?

These are some of the additional hurdles you must surmount because they are what entrepreneurship is all about. Without customers who are willing to exchange their dollars for your offerings, there is no business. Identifying these facets of marketing are even more important for the start-up venture than for the franchise or buy-a-business situations. In the latter cases existing track records can be studied or the franchisor may already have completed a comprehensive market research report for the franchisee.

NOTHING STANDS STILL

Whether you manufacture, retail, or service, your enterprise should "Think customer." The customer's needs and satisfaction should be paramount in your planning.

Years ago, companies concentrated on production and more production. This emphasis coincided neatly with the population's increasing, almost insatiable, demand for the general necessities. Following that momentum, there developed the first flush for the acquisition of the initial luxuries. Today, of course, those luxuries have long since become everyday necessities, and time has surely marched on from there.

Now, one has but to look around and the changes are overwhelming. In the past few decades, the effects of change are startlingly evident in our technological achievements, lifestyles, environmental attitudes, social and moral standards, educational emphasis, and governmental awareness.

All this simply means that there has been a corresponding change in the customer's needs and wants. It's no wonder that more than half of the products manufactured today did not exist or were not in general distribution just ten years ago. And, if you were to add in the factor of fads, it's obvious that their shooting-star-longevity has been compressed into shorter and shorter life spans.

When we refer to customers, it does involve two categories. First, there's the retail consumer of the finished product or service. The second group relates to the users of the more industrial-oriented merchandise—wholesalers, hospitals, schools and institutions, government agencies, and the almost infinite variety of manufacturing, service, and financial companies.

WHO ARE THE CUSTOMERS?

It's crucial for the small business to know who its customers are and what their needs encompass. This is especially true if your venture is developing, manufacturing, distributing, or retailing a new product. As noted earlier, an entrepreneur's terrific enthusiasm can generate a full-steam-ahead thrust into a marketplace of no demand! The entrepreneur's attitude of product benefit simply did not match the potential customer's acceptance of same.

Some sort of market research should be conducted, not only when you are introducing a new product, but in every new business start-up. It is essential for success to know what customers you are trying to reach and what assurance you have that your product or service is on target. Unlike the corporate giant that can readily absorb a marketplace mistake, the small venture can collapse into oblivion because of the losses entailed.

Although most small ventures cannot afford a professional in-depth market research, there are steps that the individual entrepreneur can take. Personal interviews of customers in the specific marketplace are invaluable in determing needs. Mail and telephone surveys are also good tools. Some community colleges with computer courses have offered consumer/market surveys to small businesses in their own geographical areas. The costs are reasonable, and the question and answer surveys are undertaken by students in their business courses. An added benefit is that the survey questions and techniques will be much more professionally prepared than if the entrepreneur had to go it alone.

Observation can be another valuable ally. In the retail and service ventures, just watching customers and analyzing the strategies of your competitors can be a positive learning tool. Does your area have the type of customers you require for the luxuries or necessities your venture may supply or for the existing or newly developed products you intend to sell?

Is the population in the affluent, middle income, or low income range? Is the area densely populated or spread out? In town or suburban? Growth or static? Most important, from your own observations and varied surveys, are there sufficient numbers within that population group to provide your venture with enough customers? And, once again, will your products or services satisfy their needs?

Once your venture is in operation, internal records of sales and demand patterns are a good reflection of customer activity and their selectivity. Your own or your sales personnel's direct contact with these buyers can provide much information and, at the same time, keep you aware of any changes that may be starting to occur.

WHERE ARE THE CUSTOMERS?

Other than your own efforts to determine customer identity and needs, there are many publications that can provide useful information. The federal government is a major source, through the Department of Commerce, which collects population demographics and market data on almost every type of business; some of that material may be pertinent to your venture or geographical region.

If you as a beginner need a nudge to appreciate research data, the

Census of Population studies is a place to start. Within the various census series offered, you can get population statistics on age, sex, race, marital status, income groups, and relationship to head of household. This can apply to your venture's operational area because the demographics data covers all states, countries, urbanized areas, cities, and places of a thousand inhabitants or more.

Also available are data on the number of families and their composition, mother tongue, school enrollment, occupation groups, and other characteristics. These census studies are issued every ten years, the latest being 1980.

Additionally, every five years, the *Census of Business* is issued. It encompasses both the retail and wholesale trades. You can check out the number of establishments, sales volume, payroll, personnel, and so on in cities of 2,500 or more. Other useful publications and studies are offered by the Department of Commerce. Check to see if one of their field offices exists in your region, and visit their library for reference and research.

Trade associations, local banks, and newspapers are also likely sources. When I relocated to the Southwest, one bank's "newcomer kit" contained a wealth of information on the various communities within the overall region. The data included types of housing, populations, income ranges, local taxes, job scales, retailers, schools, and a good deal more. The material available from trade associations, specifically in your venture's domain, would be invaluable in relation to buyer profiles, sales ratios, and marketing data.

Don't neglect your public library and, if one exists in your community, the university library. Although all these sources are considered secondary information and their data are not necessarily pinpointed to your exact requirements, they should not be cast aside. Their main benefit lies in the general direction or conclusions they may highlight. Do they conform somewhat with your other efforts concerning customer identity? Can they reinforce the findings of your personal surveys? Do they indicate factors you had not previously considered?

If your venture is geared for sales to industry and institutions, the factor of customer identity and their needs still exists. Whether it's maintenance or office supplies, raw materials or subassemblies, some thorough one-on-one research can readily establish these requirements.

The purchasing agent, however, may not be the determining person in the sale. You will have to ferret out the decision maker for the purchase of your products or services from among the production managers, engineers, designers, office or marketing managers, finance staff, and so on. Customer identity, in these cases, may require cultivating both the purchasing agent and the departmental decider.

MARKETS AND MARKET POTENTIAL

After completing the initial research of identifying the end-users of your product or service, the next step relates to market identity or market segments.

With the consumer buyer, the demographics of age, sex, marital status, income level, schooling, region, and so on are determined. In the area of industrial purchases, the types of industry, their size, location, number, and so on are also researched. Grouping these potential customers into categories of commonalities, or homogenous units, where their characteristics are similiar, enables us to identify market segments.

There may be more than one market segment that your venture can handle. At this point you must analyze the capabilities of your own operation. Do you, for example, have the finances and distribution resources to service a multi-state segment, or should you operate only within your own regional area?

There's a great difference between selling and servicing small independent retailers versus doing business with the giant chains. What are the competitive problems? Within one segment, especially if very large, you may encounter stiff, aggressive competition from bigger companies. If so, that's an area to keep away from.

Identifying market segments is only one part of the game plan. It's equally important for the new, small business to correctly judge the market that can best be served with its limited resources. Search out your competitive advantages and know your venture's limitations. Then try to select a market niche that's big enough to support your own operation, but too small for some larger competitor.

From there, the next step takes us into researching market potential. Too many beginner entrepreneurs are so anxious to put their new venture into physical operation, that they just don't make time for evaluating this vital area. If they do probe a bit, it's only to confirm their own thinking.

However, there's more to market research than that. It's essential to look out toward the market and get to know the following:

- why customers buy this product or service
- customers' buying habits
- customers' frequency of purchase
- the size of the average order
- the growth potential of the market
- whether demand is constant or cyclical
- the character of competition—weak or strong?

We all know that the large corporations and well-funded new ventures conduct lots of market research, not always successfully (for example, the new formula for Coke). As a consumer, you may be completely aware of this constant testing, but sometimes it doesn't seem to penetrate that testing is also essential to your own beginning venture. You must take the time to develop marketing awareness!

Let's consider what happened to the so-called baby boomers. Throughout the early 1980s there were numerous articles about the demographic changes. Simply stated, the baby boomers grew up! And that meant lots of changes.

The jeans manufacturer who had diversified to designer labels has now added contemporary sportswear and a line of fuller-size models. Fast-food chains have gone past the teenage crowd satisfied with hamburgers only and now offer salad bars, breakfasts, croissants, and a new variety to appeal to a changing population.

When the baby boomers first entered the work force, their choice of vehicles skewed toward the no-frill, less expensive compact cars. But not for too long. Now it's sport cars, deluxe models, high-performance jobs, pickups, custom vans, and so on.

Beverages also reflected the same trend. Beer consumption in college was terrific, but as maturity set in the new boom relates to diet drinks, wines, liqueurs, and everything light—including beers and liquor mixes.

Other industries have already felt the tides of change. So have jobs, job competition, housing, corporate policies, fringe benefits, and marketing.

We've seen flex-time, day care facilities, double-up jobs, and more liberal maternity leaves—especially in the companies who were most aware of the overall new demographics. Those are the companies who also realized that these same changes would soon affect their own markets and marketing focus.

If you think all of this market-potential idea is miles away from your proposed small business, think again. It is vital for your venture's survival to become aware of and analyze your buyer's makeup—needs, habits, age, sex, affluence, likes and dislikes, and so on. Similarly, you must understand the characteristics of your market—static or growth, constant or cyclical, competitive or open, local or regional, ease of distribution, and so on.

Having a representative picture of these marketing data give you some solid basis for judging the acceptance of your product or service and the potential success of your business. It also enables you to judge when and if you should enhance your present offerings with one or more new products or services.

Numerous books on library and bookstore shelves concentrate on all phases of marketing and marketing management. This chapter is not intended as an in-depth report, its purpose is simply to make sure you don't slough off one of the most important aspects of entrepreneurship. As brought out by Dun & Bradstreet studies, "lack of knowledge about market" is one of the most contributory causes of small business failure.

As mentioned earlier, this is one area where your industry or trade association may be able to provide some meaningful data. Check it and the other sources before you make any total commitment.

MARKETING

Marketing involves a whole spectrum of factors to consider. A dozen or so years ago, when I attended a "how to" class in starting a small business, the professor lectured on the following thoughts, which I noted then and still remember:

Marketing is the direction that takes the product (goods or services) to the concept stage (idea), on through to production, and then to the ultimate user.

    (a) to satisfy the user's needs and/or desires
    (b) to satisfy the company's objectives—profit, growth, survival.

Marketing relates to all functions and activities necessary to get product or services from producer to user, i.e., the four P's—product, price, place, promotion.

Product
    (a) Do you manufacture?
    (b) Do you buy from a manufacturer?
    (c) Do you buy from a wholesaler/distributor?

Products or services can be new and innovative, refinements of existing ones, additives or improvements to present products, or duplicates offered at lower prices because of lower costs.

Price
    (a) What is your markup?
    (b) What is your discount?
    (c) How did you arrive at your price?

A number of factors affect pricing decisions—costs, demand, and competition. Too often, small firms simply add a percentage to their actual costs for a desired markup. Using only one of these factors is inadvisable, especially where the entrepreneur does not take all operating costs into consideration.

Place

    (a) Do you move product to a central plant?
    (b) Do you have it shipped direct to you?
    (c) Do you ship to other locations?

Getting the product or service to the ultimate user within the best distribution channel is vital. A manufacturer can use direct sales, mail order, wholesalers, or retailers. A retailer sells retail, but may also incorporate a mail-order operation for certain products.

Promotion

    (a) What are your marketing objectives?
    (b) What are your advertising objectives?
    (c) How many dollars are planned for advertising?
    (d) What media do you plan to use?
    (e) What plans do you have for public relations activities?

Don't expect your product or service to sell itself, no matter how great you think it is. If you want to market successfully, you must advertise, take advantage of sales promotion, and get involved in personal selling.

Most products are sold by these marketing strategies:

1. *Product differentiation*—"Buy me, I'm different." (The consumer must perceive the difference, real or imaginery!) Good examples are the "cheapest," the "best," or most "unique."

2. *Market segmentation*—Identification of a dissatisfied segment of the market and development of a product to satisfy it.

    (a) Identify consumers and measure them.
    (b) Accessibility—how to reach them with the product and advertising.
    (c) Market segment must be big enough to make a profit.

Are these thoughts outdated? Not on your life. They are part of marketing basics, and if you examine any new creative strategy in the marketing arena, the fit into some of these basics will still be there.

I recently read a comment from someone who has developed a unique product that is selling quite well to industry. If you build a better mousetrap, the world supposedly beats a path to your door. But he said, "It's *not* true. You have to advertise, and beat a path to the world's door. And then you have to beat on that door—you have to work hard to close a sale."

That's just another way of saying, once again, don't expect your product or service to sell itself. Be aware that there have been lots of accelerating social changes taking place during the past decade. Changes that have and will affect marketing strategies and practices.

Consumerism awareness has developed to the point where court actions and government pressures have resulted in costly exposés of defective products, deceptive claims, medical malpractice, and a host of other questionable products and services.

Concern about our environmental quality has been evidenced by many a placard in the picket lines, as well as by TV documentaries, editorials, and leaflets. We all pollute, so there's plenty of blame to circulate and numerous areas to control.

What does that have to do with your little venture? Perhaps nothing. But product quality, durability, and safety may certainly relate to your business—be it manufacturing, service, or retail. If so, then it will affect your marketing—what your sales pitch stresses and presents, and how well it does it.

Additionally, your awareness of these societal changes may lead to developing an approach that creates a competitive advantage. What about developing a product or service that is a direct offshoot of these contemporary concerns?

Remember organic foods, recycled paper, reclamation centers, aerobics, cast-iron stoves, emission controls, solar water heaters, jogging footwear, water purifiers, windmills, drip irrigation, and many, many others. All are a result of the vast new interest in health, environment, and pollution.

Translating these concerns into new opportunities is entrepreneurship at its best. Marketing should follow along the same pathways, stressing consumer welfare considerations and societal interests. The small company has a lot going for it here. Cut out all the razzmatazz and point up honest benefits, dedicated service, and a true concern for your customer's needs. You'll be the winner, for there are many who are looking for just that kind of working-together relationship. Make it a plus for your venture.

ADVERTISING

All those dozens of books you can relate to for marketing will also cover advertising. Many a new entrepreneur has been thrown for a fall by a complete lack of knowledge or experience with advertising. It's a complex category, and the variety of tools available doesn't make it any easier for the beginner owner-manager.

By getting down to basics again, we can choose to go for an overview of advertising rather than a comprehensive study. This will help you achieve the initial understanding and awareness that your preplanning requires. The active operation of your venture will be the means of targeting what type of promotion can best serve your company's requirements.

The purpose of advertising is:

- to inform
- to remind
- to persuade.

Where and how you advertise relates to:

- knowing your customers
- knowing how you can reach them
- knowing how and why they buy.

Once you know your market you will also become aware of the various channels of advertising that can reach potential customers. As a consumer, you know many of them—newspapers, TV, direct mail, magazines, Penny Savers, posters, Yellow Pages, catalogs, leaflets, and so on.

The key here is twofold. Whatever medium you use must reach the greatest number of customers that make up your market. If more than one medium can accomplish this, the question of cost may be the decisive factor. TV, as one example, may be excessive in cost even within a small, regional area.

One entrepreneur servicing many of my neighbors in patio furniture rewebbing, reached each of them through the local Penny Saver. Many retail stores in my city find both newspaper and TV to be their best mediums. Service organizations invariably have listings and ads in the Yellow Pages and use direct mail effectively.

Each venture has its own needs. Expenditures for multiple mediums are not unusual. Many small firms find it very difficult to deal with advertising, and perhaps they should work with a small ad agency that can supply the needed expertise. Don't shy away from an exploratory discussion with an ad agency. If you can't afford such help initially, then your own on-the-job training, coupled with a definite concept of who your customers are and what you want to say to them, will have to do.

Even if you are going it alone you can get lots of help from the media you decide to use for advertising. Newspapers, radio, TV, and the Yellow Pages may have their respective departments assist you in writing ads, making a layout, suggesting a creative approach, or refining your copy. Print shops can offer many suggestions, especially if they specialize in direct mail servicing. Reproductions, multi-color emphasis, most economical layouts, insertions, and postal regulations, are just some of the areas about which they can supply information for your evaluation.

If you're buying from a manufacturer or distributor, check if they can provide marketing and advertising aids. For little or no charge, they may supply mats for ads, literature for direct mail, posters, and so on. They may also have a cooperative advertising arrangement, where the cost of the ad is shared and both your business name and their name are featured.

Establish your advertising goals. There are many and each venture will have differences it wishes to stress. Some typical examples include:

- the initial kickoff announcement
- promotion of a special event or sale
- increasing public awareness of your name and location
- bringing more traffic into your premises
- offering special services, such as delivery, credit, and layaway
- coupon, rebate, or tie-in offer
- announcing expansion of premises or addition of new personnel
- seasonal reminder for product or sale
- addition of new product line and demonstration offer
- promoting your image as the authority in the field
- keeping your name in front of the public.

All the above doesn't mean just winging it. Do a little homework: check your competition, try what you think will work best, analyze the results, make adjustments, and go on from there. Read up on the subject beforehand; the library is always waiting for you. You'll find ample information on the whys and wherefores of advertising, as well as budgeting methods and media selection. If possible, take a short introductory course or a seminar offered by the local office of the Small Business Administration.

PROMOTION

Promotion, of course, goes hand in hand with advertising. Here again, you know more about promotion than you think, especially as one who has been on the receiving end. In the supermarkets, the demonstrators have given you food samples. At franchise outlets, the promotional drinking glasses have been a big thing. A variety of sellers have bombarded you with games and discount cards.

Trade promotions and exhibit booths at fairs and functions are no strangers to you. "Buy one and get another at half price" or "Special sale price plus rebate from the manufacturer," are forms of promotion. Contests of every kind are another.

You, as a small entrepreneur, can easily get involved with promotional materials or events for your grand opening. Lucky coupons, live music, free balloons, sponsorship of a local happening, giant searchlights, free demonstrations, newspaper publicity, and sample giveaways for all who drop in are some possibilities for a business kickoff.

Advertising, promotion, and the other aspects of marketing are really all aimed at one simple goal—to create customers.

Even though you're just starting out and are basically a small venture, you can still be creative. Something about your product or service is different—dramatize it! Use showmanship to create and highlight that difference. Create a promotional tie-in.

Perhaps you should concentrate on attitude or image. Small companies have an excellent opportunity to personalize their approach and service for the customer. Many a consumer or industrial buyer places great value on individualized attention, problem solving, follow-through, and gratifying follow-up interest that only a small venture can offer.

There's the other kind of promotional image, too—*within* your regular advertising channels. A supermarket in town, in addition to normal sales, runs a special half-price sale on one well-known brand item. It's only one day every two or three months, but each time there's a stampede, the shopping carts are filled with that sale item, plus many others.

One furniture company runs a special offering every quarter on a specific category—recliners, lamps, couches, bedding, and so on. Instead of the same old across-the-board sale, such sales have a constant freshness, and people perceive these specials as really good bargains. Stores that have the usual "gigantic clearance sale" use less imagery.

A car dealer alternates sales ads with service ads. He recognizes the buyer fear of buying a car and then getting hooked for poor service. Full ads and TV spots that only relate to service has this dealer standing out among his numerous competitors, and creating future customers!

Truly Nolen, an exterminator, has a whole fleet of yellow Volkswagen Bugs festooned with two big ears on top, a black nose and whiskers in the front, and a black tail wagging at the rear. It only takes a few sightings of these cuties to imprint the message in your memory. When you pass the main office and see the whole fleet parked there, that's impact!

There's nothing superspecial about these examples, but they do work. As these examples indicate, you can use any medium. With the supermarket, it was newspapers. The furniture company and car dealer used both TV and the papers. Nolen used his own tools of the trade—vehicles that were a part of the job.

Here's another example of a promotion opportunity. The first time I went into a small local deli, I paid the bill with a personal check. A few months later, for the holidays, I received a Christmas card thanking me for my patronage and wishing me well. The proprietor simply made it a point to copy my address from the check when it was first presented.

Promotional ideas are endless, some almost insignificantly modest while others are outlandishly expensive. When targeted correctly, they produce results.

The town businesses, during various holidays, donate window space for children to waterpaint their own scenes of celebration. Everyone flocks to review all the windows and attend the award ceremony for the three best. The children sign each window and are responsible for removing all traces of the paint after the holiday.

One store displays the art of high school students; another sets an invitational day for display and modeling of student clothes designs. A locksmith service sets up demonstrations of various security devices during the community's charitable flea markets. Another supplies the imprinted T-shirts for the junior bowling teams.

Just as the telephone company representative shows a promotional film to the Chamber of Commerce, you can offer to lecture on your specialty to the various community organizations—whether its photography, flowers, beauty care, weight loss, natural foods, fashion, vitamins, or whatever.

Promotional prospects are all around you, and they can involve you and your sales personnel, your products or services, your location, your image, and, yes, even your pricing strategies. So use your brain cells and see what you can come up with. By all means, don't be bashful about being different. Differences stand out and command attention.

WHAT ABOUT RESULTS?

When you have identified markets and market segments, developed a marketing strategy, and taken the plunge into advertising and promotion, you must take an additional step that's essential for your success—evaluation. Did everything work? Did *anything* work?

At this point you will want to know if your strategies hit the targets and accomplished your objectives. You must analyze the results of your advertising and promotion. One of the many early books put out by the Small Business Administration includes a results-oriented listing of objectives that still has plenty of validity.

If you are a retailer, you can expect advertising/promotion to accomplish one or more of the following goals:

- bring people to the store to see what you have in the way of regular merchandise; for some of the people, it will be their first time
- attract buyers, some of them regular customers, others new, to examine what you are offering as a special
- bring in orders by phone or mail
- bring requests for estimates and for salesmen to call
- remind people of the satisfaction they have had from trading with you in the past and your hope that they will continue in the future.

If your venture is in the service area, your advertising/promotion should accomplish these goals:

- persuade people who are new in the community or dissatisfied with their present service to try your service
- keep the public informed about what you can do and what you have available
- convince people to call you in case of an emergency, rather than someone else
- bring in requests for estimates or additional information.

If you are a manufacturer or wholesaler you will want your advertising/promotion to bring about the following results:

- uncover prospects unknown to you and your sales personnel
- bring inquiries for salesmen to follow up
- get hearings for salesmen when they call uninvited because your company's name may already be recognized by the prospect
- keep customers and prospects reminded of your products between salesmen's calls
- reach unidentified persons who influence buying.

In all cases, of course, your efforts will always relate to your company's identity—where it is, what it does, what it has available, why it has special capabilities, and so on.

Additionally, your advertising and promotion will be putting forth an image for your business. As a retailer, you can make your store known for quality and service, price promotions, or the extent of your inventory. If you are in a service business, your image may reflect dependability, knowledge of the latest techniques, versatility, and dedication. As a manufacturer, your efforts can build an impression of reliability, progressiveness, and capability for problem solving.

Feedback is essential in knowing whether your objectives were achieved. Check your original plans to see if profit potential, market penetration, and customer awareness were accomplished. If not, go back to the drawing board with some new plans.

This entire chapter on customers, markets, and advertising/promotion is certainly not restricted to new start-ups. It applies equally well to a purchased business or a franchised venture. The latter two, of course, have some of these factors built into their operations, but the lessons and goals in this chapter apply in every small business. Don't neglect them!

11

Your Professional "Partners"

THE PROFESSIONALS

As noted earlier, assistance from professional sources is not only important, it is essential. The SBA, SCORE, trade associations, industry magazines, business courses, and libraries are some such sources. More visible and more familiar to you are the ongoing professionals—the ones who often become your "operational partners."

No strangers to small business owners, the accountants, lawyers, insurance brokers, and bankers will also, at one time or another, enter your own entrepreneurial sphere of operation.

Your enthusiasm and self-confidence may create the belief that you will be able to handle the start-up phase alone. After all, that's one of the main reasons for going into business—doing things your way. A second consideration may be costs, the desire to tighten up on those initial expenses and do as much as possible yourself.

But today's business problems are a great deal more complex than yesteryear's. The need for specialists and their consultations are a fact of business life. The more successful your venture becomes, the more professional advice you will require, especially if you make that wonderful crossover from small business to big business.

Let's get back to start-ups, however, and review how these specialists can offer valuable assistance to a new entrepreneur. Some of you will hang on to their every word, while others will factor that advice into your own thinking and act accordingly. Obviously, your reaction to professional advice will depend on the degree of knowledge and past business experience you possess.

ACCOUNTANTS

Any business, whether small or substantial, should have proper books and records to start off with. Recordkeeping is mandatory . . . *the IRS requires it and so does the owner/manager, if he or she wishes to know there the business is going.*

Proper accounting is one slice of the pie that will keep you moving in the right direction. An accountant can set up a simplified initial bookkeeping system that will make it easy for the owner to keep accurate daily records. As the days, weeks, and months go rolling by, those entries will keep you aware of where you're going and what shape the business is in. These same records will help greatly when tax time rolls around, even to the extent of a more reasonable fee to the accountant for the final tax returns.

If start-up levels are very small and costs are a problem, keep in mind that a neat and accurate checkbook is the simplest bookkeeping system available. An alternate suggestion is one of the account books that are available in your stationery store. Both methods, if used correctly, can help cut down the costly time-consuming labor involved when you do have to call in professional assistance.

Beginners are often deficient in management experience, and it may be cheaper to consult the specialist before the business is started. Accountants, especially CPAs, have the advantage of being involved with many small businesses. Because they've worked hand in hand with owners on diverse problems, they've had to deal with and resolve many of the basic principles that apply to *all* ventures. That kind of input, when offered to the beginner entrepreneur, can be invaluable.

Tax consequences for each of the various forms of business organization can be reviewed with the accountant in order to structure what may be best for your operation. Clarification and advice will be given in the areas of sales tax, resale certificate, employer identification number, unemployment tax, property and franchise tax, federal and state withholding forms, and so on. Some of these areas are simple, some are complex.

In the short range, the accountant can also help determine cash requirements, cash flow progression, and what the cash and return expectations would be after the first year. This will be a necessity where a business plan is required for loans or capital investment.

A number of accountants, in discussing start-ups, have mentioned they do not charge a fee for an initial, exploratory consultation. When the business does get started, there will be fees, but every effort is made to minimize these fees until the owner develops the business and the profitability. Fees are normally quoted on daily and monthly rates, depending on the complexity of the service. They should always be negotiated in advance.

In the long run, the accountant becomes a necessity. Analysis of records and financial statements can lead to business planning with an eye toward increasing future profits, tax minimization, estate planning, acquisitions, and so on. It also means advising management of problems that lie ahead if certain steps are not taken. Although much of an accountant's work involves after-the-fact statistics and situations, such analysis can result in concrete suggestions for near-term decisions that will affect survival and future growth.

Where do you go to get an accountant who will be interested in working with a small venture? One of the better sources would be your banker. He or she often works with accountants who represent small businesses, especially when loans or collateral for loans are under discussion.

Your lawyer, other business owners, your friends, the prospective landlord for your business premises—all are potential sources for locating practicing accountants already involved with small enterprises. Check several of them—their backgrounds, their accounts, what their fees will include. What is your gut reaction as to compatibility? Will it be easy to relate to each other?

As the business grows, there will be changes in the accounting services you require and fees may have to be adjusted. By that time your enterprise may be utilizing a full-time bookkeeper and your accountant's emphasis will be directed more toward taxes, pension fund, new government regulations, and financial planning for future growth.

LAWYERS

At best, consulting an attorney will force you to think more clearly about the enterprise you are about to undertake . . . simply because of the questions the attorney will ask. That may be the most important thing that can happen, especially when the decision to go ahead is made and the inevitable legal matters start to pop up.

Legal advice is another important slice of the pie, one that can sharpen your awareness of potential problems. Starting a partnership, for example, involves a simple admonition—*don't*, without an attorney. No matter the understandings you think you have with the proposed partner or partners, there are many issues that require a literal spelling out. Agreement beforehand is a must.

Who signs checks? What are the salaries or draws involved and the spheres of responsibility? How are disputes resolved? What about insurance, buy-out, book value determination, long-term illness? If one partner wants to withdraw or dies, how are payments to be made without bankrupting the company? Are there limited partners to be considered?

Depending on the participants, there may be many other additional items that could cause dissension, and they should be included in the partnership agreement. The attorney in many cases helps resolve some of the personality problems via impartial recommendations based upon accepted norms and previous contract experiences.

Incorporation agreements also require legal advice and implementation. Is it too early for that business form? Do the potential liability factors mandate incorporation? Are the costs of incorporation clear, the necessary paperwork and regulations understood?

Although personal liability is reduced when the corporate form is used, there are situations where this is not so and your attorney can advise accordingly. Specifically, in a start-up situation, the landlord of your leased premises will require both a personal and corporate signature, and that does involve you in personal liability.

When it comes to leases, it may be very advisable to have an attorney negotiate the lease, or at the very least review it before you sign. Many leases have restrictions that can affect your future operations. Can you assign the lease, sublet the premises, or have an option to renew? What about a "porterhouse formula," where you have to pay for any increases to labor, fuel, and services? Is there a tax-escalation clause? Shopping mall leases are another barrel of headaches—Does the lease call for minimum rent, or percentage of sales? How are sales checked? Are there any restrictions on competition?

Being aware of these legal elements is only half the battle. How do you hold your own in trying to negotiate? Since it's a new start-up, *can* you negotiate at all?

As one attorney said, "Securing legal advice at the beginning should be viewed as a cost of doing business and, hopefully, it will be a prudent investment that will save money in the future."

After start-up, of course, there will be many occasions where an attorney will function for the business in drawing up or checking contracts, reviewing labor laws and employment practices, validating consignment arrangements, and consulting with the entrepreneur whenever there may be questions about legal rights and obligations.

The process of locating an attorney follows along the same path as that of finding an accountant—check with your banker, friends, other business owners, trade associations, and especially with your accountant. Often a local bar association offers a referral service for an initial short consultation. Here again, compatability is an important factor. You may actually have to "audition" an attorney you will feel comfortable with and have confidence in.

Fees are another area that should be discussed beforehand, because there are a variety of arrangements that can be made. After you have that arrangement, don't hesitate to get legal advice *before*, not after, you make various decisions. Once you get into trouble, it's more costly to get out.

INSURANCE BROKERS/AGENTS

The very fact that all *businesses require some sort of insurance and protection is the very reason that a potential entrepreneur should consult an insurance agent or broker* before *the business starts up.*

This slice of the pie does affect every venture, but it is often treated a bit too lightly by the new entrepreneur. It's true that beliefs like "There's never too much insurance" or "There's no such thing as enough liability insurance" can really intimidate the beginner who sees a whole flock of dollar signs dangling around those words.

But take heart. If you are serious about starting, most insurance agents or brokers are willing, to spend some time in discussing your venture's probable needs without charging a fee. They want you to be aware of the protection that is necessary and what types of coverage are available. Without question, affordable costs may be the determining factor in what you finally select, but at least you'll know what the total score should be.

In a start-up situation, whether retail, service, manufacturing, or wholesale, these are some of the areas that may apply:

- workmen's compensation
- disability
- liability
- property
- business interruption
- all-risk (fire, theft, explosion, and so on.)
- product liability
- partnership buy-out
- group life, medical
- car nonownership.

There are tremendous variations in these areas with respect to the type and character of the venture. A retail shop, for example, will require plate-glass insurance, while a manufacturer may need boiler or machinery coverage.

Most new entrepreneurs, when leaving their previous job, have had to give up their company-sponsored group insurance for medical and life protection. Is it wise to forego this expense for a while until they get the new venture on its feet?

If you were manufacturing a small toy or packaging a household cleaner, would you think of product liability insurance? Your agent would, and he or she would also tell you that rates have sky-rocketed in recent years. Will that affect your business plan projections?

Initially, most beginners use their personal car for business and sometimes allow their employees to do the same. Protection through an employer's nonownership liability endorsement may help you avoid problems.

There are about ninety classifications of insurance coverage, covering everything you can think of. Most, fortunately, don't apply to small business ventures. Your broker or agent can tailor a package to fit your immediate needs and budget, and then give you a total proposal that can be implemented as you go along.

The main point of consulting beforehand is to determine what forms of coverage are applicable to your particular business and what is affordable as you start the venture. Make sure you get a written proposal with type of coverage, amounts, and costs for each type. Once your basic program is put into operation, riders or temporary increases can be obtained at a prorated basis of the annual rate. This is extremely important when changes occur that are temporary, such as a huge increase in inventory, renovations that may possibly create a greater liability potential for customers, initiating service at customer's home or industry premises, and so on.

When the business is established and employees are hired, many other situations will arise that require additional or new forms of coverage, such as fidelity bonds, pension plans, mortgage or loan insurance, transportation policy for shipment of goods, and auto/truck insurance for company owned vehicles.

Start your venture by consulting with an experienced professional in insurance. A broker is an independent who is dealing with several insurance companies. An agent is a direct writer who is writing policies for one company. Compare the coverage and costs of the insurance they offer and select the program that's best for your venture.

Recommendations from your accountant, banker, other business owners, and friends are a good guide to the insurance professional that is best for you. The Yellow Pages will also have a total listing of brokers and agents in your area.

BANKERS

Start-up loans are probably the highest-risk loans to make. We are not investors . . . we are creditors. We are not in for the risk-return, we are in for getting our money repaid at a reasonable rate of interest-return. With that in mind, it isn't difficult to understand why new business start-up loans are almost impossible to grant.

That's pretty blunt and maybe you're wondering whether this slice of the pie is necessary to chew on at all. The answer is a definite yes, both for the present and most especially for the future.

If you've done your research and planning, it is advisable to develop a relationship with a commercial banker to discuss financing and other business matters. A banker may not have much time to spare, so don't simply treat a meeting as a free advice session. Know the areas or specifics that you want to discuss. Pick a bank that is convenient to your proposed place of business, but make sure that it does relate to and is interested in small business.

Some of the larger banks have published pamphlets and brochures targeted toward the smaller companies. Those that encourage SBA loans are also very involved with the needs of entrepreneurs. Heed the advice that says pick a banker, not a bank. Whether the banker is a young eager beaver or an old pro, the true test is whether he or she appears willing to help by being interested in you and your new venture.

A banker is very knowledgeable about the business community in the bank's area and can often give you some guidance with relation to general business health, upcoming changes if any, demographics, and so on. If he or she is really involved in small business, there's much that can be discussed with the problems of undercapitalization, cash reserves, too much inventory and its attendant dangers, and key ratios that may apply to *your* proposed venture.

Other banking areas that will be meaningful to you include setting up a separate checking account for business, requirements for establishing a credit line, kinds of collateral for short-term loans, how personal loans are structured, interest rates for passbook-savings loans, and, finally, how the bank can help with information relative to your specialization.

There are exceptions when discussing a probable start-up loan. If the applicant is putting up 50 percent of the capital requirements, has a good personal credit rating, has had managerial experience in the field of the proposed venture and can present a well-defined business plan, full consideration will be granted to approving that loan.

Most applicants, unfortunately, don't do their homework, and their proposed plans are often farfetched or too risky for the bank or the SBA-guaranteed loan.

Nevertheless, good continuing banker relationship is vital to the future growth of your business. It's a rare enterprise that can keep rolling along without some financial input from the bank. There are short-term loans for working capital, intermediate-term loans for one- to five-year periods, and long-term loans for real estate. Somewhere along the line your business will require one or more of these accommodations.

Although commercial banks don't get involved with equity financing—investing for a piece of the action—they have developed subsidiaries that do (SBICs), or they may act as brokers in getting you together with a venture capital situation.

Staying in touch with your banker, keeping the banker appraised of your company's activities and any major changes that may occur, is good business. At the same time, it reflects good managerial judgment. Bankers are also an invaluable source for recommendations of other professionals—accountants, lawyers, consultants, investors, and local businessmen's groups. This factor can work for you when you are just starting out, and it's still viable after you are firmly established.

Choosing a bank and banker involves the bank's convenience of location and its decided interest in small business. Can it supply all the entrepreneurial services at reasonably competitive rates? Is the banker willing to talk over your plans, without rushing you out, and does he or she seem to take a real interest in establishing an ongoing relationship? Are you comfortable in this interaction?

Basically, shop around before you make the decision. However, don't neglect initial suggestions from your professional sources and other business owners. It's not unusual for your accountant to have a strong rapport with and good entree to one of the commercial bankers. This can often open doors for more meaningful assistance.

OTHERS

A number of other professionals normally aren't considered in the great majority of initial startup plans. But they do exist and some can function at this stage of the game.

Consultants are the specialized pros who function in many of the diverse management areas so necessary for a successful takeoff and future growth. Many focus their efforts in one category, while others relate to overlapping and allied areas, both consultation and implementation. Some of the categories are:

- research/product determination
- production/productivity
- distribution/marketing
- financial/cost control
- sales/marketing
- promotion/public relations
- advertising
- administration
- labor relations
- mergers and acquisitions
- underwriters.

Within the list there are other splinter areas even more narrowly defined. It's no doubt true that very few new entrepreneurs coming on board would even think about these consultants. However, if the consultants are specialists in small business, they can be exceedingly helpful in the many areas that the business newcomer will only learn about from on-the-job actualities. Determining product and market acceptance, correct pricing, effective advertising, acceptable inventory needs, multi-year cash flows, and so on can point the way to a successful operation.

Where no experience and no confidence in initial research exists, this type of consultation can get the beginner off to a good start on opening day. As growth continues, many operational areas will require this external consultancy. Numerous established business managers have agreed that a greater advantage accrues from the use of outside specialists than from the use of their own internal specialists.

Since awareness is such an important aspect of running a small business, keep in mind that these other professionals are available, and perhaps the idea of their services isn't so far out as one might think. Many a floundering venture can be saved if the negative factors can be isolated and treated in time.

One caution, however. Beware of the hangers-ons who strive to stretch out the period of consultation almost endlessly. If you decide to use a consultant, check out the reputation beforehand and, if possible, contact previous clients.

12

How Are Others Doing?

THE START-A-BUSINESS ENTREPRENEURS

Starting a business from scratch creates the greatest percentage of failures in the small business arena. Aside from all the contributory factors described in the previous chapters, common sense alone would lead you to the conclusion that such ventures face enormous difficulties.

Because it's a riskier start-up procedure, the most interesting facet of any exploration into this field lies in talking with the owner-managers of small businesses. More often than not, most of the positive or negative thoughts they express come directly from their own hands-on experiences. You may be able to read the same ideas, or listen to a lecture about them, but it simply doesn't make the same impression as when they tell you about it in their own words.

Let's see what the owners who started from ground zero have to say about their start-ups. Were they well thought out or spur of the moment? Were they flashes of new ideas or just a continuation of what the new entrepreneurs were already doing?

You may find some parallels to your own thinking. Some of their thoughts may reinforce the feeling you already have that says if and when the opportunity rises, don't wait, take it!

Keep in mind that these are not in-depth case histories with all the facts and figures that go along with such examples. The main thrust of these mini-interviews is to give you some idea of the initial thinking, the how and why of the decision to go ahead. Perhaps the observations may help you target your initiatives in determining your own best entry into entrepreneurship.

Beverly Hills Juice Club is in a storefront on a secondary street. You enter into a small anteroom, with a counter, and ring for someone to come through a large refrigerator door and take your order. The business is both retail and wholesale, with retail predominant.

Dave Otto: This is my first business venture; previously I was into music. I was looking around for something to do and I was into good health pretty much, making juices at home. I wasn't doing it for a business, just doing it for friends, people coming by; it was just a social thing. So it seemed like a good idea, maybe, and I looked around for a store. I found one that was ideally set up for a wholesale operation, even though it was a storefront. I just closed it off and started a wholesale business there.

I only sold to one store, a huge health food store over here in the Design Center—a great store. I did their juices for about three years. Then I was known as Dave, the Juice Man. How I got the present name was interesting, although some still keep the old name going—that's how I became well known.

I was located between two parts of the Beverly Hills Health Club—BH Health Club for Men and BH Health Club for Women. They were down the street, I was on the other side in the middle, and somebody one day, said "Why don't you call it the Beverly Hills Juice Club?" It was a real catchy name, it worked. Because on the logo right here, anyplace you go if you wear this logo, you will always provoke some kind of comment. Juice Club? Beverly Hills? First of all the word "club" makes it very secretive, private, you know, club is a mystery. What kind of club? And *juice* club—I mean who ever heard of that?

Then, to have Beverly Hills attached to the front of it, that gives it something extra. Most people upon hearing the name will connect it with alcohol, some type of alcohol, and then I get some interesting phone calls. I have to tell them it's health—a juice club, you know.

I think of myself as a food processor, more so than a manufacturer. With this store I'm more into retail, although a third of the business is still wholesale. My own personal approach is very strongly to good nutrition and diet. My business is an extension of my personal feelings. I don't make everything, but as much as I can. Today's listing of juices shows watermelon, cucumber, carrot, celery, mixed greens, beet, gazpacho, orange, apple, cinnamon, coconut, tangerine, wheatgrass, and some combinations of those.

My customers, I think, have a higher health conciousness than most people. There are some, however, who are just into taste, certain tastes that please them. We also have some who are cancer patients—patients who know nothing about health, other than the fact that a doctor told them about wheatgrass juice or carrot juice, both of which are good for cancer. So we get older people and a young group, mostly between twenty-four and forty.

Our operation has five people. It's small. It's run more like a mom-and-pop store. It's successful as far as I'm concerned. It's definitely successful as far as the clientele and the people in the community are concerned. I mean everybody. I'm doing what you could say was a community service.

There's no competition—there's only two or three juice companies in all of the area. Most of them are very commercial and they make high volume, but not very high quality. I'm into very low volume, but very high quality. I love perfection; that's the way I do things and I feel if you can't do it right then don't do it! If you go through all this time and effort to get that product out, you might as well make it as perfect as you can. Go for the high quality and charge the people the price for it— I mean that is what I do.

Economics was not the first consideration, so it was easy for me to go ahead and do this. I doubt if I could do this, setting it up like a business venture, as an investment. Not unless you're really prepared to work. It's mostly unskilled labor and I'm here most of the time. If you're not, it doesn't come out right. It's a lot of work, though. I'm just not into the greed and all that about life and money. If I'm happy making whatever I do, then whatever I make I'm happy. It's great.

TR Assemblies & Associates, Inc. *is a subassembly and manufacturing company. It is located in a large warehouse in a small surbaban community.*

Terri Johnston: I've never really wanted to work for someone. I was always a person who had so many ideas and I was aggresive and interested in making things happen the way I really believed it could. The only way I could do that was to be my own boss.

Right out of engineering school and engineering design I went in for sales. Knowing what I know, I thought I could be a good salesman; I liked people so well. So, my idea was to apply engineering skills to simplifying and solving manufacturing procedures that other companies could farm out.

The key to the whole contract manufacturing business is to know *where* the market is. You need to know *who* has a need for what you do. Once you've got that and once you establish a base of who *does* send work out for subassembly, then you sell them on the idea that not only can you perform for them at a competitive price they *cannot* do in-house, but it is both cost effective and profitable for them and for your company to maintain the business.

I started in my house, in my family room. On our first order, my wife and I took twenty or thirty big boxes of products and put them in the garage. Then, we took them out one at a time and set up an assembly line on one little table in our front room. She did a portion, I did another portion, and the kids watched. And we shipped on time, our first products. Perfect quality!

It made us feel good, because there was another company that had been established for five years. They had the same opportunity and the same amount of product. When they shipped, it was 100 percent incorrect and it was returned. With my knowledge of how to run the job, my wife and I produced it 100 percent correctly and it completely surprised the client.

So we first worked out of the house, built up working money and capital, and saved it. Then we used it to move into a large warehouse about three months later. Two months after we got out of the house, we had four employees at the warehouse. Now, seven months later, we have thirty full-time employees and there's still plenty of room to grow.

Here's a simple analogy of what subassembly is like. You go to the zoo and you want to feed the monkeys. Somebody has to take these nuts and put them in a bag. Somebody has to take and seal that bag, put it in a box, and ship it to the zoo. I tell them I can set up and package these peanuts for you without a large overhead and I can give on-time deliveries.

I can go to a company that makes expensive machinery and I look at a couple of wires that are sticking out of that machine. We can cut those wires for you, strip off the insulation, and put solder on the tips for you. We can do ten, or twenty, or a hundred thousand of those wires and it will be easier for us to do them. It will be done the way you want them—on time—and you will save a great deal of money because you won't have to do them in-house anymore. For a shop that has extensive equipment and engineering overhead costs, my assembly costs would be much, much less.

The same goes for cassette assemblies that may have five plastic components. We put them on a modified assembly line and can do them at less cost, with a higher quality, and a better turnaround than they can do it in their own shop. For our operations, the majority of our workers don't have to be skilled—I can train them in one day for most assemblies.

I don't have to hire a college graduate, or even a high school graduate, just any normal walk-in-from-the-street person. I will pay the required minimum wage and they will produce the required amount of product to make a profitable assembly line. They will be supporting themselves, we will be doing a good job, and the customers will be very satisfied.

I am now developing a product that we will manufacture here and there will be greater opportunities for those who have grown along with us. Offices have expanded and almost all of the warehouse space will be utilized in the near future. It's been a gratifying growth and I think there's more to come.

Deli Heaven is a fast-food shop specializing in delicatessen-type sandwiches. It's in a complex of stores and food shops across from the main gate of a university. It's mainstay is students—hungry students!

Howard Meyer: To buy an existing business would take more money than Steve and I had. We only had minimal capital—we're still in our mid-twenties, so we haven't gotten much together yet. But our intention was to get something going, a steppingstone, something that we could start moving and then sell. Get some money out of that, get something else going, sell that and so on. It might be possible to get rich off one business but we didn't really believe that.

This opportunity—well, we were more interested in its location than anything else. It was formerly a franchise operation—submarine sandwiches—but they put themselves right out of business because they served huge volumes of nothing—nothing good, anyway. We originally wanted to put a burger place into that location, but another situation changed that.

Someone we know said if you really want to do it, come up with a proposition. We did, and one guy in the group was interested. He also said he had friends who might be interested and that got us started into endless meetings with these backers. It took two months, but finally they said O.K. These investors had their own ideas about what to start, so we compromised on a second choice—a deli.

Everything was negotiable and the end was a Subchapter S corporation, with everyone being stockholders. They held the majority of stock, but Steve and I were to get 50 percent of everything and we had almost absolute control, because we would be the only ones running the whole thing. There were seven of us, in total—Steve and I the general partners, the other five making up a limited partnership. They put in $30,000, we put in $10,000.

The idea behind our layout was to keep fringe expenses to a minimum. The majority of our customers are students. Many have to eat and get back into class within a short time. We have self-service, to the extent where you walk up to a counter and give your order, thus eliminating waiters and waitresses. You don't need to leave a tip and that saves a half dollar or so on your average meal.

When your order was ready, your name was called hopefully within a total of eight minutes—five minutes to get through the order line and your name being called within three minutes after that. Originally we called out the food item itself, but it was much nicer to ask their first name when they ordered and then call it out later. People loved it and you get to know your customers, too. So the next time they might come in the door you say, "Hey, Chuck, how are you, what'll it be today?" It's really appreciated.

A contributing factor to our opening in this location was that there had been, at one time, a deli on this block. It was bought out and Arabic food took its place. So there's been no deli here to serve the many students who come from the east coast and midwestern cities—they are used to deli food and enjoy it.

We serve small quantities of very good food. People might say the sandwiches are a bit small, but people *never* say they're not good! At the beginning, we talked to every salesman in the world. The first priority was that we wanted the best. And the second was, what's the price? We made a lot of mistakes then. Salesmen would come in and swear to God they've got the best for 50 cents a pound less. You'd get it and it was garbage. We probably lost some customers there, but that's the only way you learn unless you had been running someone else's operation to begin with.

Our previous experience didn't quite do that. Steve worked during college, in restaurants mostly, first as a waiter, then a bartender, and finally bar manager. His major was accounting, so that gave us the economic background we needed. I worked part-time in a delicatessen—very part-time. All I did was stock shelves and that kind of thing. My college major was advertising communications, so I took over all the advertising and publicity. That's been fairly successful.

It's not two years yet and the business does show a profit. The only time we have problems is in the summer when our student base is out and the place becomes a break-even operation. The rest of the year it makes money. As of now the investors haven't gotten their investment out. Last year we distributed some profits—it wasn't anything to speak of. This year it looks like there'll be considerably more—probably 30 percent of their investment. There's also a possibility we may be selling the business to two of our employees and one of their parents. Naturally it will be for much more than our original investment and everyone should do well, even the new buyers.

Temporary Fill-Ins is a service for dentists. It was originally started from home; it is thriving and has grown in new directions, but in the same field. The changes have included a new office and a new name to reflect the expanded services.

Patricia Henry: I've been in the dental field for about eight and a half years and originally worked as a dental assistant and office manager. After years in that profession I got a little frustrated and bored. I had lots of ideas I wanted to implement into the office and it was stifling to be told I couldn't do it, or it wouldn't work—things like that. I wanted something different but I still wanted to stay in the same profession, it was what I knew.

When I ended my last job I was in transition. I didn't know what I wanted to do, so until something was decided I began doing fill-in work. This meant going into offices to cover for people who were sick or on vacation. It was stimulating. You had to do an awful lot of new techniques, be able to walk into an office where the procedures were different and the whole physical layout was different. It was kind of challenging—new people, new situations.

I got to do that more and more and became so busy I wasn't able to handle the calls myself. So I began adding a few more people and that just eventually grew into a business. I called it Temporary Fill-Ins. Now, I have a staff of twelve people for fill-in jobs and that includes hygenists, dental assistants, and office personnel.

It's been going about a year and a half. I specialize strictly in the dental field and from that I've grown into another business. I have my employment agency license and I'm doing permanent placements for the dental offices. And something else, too. I'm doing career development counseling and continuing education seminars in the same field.

The seminars are for continuing education in the dental profession. We have to maintain and update our licenses and skills within the profession. I have my license from the Board of Dental Examiners of the state of California. Some courses I teach myself, but most of them I organize and bring in speakers and instructors to teach specific courses. They involve clinical lectures, motivation, management practices, all the way up to the actual clinical skills and techniques of dentistry.

So there's been a name change to go along with that. The total business is now called Ultimate Potential Dental Personnel. I like Temporary Fill-Ins though, and I just keep it for that one section. Everything is more structured and formalized now. Before it was a loose, word-of-mouth situation. Today we have contracts and it's evolved into a real business. I have an office and I'm there all the time.

My staff is highly qualified. Those on the temporary fill-ins are screened very thoroughly. They have to pass certain requirements and I check all their references, past skills, employers, then I send them out on a trial probation period and get evaluations from their offices. If they aren't able to handle the situations well, then I just discontinue them from my staff.

I had no idea I was going to be in this business and where it was going and where it's grown to now. It just took off, like a tumbleweed or a snowball, gathering more and more onto itself. There are still some offices that are my favorites and I go out myself as a fill-in every once in a while, about twice a month. I like to keep in contact and keep up my own skills. And I try to stop into other offices and stay aware of what's going on in the dental community, otherwise it wouldn't work. I have to know what's going on.

Personaliz-It by Jean *is located in a large business park complex. It is a service organization that handles imprinting and engraving for individuals, corporations, schools, and organizations.*

Les Motz: This business all started with a home improvement project. We tore out the back porch and built a new kitchen and dining area. My wife, Jean, wanted to help pay for the kitchen we designed. Since I wouldn't let her go back to work she decided to do something from home. She was the instigator and founder of this business.

Her sister in California was doing a bit of hot foil-stamping work at home, not very much, so Jean contacted her, made a trip there and got one hour of instruction on operating this machine. We then bought the machine and a couple of fonts of type from her. Jean felt she could do more with it than what her sister was doing. She set it up and started in the old carport of our home, which had been blocked in for a recreation room. Jean did lots of experimenting before and while she got her first orders.

She was imprinting paper napkins initially. Then around Christmas time after the major department stores had closed off their Christmas card orders for imprinting at the factory, we began to take their boxed cards and imprint the names. In addition we contacted other people who may have been giving their customers Christmas gifts, like an appointment book. One bank had an unfortunate thing happen—they sent off 600 names to another imprinter and they came back with 180 errors. The imprinter wouldn't do anything about it until after the first of the year. Well, when you're small, you can bend with the wind and we bent with the wind and just picked up whatever was wanted.

People say, "Well, how many will you do?" We'll do one if you want to pay for it and we'll do ten thousand if we have the time. So it just began to grow. In fact, in the second year, we did seventy-five thousand Christmas cards. Our next-door neighbors came in and helped occasionally on part-time work. After a few years of that, Jean said she'd have to have somebody else come in or else I'd have to quit work. So I quit and it's gone on from there. The business got out of hand as far as the house was concerned, so we moved into this complex—even this is too small sometimes. But we do have complete air conditioning, which we need for the foils—this is not an ink printing process, it's a dry foil printing type of thing.

We do all sorts of personalized things—report covers, thesis covers, foldover desk pads, appointment books, brief cases, attaché cases, albums, guest books, aerial photos, report covers for the mining, consulting, and real estate companies. There are standing orders for many of the corporations in the area.

We got into engraving when we started to personalize and had to purchase special machinery for that. Now we do both engraving and imprinting for special projects, especially company logos, and all kinds of signs and name tags.

We are incorporated. Jean is the president and I'm the secretary. Now we have a pretty good investment in machinery, but the main thing is the expertise. Others have tried it because it looks easy, but it isn't. If you were to come in and say you'd like this done in gold, we'd say which one of the thirteen golds do you want? Also, foil does not go on everything—one foil goes well on plastic, but not paper. You've got to know your foils and your plastics.

Jean Motz: As far as accounting and management goes, Les handles all that. As for me, I knew what I wanted and I knew I had to have certain things to further myself as far as type and foil went. We made trips to the coast to find out what the foils were made of and how they were made, and who the companies were that manufactured them, especially the ones I dealt with. They took us through the plants and got to know me. I got to know their capabilities and they recognized mine. Then, when I wanted something that wasn't in their catalogs, they realized that I knew what I was talking about so they didn't turn me down. This has furthered my business, because people know they don't have to go only by the book when they come to me.

Many of the department stores and companies in town don't know anything else except "that's the way the catalog shows it." They sell goods and objects, I sell services—so we go at it altogether differently. We have accumulated much type over the years, from very small to very large, and it takes a lot of money to do that. We started with two fonts of type and now have over one hundred fonts. We have five full-time employees and do work for people in New York, New Mexico, Texas, and Arizona. My research is a constant, ongoing project and I'm learning all the time. You never quit learning about the materials—they're changing all the time and you have to keep up with it.

It might now take $50,000 to buy this business but I think it would be a good bit more than that. The problem there is that I wouldn't be selling me. And, the business *is* me! If I ever did sell the business, and that's not an impossibility, I would like to stay on as a part-time consultant. I love it!

Special Occasions *is a card and gift shop with unique offerings. It's located at a major intersection with shops, supermarkets, and extensive parking.*

Georgine Osborne: I used to be a schoolteacher and an accountant and I had worked very, very hard for other people. I really wanted to either make it on my own or fail on my own, but I wanted control of that decision.

I never even thought of buying someone else's business, or a franchise. My dad has always been self-employed and it never occurred to me to go over and pick up someone's ideas. I wanted to start right on my own and have it be a part of me. The only retail experience I had was in college and that wasn't very long.

My mother suggested visiting her friend who had an all-Christmas shop. I went and saw and was disappointed. I didn't want to do

Christmas all year long, so the more I thought about it the more I decided to start with gift items for all the seasons. Then, of course, I would need cards. In the three years I've been in business, that format hasn't changed very much and it's just grown. It was a good move.

When it came to financing, there was no bank borrowing. I had some money saved and my folks loaned me some additional funds. My research was in the library—lots of books. I needed to know what to put into fixtures, how much in inventory, and how much for expenses to last me for four months—all the overhead. I even went to the bank to get their regional statistics and I also got my traffic count for this region. When I figured what would be needed, I started with half of that.

My research indicated this area would be a great one in three years and if I wanted to be in this area, I had no choice but to take this fairly large store now. Later, nothing might be available. This shopping center was being completely remodeled and stores added. That was a good sign of future growth. And growth in the area has been steady. Even with the construction and road closings of last year, my business has increased. There were two landlord changes, some business turnovers, and with all of that the increase has been approximately 17 percent each year.

Initially I was conservative in my buying and I tried to pick a third of what I liked, a third of what I thought others might like, and a final third by the seat of my pants. Now I actually do more buying of things that I like, because then I can sell them better, with genuine enthusiasm. I also try to get a little bit of everything, to see what my customers prefer. I can always reorder, so there's no necessity to have an overabundance of things.

I've increased my card stock since the beginning, but I intend to double what I have now. Gift items range from medium to fairly expensive, and we've built up a tremendous business on helium balloons for every occasion. Gift items that are unique and creative are a definite part of the inventory.

Although I think starting from scratch is the only way to go, you can't do it that way if you need the income off that business. That's one of the major mistakes. I see so many that fail after a year and they say they were undercapitalized. They definitely were, if they needed an income from it. If I had to pay back loans immediately, I couldn't have made it. Anything I sold, I went out and bought more merchandise. I built up my inventory to a good level. I didn't have to take an income out of it.

As my business got bigger I needed help and that's the kind of money I could have taken as a salary. But getting help was more important, so even there I was putting everything back into the business. Having an employee, or two also increased the scope of my business, gave me more time to concentrate on buying, paperwork, and so on. Now, after three years, I could take a salary and the business has become a sound and profitable one.

Carson's Sports Center *is a fully stocked sporting goods store located in a shopping plaza bounded by two major streets. It is owned and operated by Dennis and Carolyn Carson.*

Dennis Carson: This is about my eighteenth year in the field. I worked in retail shops during high school and college, then went full-time into retail after college and finally into the wholesale end of it. Without that background you've got too many strikes against you.

Profit in this business is not in the selling, it's always in the buying. You make your living by selling but you make your profit by buying correctly. This is a highly competitive business, but especially so in the gun area. We have one of the largest gun operations in the nation here and he's very tough to compete with. You have to compete on more than price. You must have something more to give, some form of service. You've got to be able to talk to your customers, have the right kind of personality, too. This applies to all retail.

In any retail business, it's essential that you *enjoy* retail and that you be a salesman. Enjoy people! I made a pretty good living in the wholesale business, but I didn't totally enjoy it because I couldn't interact with the retail customer as much as I would like to. The wholesale aspect, after you develop your accounts, becomes a matter of being an order taker. In the retail business, however, you have to talk to people, you educate people, you're a teacher.

There's a very excessive failure rate in sporting goods. Although most of the owners had been in some part of the business before, working for someone else, when they decided to go on their own they failed. Reasons? Well, they didn't know how to buy, or they weren't competitive, or they couldn't create the right atmosphere in their store. One of those things. I've been here, on my own, for four years now, and today I'm just beginning to understand how to buy. But even when I started, I was still 200 percent ahead of the average guy trying to open.

Because of my wholesale experience I knew what I could bargain for and what I couldn't. I knew when to look for deals because I'd been there offering those deals. I knew their profit margin and how far they could go. In ten years I called on at least a thousand different retail accounts, so I got to see how a thousand different operations worked. I saw what their good points were and what the bad ones looked like. When we opened our store I tried to incorporate as many of the good points as I could afford.

To be successful, you need an adequate inventory, but it takes a lot of money to do that. I got lucky, I started with about $10,000 in inventory, plus about another $25,000 for fixtures, fees, and licenses. My wife and I drew nothing for one solid year. At the end of that our money was gone. But that one year got the store off the ground and we began to live on it.

When we had $10,000 worth of merchandise, we only had one or two of everything, instead of the ten or so you should have. Then I had to order on a daily basis to keep up with it. Today, right now, we have about $170,000 in inventory and there's about twelve to thirty-six pieces of a line.

But even if I had more money to start with I wouldn't have bought somebody else's problems, some existing business. Even though I hadn't owned a business before, I still felt far more capable of stocking it correctly, more so than another owner who may have had it for ten years, because I came right out of the wholesale end of it and that business included most of the lines we have here in the store.

My wife still works with me and including the part-timers, I think there's nine or ten of us now. I have the best bookkeeper in the state. Even though she happens to be my mother, she's still the best. Without proper procedures, right from the beginning, the whole thing can be lost. My bookkeeper, at this point, can tell me where I am compared to last month and last year, how we're doing so far, how much we've bought, how much more we can buy, and when I have to quit buying. She started out with us a few hours every couple of days, now it's full-time, forty-five hours a week.

I will always be involved in the sporting goods business. It's a whole way of life. I've never had another job. My hobby is sports; I hunt, fish, camp, and I just came back from five days of turkey hunting, trying out my own products. One of the things you have to sell over the counter is personality and you have to be able to talk to the customers. I subscribe to about thirty-seven different magazines and I receive seven additional trade magazines at no cost. That's part of the business too, keeping up with what's going on in the field.

I don't put in seven days a week anymore as I did the first two years. Well, actually I do put in seven days a week and twenty-four hours a day. I dream about it at night. I'm not worrying about it, I'm *thinking*. I've got so much going that I can't do it all in my regular hours.

IN SUMMATION

In their own words, these new entrepreneurs have told us about the how and why of their start-from-scratch ventures. Interestingly enough, one can detect a definite difference with this group in contrast to those who started out by purchasing an existing business.

Most of this group did some preparatory homework—some preliminary research, an evaluation of their markets, and a bit of relevant reading. In addition, a number of the new owners had a good base of previous experience in their selected field, and that's always a plus. But there were also a few other pluses. These beginners all seemed to be very highly motivated to be on their own, to keep doing it their way. They showed a determined willingness to go ahead with it, to take the risk. All in all, those positive aspects are the necessary attributes for any would-be entrepreneur.

What about another plus—the awareness factor? A number of these start-from-scratch ventures were a direct result of awareness of opportunity—spotting a marketing potential that wasn't completely covered.

Temporary Fill-Ins developed a market, but the entrepreneur had lots of experience in the field. Once you recognize an opportunity, it's the determined follow-through that makes the difference. That's what makes an entrepreneur! The Beverly Hills Juice Club found a market that wasn't overcrowded and developed an identity that reflected quality rather than high commercial output.

Check some of the others and analyze how they fit into their fields. Were their ventures a matter of luck or a recognition of opportunities? Were they breaking new ground or simply adding a different version to an existing field?

This is the kind of evaluation and observation of others that can help immeasurably in giving coherence to your own plans. In contrast to the established businesses that had an immediate cash flow, initial start was slow for many of those interviewed in this chapter. It took time, a year or two, for the ventures to take off and start returning some income and/or profits. They had to develop an identity, establish themselves in their field, and build up enough customers to make their businesses profitable.

In the case of the established entity, this vital groundwork has already been accomplished, and most authorities agree it's that fact alone that makes it desirable. But you have to total all your own pluses and minuses when it comes to choosing which way to go for your first entrepreneurial venture. Admittedly these mini-interviews just scratch the surface, but important facts can be gleaned from them. They may also serve to motivate you to get out into the field and talk to owners of other small businesses. It can be a big plus!

SECTION

III

Franchise a Business

There's a very successful business in town, one you've always admired.

The owner, a friend, suggests you both form a partnership of sorts. You will start the exact same business as hers, in the next town. You're the boss, but she will teach you all the tricks, eliminate the starting foul-ups, and help you whenever you need it.

Your investment? An advance payment for her trouble and her system, plus a small percentage of your sales.

Is that what a franchise is all about? Will it be a good deal?

13

Franchising—
Another Way to Go?

THE FRANCHISE

It's interesting to note the varied definitions for "franchise." In one instance, it may be the right or privilege granted by the government to vote, or to form a utility. Another meaning is the right to own a member team, as granted by a league in one of the professional sports. Still other definitions simply relate it to some form of license or agreement that would be operable between manufacturer and distributor or wholesaler and retailer.

For our purposes of owning and operating a small business, the more likely dictionary definition would be: the right to market a product or provide a service, often exclusive for a specified area, as granted by a manufacturer or company.

That definition relates, in part, to the present-day understanding of the term "franchise." Franchising started in the early years of this century, when the horse and buggy industry became more aware of the competition that was emerging from the manufacturers of automobiles.

The car makers and oil refiners began to license new car dealers and gas stations to sell their products. These retailers usually were given specific areas to operate in and were backed by national advertising, promotion, and, where warranted, financial assistance from the manufacturer. These marketing alliances were called licensees.

It didn't take long for other companies to make somewhat similiar arrangements. The early ones were auto parts stores, variety stores, bottlers, drug stores, and even a dance studio.

FRANCHISING

Many young adults, particularly those born during the latter days of the baby boom era, may feel that their growing-up years paralleled the first big expansion of the franchise industry. No doubt their fondest memories revolved around the fast-food shops and the ice cream stands, especially the ones that sprang up during their high school and college days.

Those were the initial years of the ever-increasing push for establishing franchise units. Dynamic growth during that period had a way of smoothing over and covering up some of the problem areas beginning to emerge in the industry. By opening many units, however, the franchisors were able to polish and perfect the operational strategies needed to make this new marketing system—for that's what it really is—a viable success.

This real growth began in the 1950s, when the owners of a variety of businesses slowly began to add units that were to be standardized, recognized, and financed by others (the franchisees) who would own and manage them. In effect, they were licensing their product, service, or method in order to obtain greater distribution. The franchisors retained the brand name, trademarks, and control over all the marketing methods, and received a consideration in return.

Some of the names that started the expansion and acceptance of this form of entrepreneurship were the following:

- United Rent-All, Inc. (1950)
- Baskin-Robbins, Inc. (1951)
- Big Boy Family Restaurants (1952)
- Holiday Inns Inc.(1953)
- Shakey's Incorporated (1954)
- Burger King Corporation (1954)
- Manpower, Inc. (1954)
- McDonald's Corporation (1955)
- Dunkin' Donuts of America, Inc. (1955)
- Hanna Carwash (1955)
- Midas International Corp. (1956)
- Seven Eleven (1956)
- Kentucky Fried Chicken Corp. (1956)
- H & R Block (1958)

- Pizza Hut (1959)
- Ramada Inns, Inc. (1959)
- Ben Franklin (1960).

There were also some early birds that helped pave the way for those who started the big push of the fifties, and they're still going strong:

- Piggly Wiggly Corporation (1916)
- A & W Restaurants (1925)
- Coast to Coast Stores (1928)
- Gamble Skogmo (1933)
- Roto-Rooter Corporation (1935)
- Culligan International Corporation (1936)
- Arthur Murray (1939)
- Dairy Queen (1941)
- Duraclean International (1944)
- Carvel Corporation (1948).

A number of other familiar names that are still healthy but no longer offering franchises include Rayco, Rexall Drugs, Hertz, Avis, and Radio Shack.

To all of the above listings, you now have to add hundreds of new names that have emerged in the past twenty years. They represent practically any product or service you can think of, from nail care to chimney sweeps, haircuts to high-tech computers, and everything in between.

Many who became franchisee-entrepreneurs in the early stages flowered with the boom and did extremely well financially. But the industry, as a whole, had some sharp up and down swings during its great growth era. Some negatives were a direct result of unscrupulous operators and get-rich-quick promoters. Others were simply a downbeat reflection of the boom and bust cycles in the nation's economy. Along the way there were many bankruptcies, caused both by excess promotion and national economic ills.

THE PRESENT IDENTITY

Without doubt, franchising has grown into adulthood. Rather than a mere license or authorization to distribute products and services, many agreements now offer a complete package. That can mean premises, equipment, inventory, national advertising, and complete systems for all management applications—a turnkey operation. The most important aspect of these arrangements is the maintenance of an ongoing, open-communication relationship between the parent company (franchisor) and the owner of the packaged unit (franchisee).

The International Franchise Association (IFA) represents a great number of franchisors. One of their statements highlights the relationship between the parties:

> *A franchise is a continuing relationship between the franchisor and the franchisee, in which the sum total of the franchisor's knowledge, image, success, manufacturing and marketing techniques are supplied to the franchisee for a consideration.*

Ever-growing numbers indicate the tremendous success that has been achieved by this new marketing concept. The overall franchise industry now accounts for more than one-third of all retail sales. Dollarwise, this is well over $350 billion annually and may soon reach $400 billion. If one were to total up every franchise outlet, including auto dealers and service stations, the final count would be more than 450,000 units.

Another measure of this industry's importance to our economic health is the number of people now working for franchises. An estimate for 1985 indicated the total would be well over 5 million. The expectation for the future is still more growth.

Although the franchise industry is now considered responsible, the normal cautions must continually be observed if you are contemplating ownership of a franchised unit. Numerous ads still offer the promises of quick and easy money and instant entrepreneurship. All too often, these offers indicate that anyone can be successful and this type of advertising does lure many an unqualified candidate into the fold. Nine times out of ten, the result is failure.

This type of promotion may apply mostly to the newer and smaller franchises, the ones without many units or extensive track records. But numerous complaints have also been filed about the exaggerated claims and insufficient training being offered by some of the more established franchisors. This is why a number of states and federal agencies have passed laws relating to full disclosure statements. These statements are in the nature of a prospectus, which is meant to give specific details and information about many aspects of the franchisor-franchisee relationship.

GET IT ALL OUT IN THE OPEN

A trade regulation rule issued by the Federal Trade Commission requires the nationwide use of disclosure statements in the sale of franchises. This went into effect on October 21, 1979, and every franchisor, in every state, must provide disclosure statements to any prospective franchisee.

The statement will contain detailed information on some twenty different subjects that may influence you to invest or not to invest in the franchise under consideration. These disclosures will help immeasurably in comparing one franchise to another and, hopefully, they'll also make you aware of what you're really getting into. The information to be supplied by the franchisor is as follows:

1. Information identifying the franchisor and affiliates, and describing their business experience.

2. Information identifying and describing the business experience of each of the franchisor's officers, directors, and management personnel responsible for the franchise services, training, and other aspects of the franchise program.

3. A description of the lawsuits in which the franchisor and its officers, directors, and management personnel have been involved.

4. Information about any previous bankruptcies in which the franchisor and its officers, directors, and management personnel have been involved.

5. Information about the initial franchise fee and other initial payments that are required to obtain the franchise.

6. A description of the continuing payments franchisees are required to make after the franchise opens.

7. Information about any restrictions on the quality of goods and services used in the franchise and where they may be purchased, including restrictions requiring purchases from the franchisor or its affiliates.

8. A description of any assistance available from the franchisor or its affiliates in financing the purchase of the franchise.

9. A description of restrictions on the goods or services franchisees are permitted to sell.

10. A description of any restrictions on the customers with whom franchisees may deal.

11. A description of any territorial protection that will be granted to the franchisee.

12. A description of the conditions under which the franchise may be repurchased or refused renewal by the franchisor, transferred to a third party by the franchisee, and terminated or modified by either party.

13. A description of the training programs provided to franchisees.

14. A description of the involvement of any celebrities or public figures in the franchise.

15. A description of any assistance in selecting a site for the franchise that will be provided by the franchisor.

16. Statistical information about the present number of franchises, the number of franchises projected for the future, the number of franchises terminated, the number the franchisor has decided not to renew, and the number repurchased in the past.

17. The financial statements of the franchisors.

18. A description of the extent to which franchisees must personally participate in the operation of the franchise.

19. A complete statement of the basis for any earnings claims made to the franchisee, including the percentage of existing franchises that have actually achieved the results that are claimed.

20. A list of the names and addresses of other franchisees.

Keep in mind that the accuracy of the information in the disclosure statement is not guaranteed by the regulation of the Federal Trade Commission. If you do discover a violation of these rights, however, legal action can be instituted and the franchisor will be subject to civil penalties.

In addition to the FTC regulation, approximately fifteen states have their own franchise registration procedures. California, in 1971, was responsible for establishing the country's first full disclosure law. As other states followed, a successful effort to make these laws uniform resulted in the Uniform Franchise Offering Circular. Where the franchisor does not comply with the state's regulations, registration of its offering may be revoked or denied. This would especially apply if misrepresentation or fraud existed in the sales of franchises to prospective franchisees.

FRAUD AND MISREPRESENTATION

As stated earlier, although the franchise industry has grown up and become responsible, the possibilities for misleading claims and blown-up promises still exist and continue to grow. It's really not too different from the boiler-room operations in the stock market, the phony make-money-at-home ads, the nonexistent tax shelters, the hole-in-the-ground gold mines, and so on.

All of these fraudulent businesses operate in legitimate fields, but they are operated by unscrupulous promoters and fast-buck con artists. Check with the U.S. Postal Service's mail fraud division and with the Federal Trade Commission to verify that complaints in the franchise field are high up on their list of fraud investigations.

There's a great deal to watch out for in considering a franchise operation. Things that don't exist have been sold time and time again. This couldn't happen with the nonexistent franchise if you observed the simple rule of investigate, investigate, investigate! Abiding by that rule would also help combat the most common deception of all: overoptimistic profit claims. In many cases, this exaggeration is deliberate—the flashing lure to reel you into the fold. Surveys have indicated that a great number—perhaps a majority—of franchisees have incomes below the average projected figures on the franchisors' statements.

Besides outright swindles and deliberate misrepresentation of earnings, there are other areas in which fraud can be perpetrated. Promises that were made, in writing or verbally, pertaining to on-line training, management assistance, extra services, product prices, and so on may never be kept. Pyramid schemes may have layer upon layer of franchise representatives, with the last few layers seeming to hold up the rest.

Celebrity names are sometimes used. When the celebrity is actively involved, the franchise can be judged on its own merits. But there have been cases where the celebrity has very little or nothing to do with the operation and often, in a very short time, the whole thing collapses—but not before a number of franchisee-entrepreneurs who got involved were eventually left holding the bag.

Granted, the poor opportunities outlined usually relate to a minority of franchisors in the field. They often will be found among the smaller, more recent franchise offerings, and even the packages that resemble franchises but aren't. That's exactly why this caution light is blinking.

The odds are against you starting a franchise operation with McDonald's or Burger King because their initial investments run into the hundreds of thousands of dollars. So it is the smaller and sometimes newer franchises that might appeal to you. The newer ones are the least likely to have a track record or any great number of existing units. They are also the most likely to relate to services or products that are just coming into being: computers, video technology, word processing, flotation tubs, environmental opportunities, and many of the small, individual service operations that can be unified or merged into a regional or nationwide chain.

With that kind of momentum in the new and future growth of this industry, the opportunities for the unscrupulous promoter can flourish. Don't walk blithely into his or her seemingly irresistible welcome. Promise yourself that you will take the necessary time and energy to evaluate carefully. Later chapters will help point the way to accomplish this.

PRELIMINARY CONSIDERATIONS

Obviously there are some preliminaries to consider if you think franchising is the route to take for your initial venture into entrepreneurship. The key question concerns the direction of your search. Where will your emphasis be?

Have you been attracted to a new franchised service or product that reflects today's lifestyle and do you believe it will be a winner?

Are you targeting your present skills and/or experience toward existing opportunities in this field?

Do you feel that because an existing franchise is not in your area, it may be a good opportunity to introduce it?

Are you open to any franchise because you feel this field offers the best opportunity for success, whether or not you know the service or product?

Do you know someone who is a franchisee and have their results convinced you to consider this field?

Have you decided to enter this field because the research indicates there is much less chance of failure than if you were to start from scratch?

Perhaps none of these questions applies, and at this stage you want to know more about the field before you make your decision. That's fine, and that's why this book has been designed for a surface exploration of all three options for entering the entrepreneurial arena.

Basic franchises now exist in almost any product or service you can name, but they all relate somewhat to one or more of the following categories:

- food service operations
- retail stores
- service stations
- automotive repairs
- car and truck dealerships
- service businesses
- wholesale distribution
- manufacturing licenses.

A quick perusal of these categories may cause you to automatically scratch off a number of them because of your own likes or dislikes. That, plus the tentative direction or emphasis you may have already decided upon, will be evaluated more thoroughly in the following chapters.

SOURCES OF FRANCHISE OPPORTUNITIES

In other than the really rural areas, every city, town, and village seems to have a representative unit of one or more franchisors. Within the larger population areas, franchises have proliferated to the point where they seem to surround all of us.

This very presence is one of the biggest means of identifying opportunities in the field. They are familiar in both name and type of operation, although many are concentrated in the fast-food and automotive service categories. Also visible are the convenience stores, physical fitness centers, motels, real estate units, automatic laundries, and others.

Franchise Directories

As you continue to search for franchise opportunities, both among known names and a great number of unknown ones, a good information source is the franchise directory. Published by both government and private agencies, franchise directories contain a listing of franchisors and the following valuable high points which the franchisor has submitted:

- home office address
- description of operation

- number of franchisees
- year business started
- equity capital needed
- financial assistance available
- training provided
- managerial assistance available
- date information was submitted.

The following excerpts are from the pages of the *Franchise Opportunities Handbook* published by the Department of Commerce.

GYMBOREE CORPORATION
872 Hinckley Road
Burlingame, California 94010
Bud Jacob, Vice President, Franchise Sales

Description of Operation: Gymboree, a quality developmental play program, offers weekly classes to parents and their children, age 3 months to 4 years, on custom-designed equipment for infants, toddlers and preschoolers. The program is based on sensory integration theory, positive parenting, child development principles, and the importance of play.

Number of Franchisees: Over 200 Gymboree centers in operation (including 5 company-owned). Franchises have been granted to over 115 franchisees covering market plans for the development of over 310 centers in 29 States and Canada.

In Business Since: 1976

Equity Capital Needed: $7,000-$14,000 fee per site depending on number of sites. Approximately $7,500-$9,000 per site for equipment and supplies; $4,000-$6,000 working capital.

Financial Assistance Available: Franchisor may assist with some financing the franchise fee, which would partially reduce equity capital needed.

Training Provided: All franchisees attend a 9 day training seminar with a follow-up visit to their location(s) after opening and once a year thereafter. Regional training programs are held on an ongoing basis.

Managerial Assistance Available: There is an annual seminar for ongoing training. All franchisees are visited annually. Phone contact regularly. Monthly written communications.

Information Submitted: March 1986

WHITE HEN PANTRY, INC.
660 Industrial Drive
Elmhurst, Illinois 60126
Arthur W. Haak, Franchising Manager

Description of Operation: A White Hen Pantry is a convenience food store of approximately 2,500 square feet. There is generally up-front parking for 10 to 15 cars. Stores are usually open 24 hours (some operate a lesser number of hours) 365 days a year. Product line includes a service deli, fresh bakery, fresh produce, and a wide variety of the most popular staples. White Hen Pantry stores are franchised to local residents who become owner/operators of this "family business."

Number of Franchisees: 320 in Illinois, Wisconsin, Indiana, Massachusetts and New Hampshire

In Business Since: 1965

Equity Capital Needed: $20,000-$25,000 (varies by location)

Financial Assistance Available: Total investment averages $41,300-$48,000. Investment includes approximately $24,000 merchandise; $5,000 security deposit; $3,000 supplies; $200 cash register fund; and $10,000 training and processing fee. A minimum investment of $20,000 is required. Financial assistance available.

Training Provided: Classroom and in-store training precede store opening. Follow-up training provided after taking over store. Detailed operation manuals are provided.

Managerial Assistance Available: This is a highly organized and comprehensive program. Other services provided include merchandising, accounting, promotions, advertising, and business insurance (group health and plate glass insurance are optional). Store counselor visits are regular and frequent.

Information Submitted: March 1986

SIR SPEEDY, INC.
23131 Verdugo Drive
LaGuna Hills, California 92653
Harold C. Lloyd, Vice President-Franchise Sales and Development

Description of Operation: Sir Speedy, Inc., is a leading franchisor of printing centers. Centers are franchisee-owned utilizing established system, procedures and techniques. Franchise prackage includes equipment, supplies, signage, graphics, market survey and training programs. Prior printing experience not required.

Number of Franchisees: Approximately 650 in 42 States.

In Business Since: 1968

Equity Capital Needed: Total franchise package is $86,000 plus working capital of $30,000. Initial investment as low as $30,000.

Financial Assistance Available: Financing available for entire package to qualified individuals, excluding working capital.

Training Provided: Total of 4 weeks initital training. This in-depth initial training includes advertising and marketing strategy, bookkeeping and record keeping, graphic design, shop organization and work flow, pricing, employee relations, and more. Ongoing regional and national seminars conventions to keep franchisees informed of trends in the industry.

Managerial Assistance Available: In-depth market surveys, site selection, assist in lease negotiations, national contract purchasing power, marketing and advertising support, accounting system, communication with all franchisees, profit management seminars, equipment evaluations, plus royalty rebate program.

Information Submitted: April 1986

SERVICEMASTER RESIDENTIAL AND COMMERCIAL CORPORATION
2300 Warrenville Road
Downers Grove, Illiois 60515
D. V. Horsfall, Vice President

Description of Operation: ServiceMaster Residential and Commercial Corporation, a subsidiary of ServiceMaster Industries Inc., offers franchising in On Location Services, Contract Services and Carpet/Upholstery Services. This encompasses carpet, rug, furniture, smooth-floor surface, housewide cleaning, wall cleaning, disaster restoration and ordor removal in homes and commercial buildings, as well as complete janitorial services.

Number of Franchisees: 3,237 in 50 States and worldwide.

In Business Since: 1948

Equity Capital Needed: Initial franchise fee is $11,500 including training manuals and aids, plus an additional $8,300 for a recommended package of promotional materials, professional equipment, supplies and tools and professional chemicals for a total of $19,800 for each of the On Location and Contract Services franchises. Initial franchise fee for the Carpet/Upholstery is $5,450 including training manuals and aids, plus an additional $5,250 for a recommended package of promotional materials, professional equipment, supplies and tools and professional chemicals for a total of $10,700.

Financial Assistance Available: Franchisor will finance qualified applicants. $8,800 minimum down payment required for each of the On Location Contract Services franchises; $4,400 minimum down payment required for the Carpet/Upholstery.

Training Provided: Home study course, 2 weeks on-the-job training with established franchisee, 1 day in the field with counselor, 1 week resident training school. Continuous training program provided for all licensees.

Managerial Assistance Available: Managerial assistance is available on a continuous basis, from the company and from the master franchise coordinator of franchisees in the field. The company makes available advertising, sales promotions, formal training, laboratory services, regional and international meetings.

Information Submitted: April 1986

CULLIGAN INTERNATIONAL COMPANY
One Culligan Parkway
Northbrook, Illinois 60062

Description of Operation: Parent company is supplier to franchisee for water treatment equipment. Franchisee sells, leases, maintains and repairs water treatment equipment for domestic, commercial, and industrial consumers.

Number of Franchisees: 845 in the U.S. and Canada

In Business Since: 1936

Equity Capital Needed: $37,500 and up

Financial Assistance Available: Franchisor has various credit arrangements available for qualified franchisees with reference to the purchase of equipment from franchisor.

Training Provided: Franchisor provides training at Northbrook, Illinois headquarters. Franchisor also provides management training and technical training through frequent visits to franchisee's dealership by company personnnel.

Managerial Assistance Available: Franchisor has continuing managerial and technical assistance to franchisee through traveling, district service, training engineers, district managers, commercial and industrial sales managers. This assistance is available to all franchisees as needed.

Information Submitted: March 1986

MERRY MAIDS, INC.
11117 Mill Valley Road
Omaha, Nebraska 68154, Dept. FOH
Dale Peterson, Executive Vice President

Description of Operation: Merry Maids is the largest company in the franchise home cleaning service industry and employs the most systematic and professional approaches to training, cleaning and management. Merry Maids' exclusive management software system is yet another important factor that has contributed to the company's position of market leadership and growth. Created exclusively for the use of Merry Maids' franchise owners, the system has been developed to streamline routine, operational procedures and provide information to assist and enhance the management process with the aid of a computer.

Number of Franchisees: 400 in 42 States

In Business Since: 1980

Equity Capital Needed: $15,500 franchise fee, plus $10,000-$15,000 to cover operational start-up including office furnishings, purchases of IBM P.C. computer, VHS video player, color television set and working capital.

Financial Assistance Available: None

Training Provided: A comprehensive 5 day training program at the merry Maids' training center is included in the franchise procedures and programs necessary to manage, develop and operate a successful franchise. Company instructors—with actual franchise operational experience—present the company's proven methods of hiring, training, marketing, selling, cleaning and scheduling.

Managerial Assistance Available: Ongoing assistance provided by both the home office personnel and a network of regional coordinators—franchise owners themselves—strategically located across the country. This assistance is further enhanced through the company's franchise buddy system in which established owners in neighboring territories are selected to monitor and counsel new franchise operations. Further assistance is also provided through seasonal regional meetings, specialized field workshops and the company's annual convention.

Information Submitted: April 1986

Although some listings may only contain a few lines of information for each heading, there's enough detail to determine if you have a beginning interest or not. One of the most important aspects of the listings is the main office address of each franchisor. With that as a base, you can write for additional details—an application, an information packet, a prospectus, or whatever the franchisor has decided will be the first step in the inquiry process.

Check your library, bookstore, SBA office, and/or the actual publisher for these directories. Some publishers of directories are as follows:

Franchise Annual Handbook and Directory
Info Press
736 Center Street
Lewiston, N.Y. 14092

Franchise Opportunities Handbook (annual)
Government Printing Office
Washington, D.C. 20402

International Franchise Association Membership Roster
International Franchise Association
1025 Connecticut Avenue, N.W., Suite 1005
Washington, D.C. 20036

Directory of Franchising Organizations
Pilot Industries, Inc.
347 Fifth Avenue
New York, N.Y. 10016

Pilot Industries also publishes two other franchising directories. One relates to opportunities for women in franchising and the other is directed to blacks who want to become their own bosses through franchising.

Business Opportunity Shows

You've seen advertisements for business opportunity shows if they're coming to your city. Usually the show is held in major cities in the large convention centers. Lately, however, there's been a trend to having such shows in the smaller municipalities and the meeting rooms of the larger motels. In all instances, franchisors set up booths and give out reams of literature and information. If the franchise consists of a mobile unit or a small manufacturing device, you may see it in actual operation.

The part-time or modest-investment type of franchise is the kind most represented at business opportunity shows. Many of the major franchisors will not be represented because they already have a waiting list of prospective franchisees. These shows are an excellent means of listening to enthusiastic claims, perusing the type of literature that accompanies them, and getting to know a bit of what this field is all about. You may even find yourself shaking your head in disbelief as to what is being offered, but that may also be the beginning of your own evaluation process.

Newspapers and Magazines

Ads of all sizes are your information signposts in these print media. In the newspapers, the place to look is the business opportunity columns. Both the Sunday *New York Times* and the *Wall Street Journal* have many offerings in this field. Some ads indicate when resales of existing franchise units are available and where they are located.

The business opportunity columns of the newspapers are a learning experience in themselves. One day's (Thursday) advertisements in the *Wall Street Journal*, for example, featured the following franchisor ads:

- American Wholesale Thermographers, Inc.
- Big Red Q Quickprint Centers
- Bryant Bureau (personnel placement)
- Budget Instant Printing Centers
- Business Cards Tomorrow, Inc.
- Byte Shop (computer retailing)
- Chuck's Contract Labor Service
- Comprehensive Accounting Corporation
- Docktor Pet Centers, Inc.
- Fantastic Sam's The Original Family Haircutters
- General Business Services, Inc.
- Good Health Medical Weight Loss
- Graphics One
- Gymboree Corp. (early childhood development)
- In & Out Photo
- Knapp Shoes
- Marcoin, Inc. (business management service)
- Maytag Home Style Laundry
- Meineke Discount Muffler Shops, Inc.
- Midas International Corp. (mufflers)
- Naked Furniture, Inc.
- Personnel Pool of America, Inc.
- (PIP) Postal Instant Press
- Sir Speedy, Inc. (photocopying)
- T-Shirts Plus, Inc.
- Trimark (direct mail marketing)
- Video Biz, Inc.
- Videocassettes Unlimited
- VR Business Brokers, Inc.

That's quite a variety of offerings. Some are familiar, others completely new. On a lesser scale, your local or regional newspaper will also feature ads, both from the franchisor and on occasion from the business brokers.

Magazines, especially those relating to business and small business, are a natural source of information, as are opportunity newsletters, on a lesser scale. Some magazines will contain business opportunity pages featuring franchisor ads, others will have the ads dispersed throughout. A few examples are *Money, Inc., In Business, Entrepreneur, Venture,* and *Income Opportunities*. Franchisors will also make use of some general consumer magazines, as well as those with a long reading-life, such as *Popular Mechanics* and *Popular Science*.

14

Is Franchising for You?

FRANCHISING ADVANTAGES

Most authorities in the small business field tend to agree on the advantages that a franchise offers. But do these advantages apply to all franchisors? My own observation indicates this perception of advantages is based mostly on the performance records of the best known and most efficiently run franchisor organizations. This also seems to be the basis of positive reactions held by many of the prospective franchisees.

But of the thousand or more franchises in existence today, only a modest percentage are household names throughout the nation. There are franchisors with only three units, others whose units are located only within one state, and a great number that operate regionally. This doesn't negate their potential as good opportunities for the new entrepreneur, but it does dilute some of the strength of the perceived benefits. Keep this aspect in proper perspective during the evaluative stages that lead to your final choice.

These are the advantages if you decide to go the franchise route.

1. The business is established and operating. Because it exists, many problem areas have already been ironed out during the franchisor's original trial-and-error period. Start-up mistakes due to inexperience have been eliminated.

2. If the product or service is nationally or regionally known, you have a built-in consumer acceptance. A successful identity has been created even before you open the doors for business.

3. Intensive training in both hands-on operations and management orientation are usually offered by the franchisor. The emphasis is to help solve all potential problems before you start out, so that profitable operations begin immediately.

4. Professional assistance is an important part of your franchise. Site selection, marketing, accounting, lease negotiations and ongoing counseling are part and parcel of many agreements. As an owner-manager, you are not working alone.

5. Advertising support is provided. Most beginners are not pros in this area and often are reluctant to do much of anything. National or regional promotion is a continual effort by the franchisor's agency at a modest or no cost to you. Your own local efforts can be guided and coordinated with the help of a franchisor representative.

6. Initial financing may be less if your franchisor provides part of it. If not, borrowing may be easier because of the franchisor's leverage. If the franchise is well known, cash flow will start on opening day and not depend on building up an image over a long period of time.

7. Centralized purchasing enables you to get a greater discount than if you were an independent business. Cost savings on supplies can be considerable because of this bulk buying.

8. If the franchise is successful, there's a resale advantage. Established franchise businesses are often easier to sell than independent ones, and command a better price. Your franchise agreement will have to be checked, however, to ascertain the conditions of a resale.

9. Standardization can be a distinct advantage to many. Everything is rigidly prescribed—storefront, signs, decor, equipment, supplies, special sales, new offerings, uniforms, bookkeeping, and complete operational and marketing procedures. Between standardization and training, all that lengthy on-the-job learning involved in a new start-up is almost completely eliminated.

10. The success rate for a franchise start-up is much higher than that for a start-from-scratch operation. Some reports indicate an 80 percent chance of success with a franchise, versus only 20 percent for your own solo venture. These statistics certainly depend on the reputation and follow-through of the franchisor.

These aspects of a franchise operation weigh heavily on the plus side. Nevertheless, a careful review of the advantages clearly points up the need for caution. To attain all the benefits, your proposed franchisor would have to rank at the top and be nationally known, well established, and provide intensive training and continual professional assistance. Naturally, a number of such franchises would be among the most expensive and perhaps have a waiting list.

Your job, if you wish to be a part of this industry, will be one of investigation and evaluation. A franchise, of itself, is no guarantee of success and prosperity. There are opportunities in the field and there are definite advantages, even with a local or regional franchisor. The material that follows will probe and examine many aspects of franchising, with an eye toward providing sufficient information for your final decision.

DISADVANTAGES

The drawbacks inherent in any type of small business start-up usually have some relationship to the benefits. As the laws of physics state, for every force, there's a counterforce.

Another saying that may apply is: "One man's meat is another man's poison." That relates quite strongly to the individual. What thoughts do you have about entrepreneurship? Do you prefer going your own way? Are you creative and do you enjoy overcoming problems with your own ideas? Are you a conformist or a maverick? All this becomes more meaningful when you look over some of the disadvantages in purchasing a franchise.

1. In a franchise, you are your own boss—but you're not. There is practically nothing you can change. Because the business exists in a specific format, that's exactly the way you are to run it. Often when new franchisees have gotten experience, they want to modify and change the systems—keep the best parts and knock out the rest. The opportunity to deviate, or to introduce your own ideas without approval is extremely doubtful, a veritable taboo.

   In most cases, you will be functioning somewhat like the subsidiary of a parent company. Certain products or prices may not go well in your local area, for example, but you don't have the flexibility or the authority to change them.

2. Standardization is the heart of every franchise operation, and it can work heavily against you if you aren't a conformist. Even good ideas, when offered, can and are turned down by the franchisor headquarters. Every sign, ice cream scoop, french fry, business report, service operation, schedule, product, or whatever must be adhered to and performed exactly. If you're secure and adventurous, this regimentation can be ulcerating and defeating.

3. Training is a vital aspect in the franchise operation. In fact, many franchisors prefer their franchisees to have no experience in that particular field. Some business background, however, is usually

welcome. Not all training is the same. Some sessions are extensive, others are surface slough-offs. Among the many complaints received by the Federal Trade Commission and state regulatory agencies, lack of sufficient training is high on the list. This may also reflect the less established franchisors who heavily promote the fact that no experience is necessary.

4. Many choose a franchise because they are beginners. They depend on the professional expertise of the franchisor, especially with regard to location. This is crucial to success, yet if you review gross and net figures in numerous units of the same franchise, there are often large variations. The same problem exists with lease arrangements. Although failures and low earnings can result from these disparities, you usually have no control over those critical areas. Even the professionals pick unsuccessful locations.

5. Costs can be extremely high. There's the franchise fee, which can be modest or way up into the six-figures range. That's for the license to use their marketing concept, their training, and their professional assistance.

   Because of standardization, the supplies, fixtures, and equipment have exact specifications and can be more costly than if you were to shop around for the best bargains in a new start-up of your own.

   Next are the franchise royalties. These can run from 3 percent to 10 percent and are most often based on your gross sales. In some cases, there may be a sliding scale of percentages linked to increasing grosses. When you've worked your way up to a $500,000 gross and there's a 5 percent royalty fee involved, that's $25,000 you have to give out to the home office. If profits are low or nonexistent, you still have to pay the royalty fee.

   There may also be co-op advertising fees for national or regional coverage. Although this does benefit the franchise identity, you still have to keep up your own local promotion. That means two advertising expenditures.

   Designated suppliers of the franchisor's choice may be more costly than obtaining bids from others. Although centralized buying is supposed to be one of the benefits, the franchisor may be getting a percentage kickback of supplier sales to franchisees. Whatever the problems—late deliveries, poor service, higher costs, and so on—you must purchase supplies from the franchisor's selected suppliers.

6. The franchise contract benefits the franchisor, and this can create

legal disadvantages for you. Sales territories may overlap that of another unit, or a similar subsidiary of the parent company may not be excluded from your marketing area. Sales quotas that are difficult to attain may cause a franchise termination. Rule infractions after you have built up the business may also cancel the contract. It may be impossible for you to sell or pull out without taking a financial beating, especially if the contract has an escape or buy-back clause favoring the franchisor.

7. What about the franchisor itself? There have been many cases of financial overextension with too many units too fast, resulting in bankruptcy. Your property or lease may become involved with the creditors or those who financed this aspect of the franchise. Replenishment of inventory and supplies would be another problem. Your unit may not be able to survive, through no fault of your own.

   Although the franchise identity is a big plus, it can also become a burden if, for example, product quality in other area units deteriorated. How badly will this reflect on your business? You may have no other choice than to ride out the storm and hope the final verdict is a positive one.

   In either case, good or bad, you have no control over these potentially destructive situations. In addition, some franchisors may be incompetent. There have been companies who expanded too quickly, anxious to grow overnight but without having the necessary capital or preparing tried and true standardization. As a result, their training and operational procedures may not be the best, and your chances for success are greatly diminished.

There's a lot of food for thought in this review of the negative aspects of franchising. However, in no way should these negatives lead you to automatically reject the franchise form of entrepreneurship. Both the plus and minus factors should be thoroughly evaluated before you plunge in. Keep in mind that many franchise operations can be easily duplicated, at much less cost. Would this be the better way to go? Is the franchise *identity* worth the added cost?

DO YOU FIT THE BILL?

Now that you've absorbed some of the advantages and disadvantages inherent in operating a franchise, you may have decided that further exploration is desirable. What are some of the other areas that should be looked into? Personal appraisal? Type of franchise? Franchisor relationship?

The answer is that you must evaluate everything! You've got to look into all the nooks and crannies that might affect your decision about being the boss in a franchise unit. A good place to start is checking out the "you" element in this environment. You may discover additional disadvantages or advantages as you evaluate yourself:

Are you healthy? The one surprise to most franchisees is the amount of hard work involved. If you intend to be active in the operation, very long hours and plenty of stress situations are a part of it. Vacations or long weekends are often difficult to get.

Can you take supervision? Although you are the boss, you are actually more like the manager of a chain operation, working under orders and giving out orders. Some franchisors keep very close tabs on all operational procedures.

Are you a self-starter? Where the franchisor doesn't sit on your shoulder and the area rep only comes when called, can you go it alone? Is hand-holding something you require to perform at your peak efficiency?

Can you supervise others? Most franchise units require personnel. In the case of fast-food and ice cream units, there are multi-shifts. Are you impatient with others? Do you dislike training personnel and are you reluctant to fire people even when necessary? Have you supervised personnel in your previous jobs? Can you communicate clearly?

Do you have previous business experience? Although most franchisors stress no experience necessary, there's lots of paperwork to handle, plus daily, weekly, and monthly reports in accordance with each franchisor's requirements. Often a knowledge of business practices or experience in a field similiar to that of the franchisor can be extremely helpful, even though you were told it wasn't essential.

What about franchise rigidity? Is this something that will bother you? Can you really follow through without ever deviating from the operational procedures that are proscribed by the franchisor? Will you be able to conform for months? A year? Five years? Although you want to be on your own, do you like the idea of having the backup assistance of those more expert than yourself whenever you need it?

This kind of analysis of your personal qualifications is the initial step you require in targeting a yes decision for franchising. In effect, the overall question being resolved is: can you work within the system?

Once you choose a particular franchise to buy, there will be a few more questions that involve the "you" ingredient. For example, will you honestly be enthusiastic about the franchised line you selected? Your original reasons for franchising might only have incorporated the basic advantages: it's all laid out for you, you don't need experience, and the chances for success are greater than if you started from scratch.

It's fine to consider the advantages. But don't get trapped into a specific line only because it seemed better, or easier, or cheaper, or required fewer hours. It should be something you believe you will *enjoy*, in addition to all the other necessary positive elements. You must ask yourself if you want to, or like to, fill ice cream cones for a goodly number of years, or make out tax reports, or sell french fries, or lube fittings, or even do aerobic dancing. Maybe, instead, it's the video or computer explosion that grabs your interest and attention.

THE FRANCHISOR VIEWPOINT

As noted earlier, there are innumerable types of franchises within the regular categories of retail, service, wholesale, and manufacturing. This can and does affect the franchisor's viewpoint of what they expect to see in a franchisee.

Some very selective franchisors have applicants submit to a series of tests involving personality and character evaluations, somewhat along the lines of the self-appraisal questions on the previous pages. Others may be more interested in your credit or financial capabilities as they relate to the monetary investment required to handle their franchise. The high-tech franchisors may relate to your skills and experience in their lines.

Reputable franchisors will take the time to investigate *you*, for they fully intend to profit from your success. They are truly interested in applicants who will make good franchisees. Generally speaking, this means selecting the person who has a high motivation personality and understands and accepts the franchise philosophy of working within the system. From the franchisor viewpoint, the success factor has already been built into their operations by the trial-and-error period that eventually led to the present polish and perfection.

There is no enthusiasm on the franchisor's part for your attempts to improve what they have standardized. Your autonomy is definitely limited—by design! The new franchisee depends on the franchisor; in fact that's why he or she has bought into the system—a system each buyer believes to be presently successful. "Why, then," moans the franchisor, "do they want to try and change things?" The answer is a simple, humanistic one. After the franchisee has gained experience and is doing well, the franchisee feels the success is mainly a result of his or her own efforts. Conversely, if things don't go well, it's obviously the franchisor's fault!

To the parent company, this is the kind of thinking that can play havoc with the entire franchise concept. In the tests and interviews that take place before the purchase, they try to weed out the mavericks who would be frustrated and unhappy working within the system.

Because of this concern, new attention has developed in women franchisees. The odds are good that franchising is a great way for them to start at the top. A lack of experience becomes a plus, because they want and appreciate the backup offered by the franchisor experts in standardized procedures, accounting, advertising, and general business management. And they themselves have lots to offer. Bringing up families and running households has already instilled many of them with the abilities for practicing effective organization, coping with details, establishing priorities, succeeding at interpersonal communication, and taking care of general emergencies. Those advantages fit very well into the franchise concept, and you will be seeing more and more women buying and running their own franchise units.

WHAT TYPE FRANCHISE?

The selection of a franchise is almost unlimited. One of the fastest growth areas in the past few years has been the service area. The 1980's have shown a 40 percent increase in franchise units that relate to services, for both small businesses and the home.

It's cheaper for small business, for example, to use outside services rather than costly internal equipment and extra personnel. At home, people seem to be too busy or too self-centered to handle chores that used to be part of their everyday routines, such as lawn and garden care, household cleaning, child care, general maintenance, and car care.

There's still more growth to come and new areas to conquer. Two key principles involve convenience and time-saving. In some cases, the importance of these aspects seems to have created a throwback to the past. Small independent stores almost disappeared when the huge chains, department stores, and supermarkets entered their areas. Today, in an effort to save time and avoid hassles, people are going back to the smaller, more knowledgeable more service-oriented entrepreneurs. Often there is less waiting for service and the complications are minimized. In many instances this has meant patronizing one of the franchise units—convenience food stores, ten-minute oil changes, athletic footwear stores, computer stores, video software stores, sports apparel stores, specialty cheese shops, health food shops, and so many others.

It's not quite a return of the mom-and-pop stores, but there is a definite resurgence of the small business in this franchise field. Additionally, this trend reflects the growth of specialization, which has permeated every aspect of our lives during the past two decades. Who can forget the comedian's gag commentary on that theme: "He's a nasal specialist now—left nostril only!"

We'll see a great deal more specialization in the near future. Just take a look at some of the franchises that have recently started or have *doubled* in the past five years.

Barter:	both personal and business, with goods or services.
Employment:	temporary placements of special skills—nurses and LPNs, dental technicians, butlers, maids, bartenders, security guards.
Housecleaning:	windows, houses, rental apartments, vacation premises, model homes, chimneys.
Car care:	instant tuneups, lube depots, rust proofing, mobile repairs, mobile wash and wax, tire centers.
Protection:	theft, fire, medical alerts.
Beauty and Health:	hair styling, nails, body care, physical fitness, aerobics, dancercise, weight loss, special cosmetics.
Electronics:	personal computers, computer software, video recorders, VHS and Beta videocassette sales and rentals, and video recording services.
Food service:	frozen yogurt, soup and salad bars, health and diet foods, cookies, tea and coffee shops, ethnic foods—Chinese, Japanese, Mexican, Greek, and so on.
Personal aids:	services that take care of shopping, organizing personal papers, arranging celebrations, delivering personal messages. Personal mailbox depots and safe deposit vaults.
Deliveries:	parcels, letters, magazines, and regional promotions for business.

Even within those categories, there are creative individuals who see additional opportunities. Theirs will start out as a small venture, and then they, or some other entrepreneur, will develop it into a new franchise opportunity.

The type of franchise to be selected depends on your own interests and then an evaluation of a number of franchisors within a few fields. By narrowing your choice down to a select group and comparing what each has to offer, the final decision may not be a difficult one. At the very least, it will be closer to the bull's-eye, specifically because you investigated and evaluated.

FRANCHISE DIRECTORY LISTINGS

As mentioned earlier, one of the better sources for initial information is the annual *Franchise Opportunities Handbook*, prepared by the Department of Commerce. A recent edition has an extensive listing of over a thousand entries of franchisors who do not discriminate on the basis of race, color, or national origin in the availability, terms, or conditions of their franchises.

Although this does not include every known franchisor in the field, it does include the greatest majority. For an initial once-over in determining the type of franchise that might interest you, this source will be your best ally.

The handbook's index, by category, has been reprinted on the following pages. Look it over. Note the extensive variety of businesses that have been structured into the franchise field. Each new edition of the handbook may include hundreds of additional businesses to choose from.

fRANChisE OPPORTUNiTiES HANdbook

UNITED STATES DEPARTMENT OF COMMERCE
International Trade Administration
and
Minority Business Development Agency

Automotive Products/Service

AAMCO Transmissions, Inc. ....
ABT Service Centers ....
Acc-U-Tune & Brake ....
Action Auto, Inc. ....
Aid Auto Stores, Inc. ....
Al & Ed's Autosound ....
Alaskan Oil Incorporated ....
American Transmissions ....
AmMark Corporation ....
Appearance Reconditioning Co., Inc. ....
Auto Care Express, Inc. (ACE) ....
Auto Oil Changers, Inc. ....
Auto-One Appearance & Protection, Inc. ....
Autospa Corp. ....
Auto Valet, Inc. ....
The Battery Bank ....
Big O Tire Dealers, Inc. ....
Brake World Auto Centers ....
Cap-A Radiator Shops of America, Inc. ....
Car Care Corporation ....
Car-Matic Systems, Inc. ....
Car-X Muffler Shops ....
Champion Auto Stores Inc. ....
Cleanco Inc. ....
Cottman Transmission Systems, Inc. ....
Detail Plus Car Appearance Centers ....
Drive Line Service, Inc. ....
Dr. Nick's Transmissions, Ltd. ....
Dr. Vinyl & Associates, Ltd. ....
Eaglespeed 5 Minute Oil Change & Lub ....
Econo Lube N'Tune, Inc. ....
End-A-Flat ....
Endrust Industries ....
E.P.I. Inc. ....
Fair Muffler Shops ....
Fantasy Coachworks Ltd. ....
The Firestone Tire & Rubber Company ....
5 Minute Oil Change, Inc. ....
Gibraltar Transmissions ....
B. F. Goodrich Company ....
The Goodyear Tire & Rubber Company ....
Grease 'N Go., Inc. ....
Grease Monkey International, Inc. ....
Great Bear Auto Centers, Inc. ....
Guaranteed Tune-up ....
Hollywood Auto Decor Ltd. ....
House of Mufflers Enterprises ....
International Cooling Experts Systems Ltd. ....
Interstate Automatic Transmission Co., Inc. ....
Jiffiwash, Inc. ....
Jiffy Lube International, Inc. ....
Kennedy Transmission ....
King Bear Enterprises, Inc. ....
Kwik Change Int'l., Inc. ....
Lee Myles Associates Corporation ....
The Lube Shop ....
MAACO Enterprises, Inc. ....
Malco Products, Inc. ....
Mark I Auto Service Centers, Inc. ....

McQuik's Oilube Inc. ....
Mechanical Man Car Wash Factory, Inc. ....
Meineke Discount Muffler Shops, Inc. ....
Merlin's Muffler Shops, Inc. ....
Midas International Corp. ....
Mighty Distributing System of America, Inc. ....
Milex of America, Inc. ....
Ming of America, Inc. ....
Miracle Auto Painting ....
Mitey, Inc. ....
Mobile Auto Trim, Inc. ....
Morall Brake Centers ....
Motra Corp. ....
Mr. Transmission, Div. ....
Muffler Crafters, Inc. ....
Multi-Start Products ....
National Car Care Centers, Inc. ....
Novus Windshield Repair and Scratch Removal ....
P&D Premier Auto Parts, Inc. ....
Parts Plus
Penn Jersey Corporation ....
Perma-Guard Car Care Centers ....
The Pit Pros ....
Plug Buggy, Inc. ....
Precision Tune, Inc. ....
Pro Car Corp. ....
Quick-O ....
Service Center ....
60 Minute Tune ....
Sparks Tune-Up, Inc. ....
Specialty Lubrication Corp. ....
SpeeDee Oil Change & Tune-Up ....
Speedy Muffler King
Speedy Transmission Centers ....
Spot-Not Car Washes ....
Star Technology Windshield Repair, Inc. ....
Stereo Workshop, Inc. ....
Steve's Detailing ....
Sunshine Polishing Systems Inc. ....
Tidy Car Inc. ....
Total Systems Technology, Inc. ....
Tuff-Kote Dinol, Inc. ....
Tuffy Service Centers, Inc. ....
Tune Omize Tune Up Centers ....
Tunex International, Inc. ....
Ultra Wash, Inc. ....
Unico Autobody & Paint ....
Victory Lane Quick Oil Change ....
Wash-O-Tel, Inc. ....
The Wax Man, Inc. ....
Wear Master Co. ....
Western Auto ....
Ziebart Rustproofing Company ....

Auto/Trailer Rentals

Affordable Used Car Rental System Inc. ....
A.I.N. Leasing Systems ....
American International Rent-A-Car ....
Americar Corporation ....
Amtralease ....
Avis Rent A Car System, Inc. ....

Budget Rent A Car Corporation ....
Dollar Rent A Car Systems, Inc. ....
Freedom Rent-A-Car System ....
Hertz Corporation ....
Holiday Payless Rent-A-Car System ....
Incentive Leasing of North America ....
Mr. Rent A Car, Mr. Lease A Car, Inc. ....
Practical Used Car Rental ....
Rent-A-Dent Car Rental Systems, Inc. ....
Rent-A-Wreck of America ....
Thrifty Rent-A-Car System ....
Ugly Duckling Rent-A-System, Inc. ....
U-Save Auto Rental of America, Inc. ....

Beauty Salons/Supplies

Americuts ....
Autumn Rose Hair Designers ....
The Barbers, Hairstyling for Men and Women, Inc.
Command Performance ....
Cost Cutters Family Hair Shops ....
Elan Hair Design Franchising Ltd. ....
Fantastic Sam's, The Original Family Haircutters ...
First Choice Haircutters Ltd. ....
First Place, Inc. ....
Great Clips, Inc. ....
Great Expectations Precision Haircutters ....
Haircrafters ....
Haircuts Co. ....
Hair Performers ....
Joan M. Cable's LaFemmina Beauty Salons, Inc. ...
The Lemon Tree ....
Lord's & Lady's Hair Salons ....
Mane Event Unisex Hair Designers ....
Mantrap Professional Hair Salons ....
Poppers Family Hair Care Center, Inc. ....
Rainy Day People, Inc. ....
Supercuts ....

Business Aids/Services

Adam Group, Inc. ....
Advantage Business Services, Inc. ....
Agvise ....
Air Brook Limousine ....
Allan & Partners ....
American Advertising Distributors, Inc. ....
American Heritage Agency, Inc. ....
American Safety and Security Film, Inc. ....
American Standard Appliance Protection, Inc. ......
An International World of Weddings, Inc. ....
Associated Air Freight, Inc. ....
ANA ....
Barter Exchange, Inc. ....
Barter Resources, Inc. ....
Best Resume Service ....
Binex-Automated Business Systems, Inc. ....
H&R Block, Inc. ....
The Bread Box ....
The Building Inspector of America ....
Business Consultants of America ....
Business Data Services, Inc. ....
Business Digest, Inc. ....

Business Investment Group of America, Inc. ....
Buy Low Enterprises ....
Caring Live-Ins Inc. ....
Certified Capital Correspondent, Inc. ....
Check Mart ....
Chroma Copy Franchising of America, Inc. ....
Chroma International ....
Classified Photo Ads, Inc. ....
Colbrin Franchise Systems, Inc. ....
Commercial Services Company ....
Communications World International, Inc. ....
Comprehensive Accounting Corp ....
Compufund National Mortgage Network ....
Concept III International ....
Contacts Influential Int'l. Corp ....
Corporate Finance Associates ....
Corporate Investment Business Brokers, Inc. ....
Correct Credit Co. Of Howell Inc. ....
Credit Clinic ....
Credit-Rite, Inc. ....
Cycle Service Messengers ....
Data Destruction Services, Inc. ....
Debit One Inc. ....
Deliverex, Inc. ....
Development Services, Inc. ....
Dial One International, Inc. ....
Dixon Commercial Investigators, Inc. ....
Dodds Management Systems, Inc. ....
Dynamic Air Freight, Inc. ....
Eastern Onion, Inc. ....
EconoTax, Inc. ....
EKW Systems ....
ESP Discount Coupons, Inc. ....
Focus On Bingo Magazine ....
Focus On Homes Magazine ....
The Franchise Architects ....
Franchise Network USA, Inc. ....
The Franchise Store ....
Franklin Traffic Service, Inc. ....
Future Search Management Corp. ....
Gascard Club, Inc. ....
General Business Services, Inc. ....
The Headquarters Companies ....
Heimer Inspections ....
HomeCall, Inc. ....
Homes & Land Publishing Corp. ....
Homewatch Corporation ....
Housemaster of America, Inc. ....
Incotax Systems, Inc. ....
Informerific Corporation ....
Int'l. Mergers and Acquisitions ....
K&O Publishing ....
K & W Computerized Tax Service, Inc. ....
Kelly's Liquidators, Inc. ....
Law Centers of America ....
Legacy One, Inc. ....
The Letter Writer, Inc. ....
Mail Boxes Etc., USA ....
Mail Sort, Inc. ....
The Management Center Inc. ....
Marcoin, Inc. ....
McTaggart Mortgage Assistance Centers, Inc. .....

Medical Insura Form Service ....
Mel Jackson Inc. ....
MiFax Service and Systems, Inc. ....
Money Concepts Int'l., Inc. ....
Money Mailer, Inc. ....
Motivational Systems ....
Mr. Sign Franchising Corp. ....
Muzak ....
Namco Systems, Inc. ....
National Housing Inspections ....
National Tenant Network, Inc. ....
Nationwide Income Tax Service Co. ....
Office Alterative, Inc. ....
The Office, Ltd. ....
Packaging Know-How and Gift Shipping, Inc. ....
Padgett Business Services ....
Pay-Fone Systems, Inc. ....
Pension Assistance Through Hicks, Inc. ....
Petro Brokerage & Service, Ltd. ....
Peyron Associates ....
Pilot Air Freight Corporation ....
PNS, Inc. ....
The Prime—PM Corp. ....
Princeton Energy Partners Inc. ....
Programmed Management Franchise Corp. ....
Property Damage Appraisers, Inc. ....
Property Inspection Service ....
proVenture, Inc. ....
Realty Counsel Brokerage Management Corp. ......
Recognition Express Int'l. Ltd. ....
Reliable Business Systems, Inc. ....
Rental Data Franchise Corporation ....
Sandy Hook Scientific Inc. ....
Sara Care Franchise Corp. ....
Sav-Pac ....
Selectra-Date Corporation ....
Sign Express ....
Simplified Business Services, Inc. ....
Sitters Unlimited, Inc. ....
SMI International, Inc. ....
Southwest Promotional Corporation ....
Sports Center Advertising, Inc. ....
Stork News ....
Stuffit Company, Inc. ....
Tax Man, Inc. ....
Tax Offices of America ....
TBC Business Brokers ....
Telecheck Services, Inc. ....
Tender Sender, Inc. ....
Tote-A-Shower, Inc. ....
Transformational Technologies ....
Trimark ....
Triple Check Income Tax Service ....
TV Facts ....
TV Focus, Inc. ....
TV News ....
TV Scene ....
TV Tempo, Inc. ....
TWP Enterprises, Inc. ....
UBI Business Brokers, Inc. ....
Video Workshop Franchises, Inc. ....
VR Business Brokers, Inc. ....

Western Appraisers ....
Widmer Office Products, Inc. ....

Campgrounds

Kamp Dakota, Inc. ....
Kampgrounds of America, Inc. ....
Safari Campgrounds ....
Yogi Bear's Jellystone Park Camp—Resorts ....

Children's Stores/Furniture/Products

Bellini Juvenile Designer Furniture Corp. ....
Lewis of London, Inc. ....
Peppermint Fudge Franchise, Inc. ....
Pregnant Inc. 4 Babys Only ....

Clothing/Shoes

Allison's Place, Inc. ....
Athlete's Foot Marketing Associates, Inc. ....
Athletic Attic Marketing, Inc. ....
Athletic Lady ....
Bags & Shoes ....
Bencone Outlet Center ....
Cherokee Franchising Corp. ....
Canterbury of New Zealand ....
Fleet Feet ....
Formal Wear Service ....
Gingliss International, Inc. ....
Hats in the Belfry Franchise Corp. ....
Jiliene, Inc. ....
J. S. Designs, Inc. ....
Just Pants ....
The Kiddie Kobbler Ltd. ....
Lady Madonna Management Corp. ....
Lanz Franchising, Inc. ....
Madeira International Corp. ....
Mark-It Stores, Inc. ....
Mode O'Day Company ....
New York City Shoes ....
President Tuxedo, Inc. ....
Sally Wallace Brides Shop, Inc. ....
Second Sole, Inc. ....
Sportique, Inc. ....
T-Shirts Plus, Inc. ....
Tyler's Country Clothes ....
Wild Tops Franchising, Inc. ....

Construction/Remodeling-Materials/Services

ABC Seamless, Inc. ....
American Energy Managers ....
Archadek International, Inc. ....
Bathcrest Inc. ....
Bath Genie, Inc. ....
B-Dry System, Inc. ....
California Closet Co. ....
Captain Glides, Inc. ....
Chimney Relining Int'l., Inc. ....
College Pro Painters (U.S.) Ltd. ....
Curbmate Corporation ....
Doctor Fix-It Inc. ....
The Drain Doctor ....

Easi-Set Industries ....
Eldorado Stone Corporation ....
Eureka Log Homes, Inc. ....
Facelifters Franchise Systems, Inc. ....
Firedex, Inc. ....
Flex-Shield Int'l., Inc. ....
Four Seasons Greenhouses, Design
  & Remodeling Center ....
GNU Services, Corp. ....
Heritage Log Homes, Inc. ....
K-Krete, Inc. ....
Kitchen Savers, Inc. ....
Lavastone International, Inc. ....
The Linc Corporation ....
Lindal Cedar Homes, Inc. ....
Master Remodelers National, Inc. ....
Miracle Method, Inc. ....
Mister Renovator ....
Mr. Build International ....
Natural Log Homes, Inc. ....
New England Log Homes, Inc. ....
Northern Products Log Homes, Inc. ....
Novus Plate Glass Repair, Inc. ....
Paul W. Davis Systems, Inc. ....
Perma Ceram Enterprises, Inc. ....
Perma-Jack Co. ....
Porcelain Patch & Glaze Company of America ......
Porcelite International, Inc. ....
Rapid Economical Construction Systems Corp .....
Redi-Strip Co., Inc. ....
Remodel Masters ....
Ryan Homes, Inc. ....
The Screenmobile Inc. ....
Service America
Smokey Mountain Log Cabins, Inc. ....
Speed Fab-Crete Corporation, Int'l. ....
SPR Int'l. Bathtub Refinishing, Inc. ....
Surface Specialists Inc. ....
Thermocrete Chimney Lining, Inc. ....
Timbermill Storage Barns, Inc. ....
Weatherbilt Homes, Inc. ....
The Windows of Opportunities, Inc. ....

Cosmetics/Toiletries

Aloette ....
Caswell-Massey ....
DermaCulture, Inc. ....
i Natural Cosmetics ....
Jacquie's Place Franchises, Inc. ....
Jean Pierre Cosmetiques Inc. ....
Judith Sans Internationale, Inc. ....
Key West Fragrance & Cosmetic ....
Syd Simons Cosmetics, Inc. ....

Dental Centers

American Dental Council, Inc. ....
Consumer Dental Network ....
DentaHealth of America ....
Dental Health Services ....
Dental Power International ....
Dwight Systems, Inc. ....

General Health Systems, Inc. ....
Jonathan Dental ....
Nu-Dimensions Dental Services ....

Drug Stores

Drug Castle Franchises, Inc. ....
Drug Emporium Inc. ....
Health Mart, Inc. ....
Le$-On Retail Systems, Inc. ....
Medicap Pharmacies Inc. ....
Medicine Shoppes International, Inc. ....
Snyder Drug Stores, Inc. ....

Educational Products/Services

Barbizon International, Inc. ....
Better Birth Foundation ....
The Carole Riggs Studios ....
Child Enrichment Centers ....
College Centers of Southern California, Inc. ....
College Preparatory Service, Inc. ....
Dawn Audio Recording Technology Institute ....
Echols Int'l. Travel and Hotel Schools, Inc. ....
Els International, Inc. ....
Gymboree Corporation ....
Huntington Learning Center ....
Institute of Reading Development ....
John Robert Powers Finishing & Modeling &
  Career School ....
Kinderdance International Inc. ....
Mac Tay Aquatics, Inc. ....
Model Merchandising Int'l. Ltd. ....
Perkins Fit By Five, Inc. ....
Personal Computer Learning Centers of America ..
Playful Parenting Franchise Corp. ....
Playorena, Inc. ....
Primary Prep Pre-Schools ....
Sandler Systems, Inc. ....
Sexton Educational Centers ....
Sylvan Learning Corp. ....
Tegeler Time Day Care System ....
Teller Training Distributors, Inc. ....
The Travel Trade School, Inc. ....
Vibralife International, Inc. ....
Weist-Barron, Inc. ....

Employment Services

AAA Employment Franchise, Inc. ....
Adia Personnel Services.....................................
Bailey Employment System, Inc. ....
Baker & Baker Employment Services, Inc. ....
Beall Associates, Inc. ....
Bryant Bureau ....
Business & Professional Consultants, Inc. ....
Career Employment Services, Inc. ....
Dennis & Dennis Personnel Services ....
Division 10 Personnel Services ....
Dunhill Office Personnel ....
Dunhill Personnel System, Inc. ....
Employers Overload ....
Engineering Corporation of America ....
Express Services, Inc. ....

Five Star Temporaries, Inc. ....
F-O-R-T-U-N-E Franchise Corporation ....
Franchise Service Corporation ....
Gerotoga Enterprises, Inc. ....
Gilbert Lane Personnel Service ....
Harper Associates, Inc. ....
Hayes Personnel Services, Inc. ....
Heritage Personnel Systems, Inc. ....
HRI Services, Inc. ....
JBS, Inc. ....
J.O.B.S. ....
Management Recruiters International, Inc. ....
Management Search, Inc. ....
Manpower, Inc. ....
The Marshall Group ....
Murphy Group ....
Nichols Personnel Inc. ....
Norrell Temporary Services, Inc. ....
The Olsten Corporation ....
Parker Page Associates, Inc. ....
Personnel Pool of America, Inc. ....
Place Mart Franchising Corporation ....
The Regional Network of Personnel Consultants ...
Retail Recruiters International, Inc./Spectra
    Professional Search ....
Romac and Associates, Inc. ....
Roth Young Personnel Services, Inc. ....
Sales Consultants International ....
Sanford Rose Associates Int'l., Inc. ....
Service Personnel, Inc. ....
Snelling and Snelling, Inc. ....
Temporaries, Incorporated ....
Thank Goodness I've Found...TGIF ....
Times Services, Inc. ....
Todays Temporary ....
Uniforce Temporary Personnel, Inc. ....
Uni/Search, Inc. ....
VIP Personnel Systems ....
Western Temporary Services, Inc. ....

Equipment/Rentals

A to Z Rental Centers ....
Apparelmaster, Inc. ....
Major Video, Inc. ....
Mr. Movies Inc. ....
Nation-Wide General Rental Centers, Inc. ....
PCR Personal Computer Rentals ....
Remco Enterprises, Inc. ....
Rental Centers U.S.A. Inc. ....
Rent-To-Own, Inc. ....
Sounds Easy Int'l. Inc. ....
Taylor Rental Corporation ....
United Rent-All, Inc. ....

Foods-Donuts

Bosa Donuts Systems, Inc. ....
Dawn Donuts Systems, Inc. ....
Dixie Cream Flour Company ....
The Donut Hole ....
Donut Inn, Inc. ....
Donutland, Inc. ....
Donuts Galore, Inc. ....

Donuts N' Coffee ....
Dunkin' Donuts of America, Inc. ....
Foster's Donuts, Inc. ....
Honey Fluff Donuts, Inc. ....
Jolly Pirate Donut Shops ....
Mister Donut of America, Inc. ....
Southern Maid Donut Flour Company, Inc. ....
Spudnuts, Inc. ....
Tastee Donuts, Inc. ....
The Whole Donut Franchise System ....
Winchell's Donut House ....

Foods—Grocery/Specialty/Stores

Alpen Pantry, Inc. ....
Atlantic Concessions Systems, Inc. ....
Atlantic Richfield Company ....
Augie's Inc. ....
Balboa Baking Co. ....
Barnie's Coffee & Tea Co., Inc. ....
Blue Chip Cookie Inc. ....
Blue Mill Enterprises Corp. ....
The Boardwalk Peanut Shoppe ....
The Bread Basket Inc. ....
Breaktime, Inc. ....
Bulk Food Warehouse ....
Bulk International ....
Buns Master Bakery Systems Corp. ....
Cheese Shop International, Inc. ....
The Coffee Beanery Ltd. ....
The Coffee Merchant ....
The Coffee Mill ....
Coffee, Tea, & Thee ....
Colonial Village Meat Market Franchise Corp. ....
Confectionery Square Corp. ....
Convenient Food Mart, Inc. ....
The Cookie Bin, Inc. ....
Cookie Factory of America ....
The Cookie Store ....
Country Biscuits ....
Dairy Mart Convenience Stores, Inc. ....
Dial-A-Gift, Inc. ....
Food-N-Fuel, Inc. ....
Frontier Fruit & Nut Co. ....
Giuliano's Delicatessen & Bakery ....
Glass Oven Bakery ....
Gloria Jean's Coffee Bean Corp. ....
Grandma Love's Cookies and Company ....
Great Earth Vitamin Stores ....
Great Harvest Franchising Inc. ....
The Great San Francisco Seafood Co., Ltd. ....
Heavenly Ham ....
Hickory Farms of Ohio, Inc. ....
In 'N' Out Food Stores, Inc. ....
International Aromas ....
Jitney-Jungle, Inc. ....
Katie McGuire's Olde Fashion Pie Shoppe ....
Kid's Korner Fresh Pizza, Inc. ....
Li'L Peach Convenience Food Stores ....
Mr. Dunderbak, Inc. ....
Neal's Cookies ....
Oky Doky Food Marts ....

The Original Great American Chocolate Chip
   Cookie Co., Inc. ....
Papa Aldos Int'l. Inc. ....
Papa John's Inc. ....
Pizza Un-Limited, Inc. ....
Quick Shop Minit Marts, Inc. ....
Sav-A-Step Food Mart, Inc. ....
The Second Cup ....
The Southland Corporation ....
Swiss Colony Stores, Inc. ....
Tidbit Alley, Inc. ....
T. J. Cinnamons, Ltd. ....
White Hen Pantry Division ....
Zaro's America's Home Bakery ....
Zip Food Stores, Inc. ....

Foods — Ice Cream/Yogurt/Candy/ Popcorn/Beverages

Baskin Robbins, Inc. ....
Ben & Jerry's Homemade Inc. ....
Bresler's 33 Flavors, Inc. ....
Brigham's ....
The California Yogurt Company ....
Candy World Treats & Gifts ....
Carberry's Homemade Ice Cream Franchise
   Systems, Inc. ....
Carter's Nuts, Inc. ....
Carvel Corporation ....
Chipwich ....
Cone-A-Copia Inc. ....
The Corn Popper, Inc. ....
Custom Leasing Co. ....
Davie's Ice Cream Shoppes, Inc. ....
Dipper Dan Ice Cream Shoppes ....
Double Rainbow Franchises, Inc. ....
Emack and Bolio's Ice Cream and Ice Cream
   Cakes for the Connoisseur ....
Ernie's Wine & Liquor Corp. ....
Foremost Sales Promotions, Inc. ....
Frosty Factory Int'l., Inc. ....
Frusen Gladje Franchise Inc. ....
The Fudge Co. ....
Galerie Group, Inc. ....
Gaston's, Inc. ....
Gelato Amare ....
Gelato Classico Franchising, Inc. ....
Gorin's Homemade Ice Cream & Sandwiches ....
The Great Midwestern Ice Cream Co. ....
Hawaiian Freeze ....
Heidi's Frogen Yozurt Shoppes, Inc. ....
I Can't Believe It's Yogurt, Inc. ....
Ice Cream Churn, Inc. ....
Island Snow Hawaii ....
J. Higby's Yogurt Treat Shoppe ....
Kara Signature Chocolates ....
Karmelkorn Shoppe, Inc. ....
Kilwins Chocolates Franchise ....
Larry's Olde Fashioned Ice Cream Parlours, Inc. ....
Lone Star Candy Mfg. Co. Of Texas, Inc. ....
M.G.M. Liquor Warehouse International, Inc. ....
Mister Softee, Inc. ....
Old Uncle Gaylord's, Inc. ....

The Peanut Shack of America, Inc. ....
Popcorn Palace and Candy Emporium ....
Popcorn Parlor Franchise Systems ....
Rainbow Snow ....
Real Rich Systems, Inc. ....
Rocky Mountain Chocolate Factory Inc. ....
Seakan Candy Company ....
Steve's Homemade Ice Cream Inc. ....
Swensen's Ice Cream Company ....
TCBY Enterprises, Inc. ....
Topsy Shoppes, Inc. ....
Tra-Hans Candies, Inc. ....
Truffles Chocolatier, Inc. ....
Twistee Treat 6 Flavors ....
Vic's Corn Popper, Inc. ....
Whirla Whip Systems, Inc. ....
White Mountain Creamery ....
Wizards Ice Cream & Confectionery Shoppe, Ltd. .
Zack's Famous Frozen Yogurt, Inc. ....

Food — Pancake/Waffle/Pretzel

Elmer's Pancake & Steak House, Inc. ....
International House of Pancakes ....
Le Peep International, Inc. ....
Mary Belle Restaurants ....
Pancake Cottage Family Restaurants ....
Perkins Restaurants, Inc. ....
Village Inn Pancake House, Franchises ....
Waffletown U.S.A. Ltd. ....

Foods — Restaurant/Drive-Ins/Carry-Outs

A & W Restaurants, Inc. ....
Across The Street Restaurants of America, Inc. ...
All American Hero, Inc. ....
Allen's Subs Int'l. Corp. ....
All-V's, Inc. ....
Andy's of America, Inc. ....
Appetito's, Inc. ....
Applebee's ....
Arby's, Inc. ....
Arthur Treacher's Inc. ....
Aunt Chilotta Systems Inc. ....
Aurelio's Pizza Franchise, Ltd. ....
Bagel Nosh, Inc. ....
Baldinos Giant Jersey Subs, Inc. ....
Bananas ....
Barn'rds International ....
Barbacoa Enterprises, Inc. ....
Barro's Pizza Inc. ....
Bash Riprock's Restaurants, Inc. ....
Ben Franks Franchising Corp. ....
Benihana of Tokyo, Inc. ....
Big Boy Family Restaurants ....
Big Cheese Pizza Corp. ....
Big Top Corp. ....
Boardwalk Fries ....
Bobby Rubbino's USA, Inc. ....
Bo-James Saloon ....
Bojangles of America, Inc. ....
Bonanza Restaurants ....

Bowincal International, Inc. ....
Boy Blue of America, Inc. ....
Boz Hot Dogs ....
Bread & Company, Ltd. ....
Bridgeman's Restaurants, Inc. ....
Browns Chicken ....
Bun N Burger International, Inc. ....
Burger King Corporation ....
Buscemi's International ....
California Smoothie ....
Callahan's Int'l., Inc. ....
Captain D's ....
Carbone's Pizza ....
Carl Karcher Enterprises, Inc. ....
Casa Lupita Restaurants, Inc. ....
Cassano's, Inc. ....
Cheese Villa ....
Chelsa Street Pub ....
Chicken Delight of Canada, Ltd. ....
Chicken George Chicken, Inc. ....
Chicken Natural Food Services, Inc. ....
Chicken Unlimited Enterprise, Inc. ....
Church's Fried Chicken, Inc. ....
Circles International Natural Foods, Inc. ....
Circus Playhouse, Inc. ....
Cock of the Walk ....
Colonel Lee's Enterprises, Inc. ....
Cooker Concepts Inc. ....
Country Kitchen International, Inc. ....
Cousins Submarine Sandwich Shop Systems, Inc.
Cozy Nook, Inc. ....
Cozzoli's Pizza Express ....
Dairy Belle Freeze Development Co., Inc. ....
Dairy Cheer Stores ....
Dairy Isle Corporation ....
Dairy Sweet Corporation ....
Daly Franchise Co. ....
Damon's Franchise Corp. ....
Danver's International, Inc. ....
Del Taco Mexican Cafe ....
Diamond Dave's Taco Co., Inc. ....
Dietwork of America, Inc. ....
Dino's USA, Inc. ....
D'Lites of America, Inc. ....
Dog N Suds Restaurants ....
Domino's Pizza, Inc. ....
Dosanko Foods, Inc. ....
Druther's International, Inc. ....
El Chico Corporation ....
El Pollo Asado, Inc. ....
El Taco Restaurants, Inc. ....
Esteban Foods, Inc. ....
Everything Yogurt ....
Families Original Submarine Sandwiches ....
Famous Recipe Corporation ....
Fat Boy's Bar-B-Q Franchise System ....
Fatburger, Inc. ....
Flap Jack Shack, Inc. ....
Fletcher's Industries, Inc. ....
Fluky's Franchise Systems Int'l., Inc. ....
Forty Carrots, Inc. ....
Fosters Freeze, International ....

Fox's Pizza Den, Inc. ....
Frankie's Franchise Systems, Inc. ....
The French Baker/Cafe ....
Frenchy's International, Inc. ....
Fuddruckers, Inc. ....
Fuzzy's, Inc. ....
Gilbert/Robinson, Inc. ....
Giordano's Int'l. Franchise System, Inc. ....
Giovanni's Pizza by the Slice ....
Godfather's Pizza ....
Golden Bird Fried Chicken ....
Golden Chicken Franchises ....
Golden Fried Chicken of America, Inc. ....
Golden Skillet International ....
Gold Star Chili, Inc. ....
Grandy's Incorporated ....
The Great Gyros ....
Greenstreets National Corp. ....
Happy Joe's Pizza & Ice Cream Parlors ....
Happy Steak Companies, Inc. ....
Hardee's Food Systems, Inc. ....
Hartz Krispy Chicken ....
House of Yakitori Japanese Restaurants ....
Huddle House, Inc. ....
Hungry Boy Delicatessen, Inc. ....
The Hungry Hobo ....
International Blimpie Corporation ....
International Dairy Queen, Inc. ....
International Yogurt Company ....
Italo's Pizza Shop, Inc. ....
Jack in the Box Foodmaker, Inc. ....
Jake's International, Inc. ....
Jerry's Sub Shop ....
Jimboy's Tacos ....
Jo Ann's Chili Bordello, Inc. ....
John Phillip Tuba Corp. ....
Joyce's Submarine Sandwiches, Inc. ....
Jreck Subs, Inc. ....
Jrs Hot Dogs Inc. ....
J. T. McCord's Restaurants ....
K-Bob's Inc. ....
Ken's Pizza ....
Kettle Restaurants, Inc. ....
KFC Corporation ....
Koor's Systems, Inc. ....
Lamppost Pizza ....
Landis Food Services, Inc. ....
LaRosa's Inc. ....
Little Big Men, Inc. ....
Little Caesar Enterprises, Inc. ....
Little King Restaurant Corporation ....
London Fish N'Chips, Ltd. ....
Long John Silver's Inc. ....
Los Primos, Inc. ....
Losurdo Foods, Inc. ....
Love's Wood Pit Barbeque Restaurants ....
Macayo Mexican Restaurants ....
Maid Rite Products, Inc. ....
Marco Pollo Restaurants Int'l., Inc. ....
Marco's Pizza ....
Marino's Corporation ....
Maverick Family Steak House, Inc. ....

Mazzio's Pizza ....
McDonald's Corporation ....
McFaddin Ventures ....
Milton's Pizza House, Inc. ....
Minsky's Pizza ....
Minute Man of America, Inc. ....
Mountain Mike's Pizza ....
Mr. Burger, Inc. ....
Mr. Chicken National, Inc. ....
Mr. Gatti's, Inc. ....
Mr. Jims Pizzeria Corporation ....
Mr. Philly ....
Mr. Steak, Inc. ....
Nathan's Famous, Inc. ....
New Meiji Franchise Corp. ....
New Orleans's Famous Fried Chicken of America .
Noble Roman's, Inc. ....
North's Franchising Corp. ....
Nugget Restaurants ....
Numero Uno Franchise Corp. ....
The Olde World Cheese Shop ....
Olga's Kitchen Licensing, Inc. ....
Omaha Steakshops, Inc. ....
The Onion Crock, Inc. ....
Orange Bowl Corporation ....
Orange Julius of America ....
The Original Wiener Work Inc. ....
Pacific Tastee Freez, Inc. ....
Pantera's Corporation ....
Paris Croissant Northeast Corp. ....
Pasquale Food Company, Inc. ....
The Pasta House Company ....
The Peddler, Ltd. ....
Penguin Point Franchise Systems, Inc. ....
Penn's Golden Nuggets ....
Pepe's Incorporated ....
Peter Piper Pizza ....
The Pewter Mug ....
Pewter Pot Inc. ....
Philadelphia Steak & Sub Co. ....
Pietro's Pizza Parlors, Inc. ....
Pioneer Take Out Corporation ....
Pizza Chalet Franchise Corp. ....
Pizza Inn, Inc. ....
Pizza Man "He Delivers" ....
Pizza Pit ....
Pizza Rack Franchise Systems, Inc. ....
Pizza Transit Authority, Inc. ....
Playboy Clubs International, Inc. ....
Plush Pippin Restaurants, Inc. ....
Po Folks, Inc. ....
Ponderosa System, Inc. ....
Pony Express Pizza ....
Popeyes Famous Fried Chicken and Biscuits ....
Primo, Incorporated ....
Pudgies Pizza Franchising, Inc. ....
Ranellis Deli and Sandwich Shops ....
Rax Restaurants, Inc. ....
Red Robin Int'l., Inc. ....
Rico's Enterprises ....
Ring Chow Systems, Inc. ....
Ritzy's America's Favorites ....

Rocky Rococo Corporation ....
Roma Corporation ....
The Round Table Franchise Corporation ....
Roy Rogers Restaurants ....
Ruggles Restaurant Franchise Corp. ....
S.A.F. California/Lettuce Patch ....
The Salad Bar Corporation ....
Samurai Sam, Ltd. ....
Sbarro, Inc. ....
Schlotzsky's Inc. ....
Scooter's Pizza Delivery ....
Scotto Management Corporation ....
Seafood America ....
Sea Galley Stores, Inc. ....
Sergio's International, Inc. ....
Shakey's Incorporated ....
ShowBiz Pizza Place
Sir Pizza International, Inc. ....
Sizzler Steak Seafood Salad ....
Skinny Haven, Inc. ....
Skipper's, Inc. ....
Skyline Food Products Co. ....
Sonic Industries, Inc. ....
Sonny's Real Pit Bar BQ, Inc. ....
Soup & Salad Systems, Inc. ....
Stewart's Restaurants, Inc. ....
Straw Hat Restaurant Corporation ....
Stuckey's, Corp. ....
Sub & Stuff Sandwich Shops Inc. ....
Sub Station II, Inc. ....
Subway ....
Super Ribs Enterprise ....
Taco Bell ....
Taco Casa International, Ltd. ....
Taco Del Sol ....
Taco Grande, Inc. ....
Taco Hut, Inc. ....
Taco John's ....
The Taco Maker, Inc. ....
Taco Mayo Franchise Systems, Inc. ....
Taco Tico, Inc. ....
Taco Time International, Inc. ....
Tark Enterprises, Inc. ....
Tastee Freez International ....
Texas Tom's Inc. ....
Tippy's Taco House, Inc. ....
Togo's Eatery ....
Tubby's Sub Shops, Inc. ....
2 for 1 Pizza Enterprises ....
Uncle Tony's Pizza & Pasta Family Style Restaurant
Vista Franchise, Inc. ....
Ward's International, Inc. ....
Watta Ethnic Food Delight ....
W.C. Frank Investments, Inc. ....
Wendy's Old Fashioned Hamburgers ....
Western Sizzlin Steak House ....
Western Steer—Mom 'Pop's, Inc. ....
Westside Deli of America ....
Whataburger, Inc. ....
Wiener King System, Inc. ....
Wienerschnitzel Int'l., Inc. ....
Winners Corporation ....
Your Pizza Shops, Inc. ....

Yummy Yogurt, Inc. ....
Zab's Development Corp. ....
Zackly's Restaurant Systems, Inc. ....

General Merchandising Stores

Ben Franklin ....
Coast to Coast Stores ....

Health Aids/Services

Aerobic Fitness Centers ....
American Health & Diet Co. ....
Beta Osteoporosis Diagnostic Center of America .
BodyComp Systems, Inc. ....
Claflin Home Health Centers ....
Concept 90 Personal Fitness Stores ....
Contempo Women's Workout ....
Diet Center, Inc. ....
Eaton Medical Systems ....
Fortunate Corporation ....
Health Clubs of America ....
Health Force ....
Homecare Helping Hand, Inc. ....
Informed Corporation ....
Jazzercise, Inc. ....
Jeneal Int'l. Skin & Health Correction Centers ....
Lean Line, Inc. ....
Life Time Medical Nursing Services, Inc. ....
Medical Networks, Inc. ....
Miller Medical Service ....
Nu-Concept Body Wrap, Inc. ....
Nursefinders ....
Nutri-System, Inc. ....
Omni Health International, Inc. ....
Our Weigh ....
Physicians Weight Loss Centers of America, Inc. .
Respond First Aid Systems ....
Slender Center, Inc. ....
Sutter Medical Management Co., Inc. ....
Take Time Inc. ....
Thermographit Medical Associates, Inc. ....
Thin Life Centers ....
T.L.C. Nursing, Inc. ....
Total Lifestyle Corporation ....
United Surgical Centers ....
Victory International, Inc. ....
Waist Basket International ....
Weigh To Go, Inc. ....
The Weight Place, Inc. ....
Women At Large Systems, Inc. ....

Hearing Aids

Miracle Ear ....

Home Furnishings/Furniture-Retail/ Repair Services

Abbey Carpet Company ....
Amity, Inc. ....
Carpeteria, Inc. ....
Carpet Town, Inc. ....

Center Third Mattress Stores ....
Chem-Clean Furniture Restoration Center ....
Chem-Dry Carpet Cleaning ....
Cleanmark Corporation ....
Crossland Studies of America Inc. ....
Decorating Den Systems, Inc. ....
Dip 'N Strip, Inc. ....
Duraclean International ....
Expressions ....
Fabri-Zone of America, Inc. ....
The Floor to Ceiling Store ....
G. Fried Carpetland, Incorporated ....
Groundwater, Inc. ....
Guarantee System ....
Hillside Bedding ....
Howard Kaplan's French Country Store ....
Indoor Magic, Inc. ....
John Simmons, Inc. ....
King Koil Sleep Products ....
Langenwalter-Harris Chemical Co., Inc. ....
Murphy Beds of California ....
Naked Furniture, Inc. ....
Nettle Creek Industries, Inc. ....
Off-Track Bedding ....
The Pine Factory, Ltd. ....
Pro-Tection National, Inc. ....
Rainbow International Carpet Dyeing and
    Cleaning Co. ....
RecRoom Shoppe of Omaha, Inc. ....
Repele International ....
Scandia Down Corporation ....
Siesta Sleep Shop, Inc. ....
Slumberland, Inc. ....
Spring Crest Company ....
Stanley Steemer International, Inc. ....
Steamatic Incorporated ....
Storehouse, Inc. ....
United Consumers Club ....
Wallpaper Plus Inc. ....
WFO Franchises ....
Window Works, Inc. ....
Workbench, Inc. ....

Insurance

America One, Inc. ....
Dental Insurance Service, Inc. ....
ISU Corporation ....
Marketforce International, Inc. ....
Pridemark Corporation ....
Systems VII ....
Underwriters Adjusting Company ....

Laundries, Dry Cleaning-Services

A Cleaner World ....
Bruck Distributing Co., Inc. ....
Clean ''N'' Press Franchise, Inc. ....
Coin Operated Norge Village ....
Coit Drapery & Carpet Cleaners, Inc. ....
Dryclean—U.S.A., Inc. ....
Duds 'N Suds Corporation ....

The European Dry Cleaning Boutique ....
Golden Touch Cleaners, Inc. ....
London Equipment Company ....
Martin Franchises, Inc. ....
Payless Quality Cleaners of America, Inc. ....
Speed Queen Coin Operated Laundromat and Dry
    Cleaner, Inc. ....
Wash-Bowl, Inc. ....

Lawn and Garden Supplies/Services

Barefoot Grass Lawn Service, Inc. ....
ChemLawn Services Corporation ....
Green Care Lawn Service, Inc. ....
Johnson Hydro Seeding ....
Lawn Doctor Incorporated ....
Liqui-Green Lawn Care Corporation ....
Nitro-Green Corp. ....
ServiceMaster Lawn Care ....
Spring-Green Lawn Care Corp. ....
Superlawns, Inc. ....

Maid Services/Home Cleaning/Party Serving

Classy Maids U.S.A., Inc. ....
Daisy Fresh, Inc. ....
Day's Ease, Inc. ....
Domesticaid Inc. ....
Maid For A Day Corporation ....
The Maids International ....
Maids-On-Call ....
McMaid, Inc. ....
Merry Maids, Inc. ....
Metro Maid Light Housekeeping Services, Inc. ......
Mini-Maid Services, Inc. ....
Molly Maid, Inc. ....
Servicemaster Residential and Commercial Corp. ..
Servpro Industries, Inc. ....

Maintenance — Cleaning/Sanitation-Services/ — Supplies

Acoustique Care Inc. ....
All-Bright Industries Corporation of America ....
Americorp ....
Ceiling Doctor ....
Cheman Manufacturing Corp. ....
Chem-Mark International, Inc. ....
Clentech-AcousticClean ....
Colormate, Inc. ....
Coustic-Glo Int'l., Inc. ....
Highlands Maintenance Systems ....
Jani-King, Inc. ....
Lien Chemical Company ....
Mr. Maintenance ....
Mr. Rooter Corporation ....
National Maintenance Contractors, Inc. ....
Protech Restoration, Inc. ....
Restorx, Inc. ....
Roof-Vac Services, Inc. ....
Roto-Rooter Corporation ....
Sparkle Wash, Inc. ....

U.S. Rooter Corporation ....
Value Line Maintenance Systems ....
Western Vinyl Repair ....
West Sanitation Services, Inc. ....

Motels, Hotels

America's Best Inns, Inc. ....
ClubHouse Inns of America, Inc. ....
Days Inns of America, Inc. ....
Econo Lodges of America, Inc. ....
Family Inns of America, Inc. ....
Hampton Inn Hotel Division ....
Hilton Inns, Inc. ....
Holiday Inns, Inc. ....
Master Hosts Inns ....
Midway Hospitality Corporation ....
Prime Rate, Inc. ....
Quality Inns International ....
Ramada Inns, Inc. ....
Red Carpet Inn, Inc. ....
The Residence Inn Company ....
Rodeway Inns International, Inc. ....
Scottish Inns ....
Sheraton Inns, Inc. ....
Summit Hotels Int'l., Inc. ....
Super 8 Motels ....
Tourway Inns of America, Inc. ....
Travelodge International, Inc. ....
Treadway Inns Corporation ....
Woodfin Suites, Inc. ....

Optical Products/Services

American Vision Centers ....
America's Docotrs of Optometry, Inc. ....
D.O.C. Optics Corporation ....
First Optometry Eye Care Centers, Inc. ....
NuVision, Inc. ....
Pearle Vision Centers ....
Texas State Optical (TSO) ....

Paint and Decorating Supplies

Davis Paint Company ....

Pet Centers

Docktor Pet Centers, Inc. ....
Lick Your Chops, Inc. ....
Petland, Inc. ....
Pets Are Inn, Ltd. ....

Printing

AIC International ....
Alphagraphics Print Shops of the Future ....
American Speedy Printing Centers, Inc. ....
American Wholesale Thermographers, Inc. ....
Business Card Express
Business Cards Overnight ....
Business Cards Tomorrow, Inc. ....
Copycat Copy Centers of America ....
Franklin's Copy Service, Inc. ....

Real Estate

Recreation/Entertainment/Travel-Services/Supplies

Retailing—Art Supplies/Frames

Retailing—Computer Sales/Services

Retailing—Florists

Silk Plants, Etc. ....
Wesley Berry Flowers ....

Retailing — Not Elsewhere Classified

Adele's Enterprises, Inc. ....
Adventureland Video ....
Agway, Inc. ....
American Hardware Supply Company ....
Animation Station ....
Annie's Book Stop, Inc. ....
Applause Video ....
Armchair Sailor Int'l., Inc. ....
Balloon—Age ....
Bath & A-Half Franchise Systems, Inc. ....
Bathtique International, Ltd. ....
Beyond/Viva Franchise ....
Blind Designs, Inc. ....
Bowl and Board ....
The Box Shoppe, Inc. ....
Budget Tapes & Records, Inc. ....
Butterfields Development, Inc. ....
Cartoon Junction International ....
Chad's Rainbow, Inc. ....
Colonel Video ....
Consumer Products of America, Inc. ....
Cook's Corner ....
Copy Mat ....
Create-A-Book ....
Curtis Mathes Corporation ....
Delphi Stained Glass Centers, Inc. ....
Descamps, Inc. ....
Energy Saver Store ....
Every Brand Appliance & Furniture Co., Inc. ....
Fan Fair Development Corp. ....
Friedman Franchisors ....
Goodwill Candle & Incense Franchise Corp. ....
Happi-Bather ....
Happi-Cook ....
Happi-Names ....
Have A Heart, Inc. ....
Heritage Clock and Brassmiths ....
Heroes World Centers, Inc. ....
The House of Watch Bands Franchise Corp. ....
The Incredible Machine, Inc. ....
Intile Designs Franchise Systems, Inc. ....
Island Water Sports ....
Jet Photo Int'l., Inc. ....
Just Closets Franchise, Inc. ....
Kits Cameras, Inc. ....
L'Dream ....
Lemstone Book Branch ....
Little Professor Book Centers, Inc. ....
Loeschhorn's For Runners ....
Mehta Holdings, Inc. ....
Merry Go Round Stained Glass Ctrs. ....
Miss Bojangles ....
Mobility Center, Inc. ....
Moto Photo, Inc. ....
Movies & More Franchise Corp. ....
Mr. Locksmithy Convenience Ctrs. ....
Namesakes—Personalized Gifts ....
National Video, Inc. ....

Heighborhood Video & 1-Hr. Photo Center, Inc. ....
Pak Mail Centers of America, Inc. ....
Palmer Video Corp. ....
Passing Fancy ....
The Perfumery, Inc. ....
Pinch A Penny, Inc. ....
P.O.P. America Corp. ....
The Pro Image ....
Pro Video, Inc. ....
Radio Shack ....
Receptions Plus, Inc. ....
Re-Sell-It Shops, Inc. ....
The Science Shop, Inc. ....
Silver Screen Video ....
Software City ....
Sooter Studios/Super Foto ....
Sport About, Inc. ....
Sporting Life, Inc. ....
Sporting Life, Ltd. ....
Sports Arena, Ltd. ....
Sport Shacks, Inc. ....
Standard Tile Supply Co., Inc. ....
Starlite Video, Inc. ....
Strictly Business Books ....
Superstar Sneakers & Sports, Inc. ....
The Tinder Box International Ltd. ....
Video Biz, Inc. ....
Video Data Services ....
Video Update, Inc. ....
Video USA ....
Weather or Not Parasols, Inc. ....
Wedding Bell Bridal Boutiques ....
Whit's Studio ....
Wicks 'N' Sticks, Inc. ....
Wide World of Maps Franchise Corp. ....
Wild Birds Unlimited, Inc. ....
William Ernest Brown Ltd. ....
World Bazaar ....
World of Laminating ....

Security Systems

Chambers Franchised Security Systems, Inc. ....
Dictograph Security Systems ....
Dynamark Security Centers, Inc. ....
The Security Alliance Corp. ....
Sonitrol Corporation ....

Swimming Pools

California Pools, Inc. ....
Caribbean Clear, Inc. ....

Tools, Hardware

Ad A Boy Tool Rental, Inc. ....
Imperial Hammer, Inc. ....
Mac Tools, Inc. ....
Tool Shack ....
Vulcan Tools ....

Vending

Canteen Corporation ....
Ford Gum & Machine Co., Inc. ....
Mechanical Servants, Inc. ....
Snackpacker ....
Westrock Vending Vehicles Corp. ....

Water Conditioning

Culligan International Company ....
Rainsoft Water Conditioning Co. ....
Watercare Corporation ....

Miscellaneous Wholesale/Service Business

Addhair Technologies, Inc. ....
Ads & Type Overnight ....
All State Welding and Industrial Products ....
Almost Heaven Hot Tubs, Ltd. ....
The Armoloy Company ....
Armorized Glass, Inc. ....
Armor Shield, Inc. ....
Asi Sign Systems, Inc. ....
Astre Appliance—Tech ....
Ballon Bouquets, Inc. ....
Chemstation International, Inc. ....
Composil North America, Inc. ....
Fire Defense Centers ....
Fire Protection USA/Inc. ....

Foliage Design Systems Franchise Co., Inc. ....
Great Expectations Creative Management ....
Green Keepers Int'l., Inc. ....
Hair Replacement Systems ....
Heel Quik ....
International Frog Pond, Inc. ....
Jefflease, Inc. ....
Machinery Wholesalers Corp. ....
Meistergram ....
Mid Continent Systems, Inc. ....
Oxygen Therapy Institute, Inc. ....
Qual Krom Franchising, Inc. ....
The Sports Section Photography, Inc. ....
Stained Glass Overlay, Inc. ....
Starving Students Franchise Corp. ....
Tan Corp., Inc. ....
TanFashion Franchising, Inc. ....
Tan Me, Inc. ....
Tempaco, Inc. ....
Together Dating Service ....
The Ultimate Tan ....
United Air Specialists, Inc. ....
United Dignity, Inc. ....
United Worth Hydrochem Corporation ....
Watsco, Inc. ....
Wee Win Toys & Accessories, Inc. ....
Your Attic, Inc. ....

That's quite a listing, isn't it? You may have only recognized about 10 percent of those with extensive exposure, but it's easy to see there's something that can suit everyone, based on previous experience, or just personal likes and dislikes. A later chapter in this book will have interviews with some of the franchisees who have purchased a number of the listed franchises.

15

The Who, What, and Why of Franchising

STARTING THE INVESTIGATION

You should precede the decision to buy into any franchise with a series of evaluative steps. Admittedly, franchises are popular, and their success rate is far superior to that for starting a business on your own. But at the same time, this doesn't guarantee that your purchase of one will immediately put you into the winner's circle of great profitability.

Even the top-rated franchises can make mistakes. I recall reading about a Burger King franchisee who now has some dozen or so units in the Oregon area. He reported that his first one, in another state, turned out to be an absolute disaster. The location, in the back of a shopping center, was the big problem. It took a few years of sixteen-hour days before he could report any degree of meaningful profit. That certainly wasn't representative of what many potential entrepreneurs think a fast-food franchise stands for—they envision an overnight, fantastic success.

In fact, a new McDonald's in my own neighborhood has been issuing periodic two-for-one coupons during the past six months. The surrounding area is not densely populated; growth is still gradual and this factor may have been taken into consideration with the location selection and their business projections. Setting up a fast-food unit in anticipation of population growth is fine—providing both parties know that, going into the deal. It may have been vital, for example, to build earlier than necessary, specifically to tie up that particular location. But that may mean that big profits will not be forthcoming in the short term.

Although known franchises generate immediate income, there are circumstances that can slow down the projected expectations almost to the same snail's pace that a brand-new, independent venture encounters. Investigate before investing is a valid admonition, even with franchises. They may have developed all the answers and taken the guesswork out of many of the unknowns that face the small entrepreneur, but the venture doesn't stop there. You still have your job to do. You're the one who has to determine if a particular franchise is the most suitable for your objectives and the desired success.

THE NONFRANCHISES

While perusing the franchise offers in the various media, your initial direction will hopefully lead you to the few real situations that tend to fit all your criteria. Within that preliminary probing you may run across a number of variations in this field, such as franchises that are *not* franchises.

One version of the nonfranchise may be reflected in those ads which claim that a small investment will return you big profits. That's when you may meet the supersalesman, contract in hand, who has this wonderful equipment that makes money for you hand-over-fist. Vending machines, electronic whiz-bang games, computer artist machines, and coin presses are examples of such equipment. Some work well, others are in constant disrepair. What you may eventually own is a batch of costly equipment—not a franchise.

Other business opportunities, however, bear some resemblance to franchises but are not complete franchise situations in any sense of a "turnkey" operation. Distributorships and dealerships can fall into this category. Snap-on Tools, for example, centers around mobile sales of auto and home tools. Wash-On-Wheels is a distributor of mobile power washing dealerships. Neither entrepreneurial opportunity requires franchise fees or royalties, although they do offer some type of training.

Coin-operated automatic car washes, carpet cleaning, solar energy products, water purification, hot tubs, rack merchandising, indoor golf, and furniture stripping are among the many other types of business opportunities available. Most do not offer any financing arrangements or charge any fees, but they do provide some training and other generalized assistance. You are more on your own than with any franchise, yet many such businesses show a higher return on investment than franchises.

Some states do require that business opportunity offerings also follow their full disclosure rule, but there are many ways to get around this requirement. Because similar types of business do exist in the franchise arena, one of your first steps in the beginning analysis can be to make sure that you are investigating a *franchise*, if that's your objective, and not some nonfranchise business opportunity.

INITIAL CAUTIONS

A number of acknowledged go-slow signals should be factored into your thinking during the first explorations of this field:

1. Don't ever think of franchising as the easy roadway to quick money.
2. If you intend to be active as an owner-manager, be aware that there's a great deal of hard work and long hours involved.
3. Be true to yourself and make sure your prospective franchise matches or complements your own lifestyle.
4. Avoid offers of "fad" franchises that may be here today but gone tomorrow. Your product or service should relate to major market trends.
5. Don't consider any pyramid-type or multi-level marketing scheme. This involves selling distributorships to others, who then divide and subdivide them for sale to other purchasers.
6. Shy away from those who offer promises of high profits with only minimal efforts on your part. Especially avoid those who guarantee that you *can't* lose!
7. If pressure is exerted to get you to sign a contract quickly, make a hasty retreat. A reputable franchisor prefers the time to check you out and will also encourage you to check its own reputation.
8. If a franchisor representative fails to answer your inquiries directly and dodges the specifics, that's also a good time to leave. He or she is more interested in selling franchises than in establishing a healthy relationship.
9. Be skeptical of any franchisor who tries to discourage the use of your own attorney or accountant to review its contract and income projections.
10. Triple check or avoid those offerings that have a very high franchise fee and little or no royalties. They may be more interested in getting you involved in furnishings and equipment, with no follow-through thereafter.

11. Confirm that the product or service offered by the franchisor has a high quality standard. If you aren't familiar with it, check with others who are.

Many of these initial guidelines will tend to weed out a number of unsatisfactory franchise offerings that are best avoided, thus saving you lots of valuable evaluation time and effort.

PRELIMINARY STEPS

Your personal knowledge of certain franchises, or your initial perusal of ads or run-through of one of the franchise directories has probably resulted in a hankering to know more about three or four of them. That's the time to write or call their home offices for additional information. Incidentally, it may be a good idea to also ask for this material from competitive franchises, so that you can compare the different offerings.

If you are interested in automotive lube services, for example, there are a number of them: Jiffy Lube, Auto Lube, 5 Minute Oil Change, Econo Lube N'Tune, and so on. Instead of getting the franchisor details on one, get in touch with two or three and see if their terms differ— perhaps to your benefit. The same is true for pet shops: Docktor Pet Centers, Petland, Pet Master, and so on. Whether it's campgrounds, soft ice cream, print shops, equipment rentals, or video services, there are competitive franchises. By investigating more than one in the area of your interest, you will be way ahead of the game in judging franchise fees, royalties, territories, and other contract terms.

The initial information packet that comes back to you from the franchisors will be glowing in full color with the wonders of their product or service and their organization. Don't worry, *you* won't be neglected. There will be ample attention paid to you, the prospective franchisee. The descriptions of the wonderful opportunities that you will enjoy by joining their franchise family will be many.

You will become your own entrepreneur, possessed of new skills and confidence, as a result of their training. You will be able to build a future for yourself and your family. If you are willing to work for it, you can profit from *their* formula for success. That success will be achieved a great deal sooner than if you were to start your own independent venture.

Much of what is printed has some validity, especially if the franchisor is a well-established one and the product or service a readily accepted one. Let's check one franchisor's informational packet to see what it contains. Obviously some will be more complete than others, but the character of the information should be fairly similar.

FRANCHISOR INFORMATION

When I called and requested one franchisor's literature, this is what I received:

1. A very attractive, twenty-page, color brochure introduced the company and gave the background of its field. It also generally indicated what the franchisor will do for the franchisee initially, and as a follow-up later.

2. Six additional pages spelled out more of the details on location selection, accounting, ongoing support, advertising and marketing, training, and future plans.

3. Reprints of numerous newspaper and magazine articles about the franchisor, where and when it started, and its progress in the field were included, along with specifics as to the costs of the franchise. The costs included franchise fee, equipment, inventory, and working capital. Royalty fee, financing assistance, and size of premises were also defined.

4. A list of company-owned and franchisee-owned locations provided phone numbers and owner names. In this case, there were about sixty units.

5. A twelve-page bimonthly newsletter featured franchisee activities, industry conventions, common problems and their solutions, and varied tips relating to technology and customer behavior patterns. Reports and reviews within the industry that may relate to the franchisee's business were also included.

6. A very comprehensive four-page questionnaire to be filled out by the prospective franchisee requested personal history, reason for selecting this franchise, the geographical location preferred, references, financial breakdown of net worth, and income statement, as well as other information to determine interest and qualifications.

This information packet was quite comprehensive; the amount and depth of this type of material will vary from one franchisor to another. But, all in all, you now have something to work on. If you studied this kind of information from two or three competitive franchisors in the same field, your understanding of the franchising world would be off to a great start.

FRANCHISOR'S PROFILES

How and what do you check in relation to the franchisor? That initial prospectus you received from them may answer some of the questions that should be asked about the franchise company itself.

How long has the franchisor been in business?

It stands to reason that if the franchisor has been around for a number of years, this could be a definite plus sign. Longevity should indicate a quality product or service, as well as some favorable management practices in the franchisor-franchisee relationships. The seniority factor also facilitates other checkpoints. If the franchisor is publicly owned, you can get a stock report and look for growth or negative trends in sales, profits and earnings. It will also be easier to get information from Dun & Bradstreet and the Better Business Bureau.

If the franchisor is new, you must evaluate the feasibility of their product or service and determine that the offering is not a fad and there is a market for it. Financial stability and management capabilities also require an evaluation. The franchisor's existing outlets may provide some track records in this area.

Is the franchisor a subsidiary of a larger company?

In the franchise field, a recent trend involves large corporations operating franchisors as subsidiaries. The large corporations are usually reluctant to start from scratch in this growth industry, but they do want to participate. The simple solution is to buy an ongoing and successful franchise. If the franchisor you are considering has a parent company, this could be beneficial in relation to the financial stability of the franchise. Check the parent company also.

Is the franchisor national, regional, or local?

The national and international franchisors obviously have the greatest recognition value. This usually indicates they are older and well established. The odds, in those cases, also favor higher franchise fees. Regional or local identity does not indicate a *lesser* potential for high profitability. There are many excellent regional franchisors. They and some of the newer franchisors have great prospects for future expansion into national reputations. Check the state consumer agency, the Better Business Bureau, and the Chamber of Commerce for any information they may possess.

Does the franchisor own any of the franchised units?

There are a number of pluses and minuses on the question of franchisor ownership of individual units. If they do own some outlets, they can stay abreast of market changes, competition, and customer preferences. They can also be aware of any new problems that may develop in the general everyday operations and provide solutions for their franchisees. Additionally, experimentation with new products or management practices can take place in the company units. When perfected there, they can then be offered to the franchisees.

Many of the large franchisors own a fairly good number of their outlets. Some examples include McDonald's, Pizza Hut, Bob's Big Boy, Howard Johnson, and many others. Some independent owners of outlets worry that they may be pressured to sell after they have built up a very successful operation. Others are fearful that this company ownership may indicate the franchisor is taking back units because of minor contract violations or nonfulfillment of quotas. This latter situation regarding violations—if they are major—could be a positive factor, because it shows the franchisor is determined to keep up quality standards. Make sure you understand the contract's clauses in relation to buy-back terms and any stipulations concerning the sale of your own franchise unit.

Is the franchisor offering an exclusive or nonexclusive territory?

Some franchises are nonexclusive. In others, the exclusive territory may only be a few square blocks in a large city. And, still others may relate to demographics, rather than geography. Additionally, this will also differ because of the franchise character—one may be a business service, another a retail product, another a fast food, and so on. Each has its own standard of what constitutes saturation and encroachment. The important factor here is that you are aware of and understand what is being offered.

The franchisor's size and age also affects territory considerations. If a franchisor is large and well-established, the assigned territory will be well-defined, because of the franchisor's experience and knowledge with relation to the number of outlets required in any region. If the franchisor is small and new, it would not be unusual for a well-financed franchisee to reserve a large territory or even a whole state on an exclusive basis.

EXISTING UNITS—YOUR BEST SOURCE

If the initial material you receive from a franchisor includes a listing of franchisees, that can be the basis of your next steps. If not, you may have to call or write the franchisor for the locations of their units in your geographical area. Then visit as many as you can and check the following.

What do the premises look like? Is the place attractive, clean, and roomy enough to accommodate the operations? Is it easy to get to and are there ample parking facilities?

The condition of the premises is important in all types of ventures from ice cream stands to income tax and quick copy centers. The well-known fast-food franchisors were the leaders in promoting pleasant environments. Their initial reasonable prices and uniformly clean facilities were the positives that weaned people away from the many independent fast-food eateries that ranged from pretty clean to downright dirty. When you add the other pluses of ease of access, plenty of parking, and specialization, you have the success basics of all the more recent franchises—convenience and time-saving.

Since the great majority of franchises relate to retail and service operations, there's much more you can accomplish with your visit to the franchise unit.

What are the prescribed hours of business? Is there sufficient help and are they knowledgeable and courteous? Are the customers varied or of a specific group? Is the buying pattern general or concentrated in a few areas?

Some of the answers regarding everyday operation depend on the length of your visit to each franchise unit. If it is a retail operation, it will pay you to observe this activity during the busy periods, for that will be the best opportunity to gauge the character of the customers, as well as the employees who service them. The customer profile is important and their buying patterns may be significant. Will one or both of these relate positively to the locality in which you wish to set up a franchise unit?

Occasionally the products or services contemplated may simply not be the perfect match for the selected neighborhood. This may be due to the franchisor's price structure, or to the lack of flexibility and diversification in the prescribed product offerings. As an independent you would be able to change things in accordance with your customers and their needs, as well as in relation to competitive influences. This might be impossible with a franchise, so make sure that the franchise you are considering fits the area in all these aspects.

Meet with and *talk* to the franchisees of the units you are visiting. Tell them you are considering purchasing and joining that franchise— would they share their evaluations with you?

Visits to other franchise units are such an obvious evaluative step you must take that many may wonder why I include it at all. It's stressed simply because so many prospective entrepreneurs don't do it at all, or only talk very casually with one franchisee. That's not the way to do it! At this stage, forget the books, articles, professors, and slick prospectus of the franchise offering. Everything you would want to know is available from the existing franchisees in their actual operations. Who else could tell you about the reality of the franchisee-franchisor relationship? If you want the answers, you have to ask the questions.

Did the franchisor select the location and was it a good one?

Were the original equipment and supplies up to the promised standards?

Was the training excellent, good, or passable? Was it sufficient for a successful start-up?

Has the management assistance been one of a continual, ongoing partnership?

Have the gross sales and profits been somewhere in the range of the franchisor projections?

If you can get this kind of feedback from a number of franchisees, you will certainly know a great deal about the franchise you are considering. It's easy to see why this evaluative step can pay big dividends and why it's mandatory for you to complete it before making a final decision.

OTHER CONSIDERATIONS

Some additional considerations have been touched on earlier, but they're worth repeating. There are well over a thousand franchises available, and the percentage of high-profitability winners is very low. That's reason enough for thoroughly checking the franchise of your interest.

Keep in mind that there are many inadequate franchisors, with inexperienced management teams. They're striving to learn and smooth out operational procedures, training, finance, and so on. Some of these franchisors only have one pilot operation, the model that's shown to eager prospects who want to get in on the ground floor. They're trying, but not yet succeeding.

This is also the kind of operation, however, that's often been set up by the con operators. They'll fly you to the model, swamp you with the glowing forecasts, and pressure you to sign up. Next thing you know, there's a TV or newspaper exposé of the entire scam, along with stories of dozens of people who lost their savings.

Some legitimate franchises may be in a shrinking or saturated market. Others are dormant or going nowhere after selling a small number of outlets. In some unusual cases, all the franchisor wanted was just modest growth within a specific regional location. Is that what you want?

If possible, look for a product or service in a growth market. This is not necessarily restricted to computers, energy, video, and other technological changes. Instead, it could be something unique, or a different way of selling something familiar. With changes in lifestyles, the twin factors of speed and convenience have come rushing to the forefront. That means all kinds of home services, self-improvement courses, increased child care, equipment servicing, rental centers of all kinds, small business services, and new breakthroughs still to come.

Keep away from the fads or the luxury items that only the well-to-do can afford. They may work out for a short time, but that's not the entrepreneurship you had in mind. The product or service you intend to offer should be a quality one, with good consumer acceptance.

Part-time franchises are tough, most are not successful. If you can only devote a fraction of your time to the enterprise, you may be better off with a simple business opportunity or simply a small independent operation. Franchisors usually want total involvement, even preferring that the venture become a family affair.

You will usually find the high-profitability winners among the national and strong regional franchisors. They are easy to check. But for the majority of less well-known franchisors, there is no quick method of evaluation. If you do your job correctly, checking a franchisor's program, potential, and actuality will take a great deal of time and effort.

The initial steps outlined in this chapter are a major part of your investigation, especially the direct contact with other franchisees. Their relationship with the franchisor is the reality of what you are evaluating. Not only the answers to your specific questions will be enlightening. Their encompassing peripheral discussions, their attitudes, their sense of satisfaction or frustration—all these will serve to reinforce, one way or the other, your own conclusions about the franchisee's relationship with the franchisor.

Once again, the main emphasis of these direct contacts is to visit more than one franchisee-owned outlet. Three or four would be better. This would also give you an opportunity to see the kinds of locations that were selected and the attractiveness, in different areas, of the franchisor's premises, layout, and design. All the information you gather from talking to these independent owners of the franchise can result in a feel for the franchisor's competence and integrity.

Once you've established that the franchisor does have these qualities, then pursuing this opportunity further would seem very worthwhile.

If the initial information packet you received from the franchisor did not contain the disclosure statement, now is the time to request it. The twenty different subject areas that the statement covers were listed in Chapter 13 of this franchising section. A quick condensed reminder of the information to be supplied is as follows:

- the principals involved and their business experience; lawsuits and bankruptcies, if any, in which any of the management has been involved; identification of franchisor affiliates and their background
- franchise fees, other payments, royalties, purchasing restrictions, and any financing assistance for buying the franchise
- any restrictions on goods or services to be sold and on customers that can be serviced; territorial protection, buy-back terms and franchise-outlet sale conditions
- descriptions of training program, site selection, franchisee participation terms, and statistics on present, future, or discontinued franchises
- franchisor's financial statement, franchisee earnings claims and their actual results, and a list of present franchisees.

Here again, it would be sensible to get the disclosure statement from a competitive franchisor, for comparison purposes. There may be significant differences, or at the very least you may gain some knowledge that could be used to negotiate the contract of your selected franchisor.

16

Setting the Terms

THE AGREEMENT

The franchise agreement is the key to a continuing relationship. It stands to reason, then, that any and all verbal promises or understandings must be *written* into the contract. This applies to both the franchisor and the franchisee.

The further essence of the agreement relates to the two basic fundamentals of that continuing relationship.

1. It will define in great detail how the franchisee is to run the business—what he or she will be responsible for and obligated to do.
2. It will also confirm the franchisor's offering—what the franchisor will supply initially and what the exact character and extent of the continuing assistance and services will be.

Without question, this contract should be reviewed and discussed with your attorney before you sign it. If possible, the attorney should be one who has had previous dealings and experience with franchise agreements. If not, perhaps a franchise consultant can be engaged for this purpose. The attorney should also examine any other legal papers that may be involved, such as the lease, equipment purchase agreement, and financial instruments.

From the franchisor's viewpoint, the complicated contract that is offered the franchisee is made to protect the franchise company. Additionally, it spells out in great deal the obligations of the franchisee and what penalties, if any, are involved for nonfulfilment.

Is the contract fair and reasonable? The most common view is that the contract is completely weighted in favor of the franchisor. And usually it is. But it's the franchisor who has more to lose in the long run. Considerations regarding quality standards, business hours, premises, banking, records, inventories, and termination affect *all* the units, not just the one signing up. To keep the whole a success, all the parts have to work in unison, and this, basically, is what the franchisor is trying to protect. Even if something in the agreement seems unnecessary, there may be a valid and justifiable reason for its inclusion. Ask for an explanation.

Keep in mind, however, the inherent differences between established franchisors and franchisors that are just starting to grow. Their agreements will reflect that difference in status. Negotiation may seem to be a lost cause, especially with those established franchisors who refuse to make changes. Still in all, there is no one standard contract, and variations exist in some areas that may be possible to change.

Locations and community regulations will differ, and the ownerships of premises are variable, for example. Depending on the character of the franchise, your management background or technical expertise may call for some kind of adjustment in your favor. In the smaller communities, your local reputation may enhance the franchise company's entrance and acceptance. You and your attorney should try to negotiate wherever possible to ease terms that seem unreasonable and to gain benefits wherever you may have advantages to offer.

By the time this stage of submission of a contract agreement is reached, the two parties to it will have had prior meetings. The franchisor will have evaluated the prospective franchisee and answered in greater detail any questions that still remained. Both are ready for a binding commitment and both are expected to adhere to this mutual dependency for the duration of the contract.

CONTRACT TERMS

The structure of the contract terms will differ among various franchisors in the description and sequence of each of the signer's obligations. What follows, therefore, is only a partial listing highlighting those major areas that initially concern the franchisee.

Costs

Since the franchisor usually specifies "total equity capital needed," it's important that the franchisee be informed of its breakdown. Is the franchise fee, for example, a single one-time payment, payable upon signing of the contract? Does it, in effect, relate to the right to use the franchisor name, licenses, and operating procedures? Will it also include the initial specified training and site selection?

Will there be construction costs of the premises or, if not, will there be lease deposits? What are the anticipated costs for designated fixtures, equipment, and initial supplies. Is any of the equipment to be consigned on a leasing arrangement by the franchisor or its supplier?

Does the franchisor, in any of the above costs, participate as a financing source, or is it up to the franchisee to arrange his or her own sources of financial assistance? If the franchisor does assist in financing some costs, what is the interest charge?

What about royalty fees? This figure, a percentage of gross sales, can run from 3 percent to 8 percent. What services do they include? Will they relate to ongoing assistance in the areas of management, computerized accounting, operations, research, and inventory? When needed, will the area representatives be available on call, or is there a periodic schedule of their automatic visits? Is assistance with the franchisee's local advertising included? Will there be additional percentage fees of gross sales for national or regional advertising and marketing that is initiated by the franchisor? Are any of the royalty fees on a sliding scale? Can they be adjusted during any period of the contract's life?

Is there a suggested figure as to the recommended amount of working capital required by the franchisee? Normally, this amount would be needed to cover operating expenses until the franchise outlet starts to turn a profit. The franchisor projections and experience with other franchisees should be able to approximate this timetable fairly accurately.

As you can see, this area of costs can be vital to the franchisee's potential of profitability and success. Make sure you are aware of the total costs involved in your proposed venture.

Site Selection and Territory

Because of the many factors involved in the selection of a *location*, the primary effort should be left to the franchisor. Some franchisors do have a specific department to handle this aspect, which can involve zoning laws, building codes, utilities, real estate taxes, lease arrangements, traffic patterns, and consumer accessability. The franchise character of retail, service, or manufacture will also determine what constitutes the prime location.

Responsibility should be clearly indicated with reference to the costs and decisions involved. Who will negotiate the lease or purchase the site, and equip the franchise unit? Does the franchisor already own the land or building? If the franchisee owns it, will he or she retain it, sell it, or arrange a sale and lease-back deal? Is the selection of a location subject to the franchisee's approval?

The contract provisions concerning the franchisee's territory can often be questionable. Exclusivity, as indicated earlier, can mean a half dozen square blocks in a metropolitan area, a portion of a county, a town or small city, perhaps even a state. Here again, size of territory often depends on the type of franchise involved—fast food, home services, small business service, retail, and so on.

One Baskin-Robbins owner expressed concern when another unit was opened in a location that he felt was too close to his own. Six months later, however, his conclusion was that he had lost some customers, but gained a good deal more. Perhaps it was the extra exposure, or a greater consumer growth in his own area, but the end result was positive.

Generally speaking, if a specified territory is indicated, exclusivity means the franchisor will not open another unit on a location within that territory. Check this carefully, for there have been misunderstandings as to what the terms "exclusive" and "nonexclusive" really mean, from the franchisor's viewpoint. Make sure you are both in agreement and that your lawyer also agrees! If the franchisor is owned by a larger corporation, also make sure that company doesn't own a somewhat similiar franchise that can then be located in your territory.

Training

Training or lack of it has been the basis of many complaints to the Federal Trade Commission and state agencies. The common complaint that has surfaced is "insufficient training." Because the franchisor's success is definitely tied to the success of its franchisees, training should be of paramount importance to them. Obviously, to some it isn't. Take heed, then, and check what the training consists of. Your best bet, of course, is to have checked this category with those franchisees you previously interviewed.

Usually the training is conducted at the franchisor's training center or main headquarters. Nine times out of ten, transportation and lodging will be at your expense. The instructional courses themselves should be included in the franchise fee. Determine and clarify the extent of the training. Will it include basic accounting procedures, general operations, and personnel hiring? If necessary, will you be working in an actual franchise outlet, and for how long?

The Baskin-Robbins franchisee mentioned earlier received both management instruction and operational on-the-job training. He confirmed that when he walked into his own outlet on the first day, he handled the day's work easily and knew every piece of equipment in the store. That invaluable knowledge was a result of having cleaned and operated each and every one of those units in an actual, on-site, working franchise outlet. This kind of training is a tremendous confidence-builder when you first open the door for business.

After the initial training, will there be any refresher courses at the company headquarters? Such courses may be necessary in the event new products or sales techniques are developed and put into operation. Depending on the type franchise, will there be any training or instruction on the premises of the franchisee's own outlet when the outlet commences operations?

Operations and Assistance

The franchisor will usually provide a management and operations manual that details the system to be followed in the actual running of the business. Company policies and methods of implementation are spelled out clearly. Condition of premises, signs, logos, displays, and trademarks are also defined and they must meet with the franchisor's approval. If not adhered to, the franchisor may restore them to order and charge the franchisee accordingly.

Business practices, hours, personnel hiring, recordkeeping, inventory procedures, and many other operational areas will be targeted to the specific guidelines established by the franchisor's operating policies. In a large sense, the manual capsulizes what the franchise character is all about—its identity and its system of distribution.

The contract will call for the franchisee's best efforts to maintain quality standards and maximum efficiency, and the franchisor's reputation and goodwill. This is the aspect of a franchise wherein you owe a specific responsibility to all the other franchisees and their participating consumers.

What is the nature of continuing assistance, as described in the contract? Will there be seminars and workshops when new marketing techniques are developed? When new personnel are hired, will the franchisor supply training courses for them? If management problems arise, can the area representative be called for advice and guidance? Are periodic visits scheduled to anticipate problems? Will there be franchisor support in capital equipment maintenance and recordkeeping practices?

Many franchisors have newsletters, filmstrips, and audio tapes that keep their franchisees up-to-date on activities that relate to consumer motivation, local publicity, solutions to recurring minor problems, and regional promotions. Area comparisons of sales figures attained by other franchisees are reported, and this can often cause the lesser units to check their operations for problem areas. Equally important are reports of developments by competitors of your franchise system. Do all or any of these exist with your prospective franchisor?

If you are required to advertise locally and take part in specific contests or promotions, will there be some form of guidance and assistance from the area representatives? Do your own local advertisements have to be cleared by the franchisor? All this should be apart from the normal advertising and marketing programs initiated by the parent company for which you may already be paying a percentage-of-sales fee.

Contract Terminations

You should be alert to a number of factors regarding contract terminations. Initially, check the duration of the agreement. The great majority seem to be for a ten-year term. If the contract relates to a specific location, make sure the lease agreement and the length of the contract are the same. Perhaps both these factors should be included in the same agreement form.

What about renewal terms and conditions? Are they spelled out now, or deferred to some far-off later date? Many a franchisee has been so intent on getting started that this factor did not seem important at the time. Suddenly it *is* time, and lo and behold, there's no condition of renewal in the contract. That can be quite traumatic, unless and until the relationship gets squared away again. Make certain that renewal rights are clearly spelled out and that you understand the options involved. If the renewal terms are there, double check whether there's any *additional* license fee and whether you have to start a new contract from the very beginning again.

Also check the terms regarding termination or cancellation. Obviously there will be certain conditions that would require termination, and many misunderstandings could be avoided if all reasons for revocation were listed under this heading. Too often, however, some additional reasons are integrated throughout the contract under various categories.

One franchisor will terminate the contract when the following conditions occur:

- filing of any bankruptcy proceeding, voluntary or involuntary, by the franchisee

- attempted assignment of the agreement without prior written consent of the franchisor
- franchisee's failure to pay all amounts due under the agreement
- failure to perform any other obligation of the agreement and failure to meet the specified quality standards
- franchisee's default under any lease or sublease agreement covering the premises in which it is located
- franchisee's default in payment of any amounts owed by the franchisee and guaranteed by the franchisor.

In some of the situations outlined above there may be a grace period, or a notice for the default to be corrected within a specified number of days. There may be other conditions that fall under the phrase "failure to perform any other obligations." Those are the areas for your attorney to note and explain to you.

Not to be neglected are the terminations that come about because of failure to meet sales quotas, or the obligation to achieve minimum purchase levels. Can you determine their reality? Franchisor projections are often based on the results of their own company outlets or top franchisee's achievements. New units may require a year or two before they can reach satisfactory performance levels. Are these standards reasonable? Will minor infractions of any obligation result in threats of contract cancellation? A number of the states already have termination statutes to protect franchisees from unfair practices in this area. The federal government is also trying to set uniform standards for termination procedures.

The most important aspect of this termination category, when exercised by the franchisor, concerns what the franchisees are left with. Their investments in time and money to build up their units may be in great jeopardy. The franchisor will immediately strip them of any and all uses of trademarks and all aspects of the system. In addition, there's usually a noncompete clause restricting the ex-franchisee from continuing in the same business from that location or any other site close to another franchisee. You and your attorney will have to carefully evaluate these conditions and check if and how the buy-back clause applies in that situation.

Buy-back

A number of applications must be checked in the buy-back category such as death of the franchisee, transfer of ownership, termination b the franchisee, or termination by the franchisor. Each will have specific conditions and options. In cases of disagreement, there may also be a description of the arbitration procedures.

If you find, after a few years, that this franchise is not for you, can you sell it easily? Your contract may say no, not easily. The franchisor contract may specifically state that the proposed new owner must meet company qualifications, and must sign a new franchise contract. It may also be mandatory that the new owner complete the franchisor's training program. Some contracts may have other restrictions, or may have a clause that gives the franchisor the first crack at buying back the franchisee's outlet.

One of the main points to check is what formula is being used to determine the value of the business when purchased by the franchisor. Where the contract is terminated for infractions, or the franchisee is unsuccessful in running it, how is the buy-back price evaluated? Is it only based on book value?

What about the successful franchisee who is pressured to sell because the company wants to operate the outlet itself? Will the price reflect all the time and effort put in by the franchisee? Will a goodwill factor be added to the book value?

In the event of the franchisee's death, do the heirs face the same restrictions if they want to sell? Under what conditions can they elect to continue operating the outlet? Here, as in all instances that arise involving ownership transfer, if the franchisor is reasonable and conditions are clearly indicated, the problems should not be insurmountable. Just confirm that the contract agreement does contain the what and how of these occasions and that all concerned understand them.

MORE CONTRACT TERMS

The categories detailed above do not make up the entire agreement, but they do relate to the prospective franchisee's major concerns, the conditions that will govern both the entrepreneurial entrance into and exit out of the franchise industry. At the same time, they will be of primary importance in determining the success or failure of the endeavor.

Most of the obligations covered were those that the franchisor is responsible for—training, site selection and territory, operational procedures and continuing assistance, as well as transfer and termination conditions. Also important is the flow of company products, services, or supplies that the franchisor must make available on a continuing basis.

That also includes any of the trade secrets that are a part of the franchisor's system.

Clauses covering these specifics, along with decor, logos, fixtures and equipment, should be clearly defined. If there are restrictions on purchasing supplies because of franchisor specifications, they should be indicated. In some cases the franchisor will allow the use of alternate sources, but only upon submission of samples for their final approval.

Advertising and marketing, both locally and regionally, will usually require franchisor approval. It must feature the franchise logo and trademark, and there may be requirements for joint efforts with other franchisees in the same regional area. Check these clauses to determine cost arrangements and mandatories, if any. For example, there may be a stipulation for minimum insertion of ads in the local Yellow Pages, or a definite obligation to purchase displays and ad mats from the franchisor.

When it comes to franchisee obligations, the various fees and costs connected with the franchise purchase were previously discussed. But there are more aspects to be taken care of within the legal framework of the agreement. You are committed to keep true and accurate books of account that shall be open at all times to the franchisor's reasonable inspection. The books are also subject to audit. The bookkeeping system will usually be one that is furnished by the franchisor and frequent periodic reports of the outlet's receipts and expenditures must be supplied.

Expenses and taxes of the outlet are the franchisee's sole responsibility. So are worker's compensation, liability insurance, and all other federal, state, or local laws and regulations that require licenses or payments of any kind. You will also notice a clause in which the franchisee agrees to indemnify and save franchisor from and against liability of any kind. Normally this will involve the expenses of a large public liability insurance and property damage insurance. In these policies, the franchisee is required to include the franchisor as an additional insured.

Usually a noncompetition clause prevents you from having any interest in a business of similar nature, or sometimes *any* other type of commercial business. And so it goes, on and on. Stipulations will often include where to bank, suggested prices for products and services, credit policies if any, quality standards, mandatory inventory levels, approval of hired personnel, and business hours.

These specifications are not at all surprising when you remember that the purchase of a franchise means buying a mandated system. The main thrust of this chapter is to provide you with an awareness of what to expect in your agreement. Take ample time to study each and every clause with your attorney. Negotiate, if possible, any area that seems overly weighted against you. Keep in mind, however, that the contract was designed to protect the franchisor.

Also keep in mind that you are making a firm and binding commitment for a long period of time. It's not something you can get out of arbitrarily without some legal action or penalties. Although the same holds true for the franchisor, *you* are more likely to take the beating of a financial loss.

17

They Can Tell You— How It Worked for Others

THE FRANCHISE ENTREPRENEURS

Starting new ventures and buying established businesses has been going on since the early days of barter and trade, supply and demand. The business newcomer on the street during the last three decades, however, has been the franchising industry. And it's been growing by leaps and bounds.

Just when you think the franchise boom has leveled off, it takes off again in new franchise setups that weren't dreamed of just five years ago: haircuts, real estate, video, business services, computers, household help, and a variety of others. If it isn't here yet, it will be coming soon.

Such an explosion can only result from core benefits that must be inherent in the franchise system. Who reaps the benefits and advantages? Apparently the consumers benefit, for they have supported and encouraged this growth. The franchisees benefit, for these entrepreneurs have purchased the rights to each of the systems and operated them successfully in strict accordance to that system. Some of the well-established franchises have long waiting lists of willing buyers.

Are there failures? Yes, definitely, but *many fewer* than for any other type of new business start-up. Perhaps it's because the franchisor will teach you, help you, supply you, and mold you into a team member of an already successful organization. That support sounds great—is that why people buy franchises rather than start out on their own?

The built-in support system does seem to be the main reason that people buy franchises. Perhaps the new franchisee's lack of knowledge and experience was the deciding factor. For many who want to own their own business, the fear of failing and losing their investment is the main focus of their decision-making process.

Whatever the reasons, the interviews that follow reveal the same initial thoughts and uncertainties that you possess. Let's listen to some of the owners tell us about their reasons for going the franchise route to entrepreneurship. Did everything work out well? Were they able to handle all the situations without prior experience? Are they generally satisfied?

Mail Boxes Etc., USA *is a multi-service store in a shopping center anchored by a large supermarket. Private mail boxes, shipping, telegrams, passport photos, packing, business cards, and copying are just some of the services offered.*

David Wunsch: This is my first entrepreneurship and probably the reason I got into it was flexibility and freedom of choice—be your own boss, that type of thing. Previously I had been in medical administration, and although I have a degree in business and have taken marketing classes in the past, I felt that a franchise would offer the support I needed.

I looked at several alternatives and when the first store of this type was opening here, I saw all the promotional materials they displayed before the opening. I was intrigued and wrote to the franchisor headquarters for more details. They sent me all the literature and their history, which I studied thoroughly. The franchise was only five years old but it was growing rapidly.

Basically, this was a new concept for the country—sort of a Seven-Eleven type of postal business. There were fourteen stores of this franchise in another city of this state, so I researched that by interviewing six of them. All of them were genuinely satisfied with the franchisor and the support they received. The majority were happy with the income level they achieved, but a few were disappointed in that they had been among the early ones and there was not the marketing help at the beginning that is now available.

I went into escrow for an outlet here over a year and a half ago. It was up to me to obtain all the financing from the various lending institutions, for they offered no assistance in that area. Today, however, they do have some financing and extended marketing surveys available for their franchisees.

The offer for assistance to choose a location came from the area representative, not the corporate office. However, I felt it lacking, so I spent three months doing my own research and demographics, and finally chose this location.

The diversification is what intrigued me in the whole concept. You are not tied into one product or service—there are *thirty* different services we offer, and you're not tied into one profit margin. That margin can range from as little as 8 percent almost up to 90 percent. We pay a royalty of 5 percent and an advertising fee of 2 percent. The franchisor matches your advertising fee, and the matched funds are available to you when you do your own advertising.

Since we now have seven stores in town, we have a cooperative advertising association and we receive those funds. Over and above that, we contribute an additional amount monthly and can do a lot more things than if we acted individually. We meet monthly and share both the successes and the problems.

My training was done at the corporate headquarters and the initial training was a period of two weeks, six days a week, from six in the morning to about ten at night. It was a very compact time because you had to go through so many facets—remember the thirty different services. Following that period, there was in additional in-store experience of no less than four weeks, and more if you wanted it, with another franchisor that had been in business for at least a year. All this, naturally, is prior to opening your own shop.

The area representative is usually within your own area and he operates his own store in addition. Therefore, you can get good support that way and also through the group in your own region. Yearly, the corporate office offers seminars and additional training for those who desire it.

After a year and a half, I feel comfortable with the franchisor support—more on the local level than on a corporate basis. I'm satisfied with the concept and what we're offering to the public. My only disappointment relates to growth, and maybe I'm not giving it enough time to develop. My returns do follow pretty well with their projections, but I did hope for more growth after the first year than I have experienced.

As the parent company grows, I see more national advertising coming along down the road. And even locally, you still couldn't do as much if you were operating as an individual. So if it's your first venture, I think I would still recommend a franchise because of all the backup. So far, anyway, it's working for me.

Duraclean by Ritchie *is a carpet cleaning service business. The facilities are located in a small complex of offices and business firms. The building faces onto a busy avenue, with ample parking in the front.*

Barry Ritchie: After college I worked for several years as a salesman for a variety of companies. Then I started to get frustrated with sales. You would have a territory, build it up, and then they would move or curtail the territory, which is quite characteristic of what your commission-type sales personnel go through. So this prompted me to go into my own business.

Ever since I was a youngster, I kind of had the idea of my own business. Then I would think of the more glamorous types—the neat clothing stores or furniture stores, and so on. Of course, money was kind of nonexistent, as far as getting into those opportunities.

While in college, one of my professor friends had a carpet cleaning business left to him. He sort of laughed about it and wondered how he was going to handle it. Well, after two months, he quit his teaching position and made carpet cleaning his profession. He did very well with it.

Although I had no intention of carpet cleaning, when I ran across an ad for Duraclean in the back of a magazine, it stimulated thoughts of my old professor friend. I sent for information and checked it out a bit. It was relatively inexpensive to get into it, no more than if I set out on my own as an independent. But, I had no expertise or knowledge of any kind and since they offered some training, it seemed like a good idea.

My dad was living in this area and he wanted me to leave North Dakota and settle here. It seemed to me that the field of carpet cleaning might be better in an area where it could be done all year round, so I moved to the Southwest. I didn't talk to anybody with a Duraclean franchise before I actually purchased it. They were a large organization, twenty-fifth in the field of franchising, and their process seemed pretty good to me.

I went ahead and purchased the franchise. There was a full week of training at their headquarters. It was a comprehensive week, no sloughing off, plus you also had a full week with another Duraclean dealer, on the job, before you even went to the training school. You don't pay for the classes, but you do pay your own expenses while you're there.

During the week at the dealership, they touched on all phases—the cleaning, the problems, identifying fibers, the accounting, the whole ball of wax. The school brought it all out again, sort of brought it forward. When you are finished with the school, you feel you can go out and conquer the world. It was more of a motivating experience. And in my years with Duraclean, I have discovered that's probably the most important aspect of the business, the motivational aspect. Keep yourself motivated and you're going to grow continuously.

The first year was very tough. Many times I wondered what the heck I was doing in this business. But I did have help from my father. It wasn't too terribly long into the first year that I realized a profit in the operation. It wasn't a significant profit, not enough to change jobs, for example, but it was a profit.

As a Duraclean representative, you are a sole individual proprietor. Any problems you have, you are sort of expected to handle yourself. They will, however, help in special cases where you want to utilize them. If you couldn't get a stain out and you were able to send a sample to them, they will let you know how to handle it. Occasionally they send you referrals; businesses or individuals that see a Duraclean advertisement and want the name of the local representative.

There isn't a fee for national advertising; its really incorporated in our royalty fees, which are based on a percentage of our gross sales. The more work you do, the less percentage you have to pay—it's a sliding scale. Within the original franchise fee, you do get their specialized equipment. If you require a truck, that's your extra expense. Initially I just used the back of my Plymouth sedan, the equipment isn't that bulky.

Any additional equipment you need because of a growth in your business is supplied free. And that's a big advantage over being on your own and having to buy new equipment. We purchase all our chemicals from Duraclean; that's one way they get their money back. But those chemicals are competitively priced with others like it that I can buy here. And I did try the others, but they aren't as good as Duraclean's.

In this particular case, I would recommend going into a franchise. Maybe in any case! Since I had no experience, I would have had to work in the business for a while to get practical experience. In that situation, the business I opened would have to relate to the type of cleaning I learned as an employee.

With Duraclean, I got the training quickly and I'm involved in a type of cleaning that I feel is specialized and superior. We get lots of national exposure through the ads that show endorsements from businesses and major retailers that recommend the Duraclean process. It's fifty years of experience that a new dealer has behind him in comparison to any other franchise or independent owner. Who else in this area can say their system cleans the Hyatt Regency in Chicago, a palace in England, and a castle in Ireland?

In respect to territory, Duraclean will limit the number of franchises in any given community. I don't know their exact formula, but I do know that right now there are only two Duraclean franchises here.

I don't go out as much on actual jobs. I have five people working now and two trucks. We handle the residential trade mostly, about 90 percent. At one time it was the opposite, but I've gotten out of the commercial market. You get too dependent on a few large accounts, and then the one in charge leaves and you're out also.

I don't think you ever get satisfied with your progress, but I'm making a decent living and there's still room to grow.

SUBWAY Sandwiches & Salads *is a food franchise. It is located in a free-standing building with another tenant. Around it are additional shops and ample parking. It faces a main intersection and is very visible.*

Jim Sabo: I'd worked for one company for about eighteen years and I finally decided I would be a better boss than any of the ones I had. So I quit there to go back to the university. Right after starting that, I read a little newspaper ad about a seminar on SUBWAY Sandwiches franchises. My wife and I decided to attend that session and we were very impressed by the simplicity of the concept.

We were interested and we went ahead to visit the stores that existed in an adjacent city. We talked to the owners, looked at the decor, at the operations, and decided to look into it a little more. The three franchisees we spoke to all told us it was hard work, but that didn't frighten me because I am a hard worker.

It was the product that really sold me. I'd previously eaten at what I felt would be their competitors and I thought the SUBWAY product was better. It's fast, but it's not fast food—all the meats are sliced daily, they bake their own bread, and I think everything is fresher. It's a deli type, but I wouldn't call it a delicatessen or a fast-food restaurant.

Before I decided to go with SUBWAY, I called owners in other states and looked into what the real financial investment would be, as opposed to the brochures. I'm sure they try to be very accurate, but there's a difference in markets where the franchise is known and the financing may be easier to obtain. It was a rude awakening to look at the projected bottom line for an inexpensive franchise and at what the bottom line actually is.

We did decide to get an outlet and went to train in the corporate headquarters, as well as in the corporate-owned stores in the vicinity. The intensive training was for two weeks. The school is included in the franchise fess, but we paid our own transportation and lodging expenses.

Their area representative gave us ideas to look for regarding location and we must have looked at hundreds before I chose this one. It finally comes down to the lease arrangements, and there were lots of details there that I hadn't realized—they were a great help there. The legal staff at the headquarters is just a phone call away whenever you have any questions. But they don't help with any of the financing; we had to do that ourselves.

They really don't make projections for you. You can talk to other owners and check their expectations, and I also asked my accountant to figure out what would be a good return for this type of business. I found the return is good if you don't make mistakes. We've been open a year now and we have made lots of mistakes. Now that we've learned all the ropes, I hope our costly mistakes are all behind us. After our first three months, things seemed to be going real well and I was able to negotiate the rights for our whole region. The area rep helped there with his recommendation. He knew how we worked and our small store became a good showplace for others who were interested.

Although they don't give out large territories anymore, we were approved. Our second store is now open and my wife relates to that one. SUBWAY is not interested in the investor type who wants a large territory; they prefer the owner-operator situation, even if later you have to staff with managers and you are still active. You have to care about the business and the customers you have, otherwise you won't make out. The competition around here is stiff and what we have going for us is how we run the business and what product we offer. We want to keep that in our favor.

SUBWAY has been in business about twenty years; I think they're in every state except the Dakatos and one or two others. The last I heard, there are over one thousand stores in forty-five states and five countries. Most of the things are structured where they have to be, but they also allow for some flexibility. They have the structure for the logos, equipment, product, suppliers, and so on, but they do give us a little leeway. Through labor-saving methods that we incorporated and vendors that we've dealt with, via SUBWAY, we can save and still make a good product.

Although I had professional assistance before I signed up, it was the other owners that I depended on—they had no reasons to mislead me. At first they were cagy, thinking I wanted actual figures, but I simply asked if I could make a living with one SUBWAY. They said yes, but most were multi-unit owners, and that makes sense. Even the corporate office recommends that you talk to the franchisees.

As far as franchising goes, study your franchisor for a long time. I did that without realizing it. I had kept up with the industry by reading *Venture, Entrepreneur, Money*, and sometimes *Forbes*. I noticed SUB-WAY was up on top in a lot of categories for many years. When I did get interested in that franchise, I went back to those issues I saved and reread those magazines for articles that related to SUBWAY.

Make sure that the franchise you're interested in has a track record of success and growth. There was one somewhat similar type franchisor that had been operating for ten years and only had fifty-one outlets. Maybe they wanted to stay small, or perhaps they weren't aggressive enough. Whatever it is, check them thoroughly. Talk to those other owners; they can give you invaluable information. With a good franchisor, you can learn from their mistakes without having to pay for them yourself.

Dairy Queen, one of many in this area, is in a freestanding building with ample parking and drive-through facilities. Easily recognizable, the location is about two hundred feet off a busy main avenue.

Lyle Huntsinger: Before I settled in here, I lived in Milwaukee and worked for the fire department for fourteen years. My brother-in-law lived here and we always wanted to move here, but I never had any type of work or anything that could make me relocate here. Knowing the former owner and hearing that he wanted to sell this Dairy Queen outlet, my brother-in-law called to see if I would be interested. My first reaction was to say "You're crazy, I've never run a business in my life, I don't know anything about it." I never even had any thoughts about ever going into a business of my own.

Eventually he talked me into coming down to at least look into the thing. So my wife and I did. We talked to another owner who explained the pros and cons. I talked it over with my brother-in-law and he had me contact two other friends of his who had Dairy Queen franchises. They were particularly helpful and they sat down with me, showed me their books and how things could work out where it might even increase my income.

Well, my wife and I did decide to move here and buy the business. The fact that it was a franchise was a contributing factor, because the failure rate was very low in this field. It made it sound like a pretty safe thing to go into. We have seven kids and my primary thought was to improve my income to raise and support my family.

The fact that everything is laid out for you helps make it easy. The name Dairy Queen is there; people can identify with it. So I don't have to do anything extraordinary saleswise, and all I had to do was learn to operate the business. The former owner stayed with me for one month and he broke me in. One of the main parts of this business is learning how to tear down your various machines, clean them, put them back together again, and be able to take care of any breakdowns. The business part of it you kind of learn as you stumble along. You learn most from trial-and-error.

I didn't go to any training school. International Dairy Queen has one, but this unit is part of an *area* franchise. They own the rights to all of Tucson and southern Arizona. But I don't go to them for any help. Any help I do get comes from the other operators in this vicinity. When I was new and had a problem or needed something, I could call just about any one of the older operators and they'd be glad to help me out.

All the local operators do get together and we have advertising meetings. At the beginning of the year, we determine how much we are going to put into advertising and what type we want to do. International Dairy Queen also has a national program, but we don't necessarily have to go into it. We will buy part of their program, like TV ads that are done professionally. Right now we are giving out some scratch-off game cards that came from them.

Everything we buy has to be Dairy Queen approved; we can't pick up some substitute that might be cheaper elsewhere. Our area distributor can supply the product, toppings, cones, cups, everything we need to maintain quality. Unlike Baskin-Robbins, which measures things by size of the scoop, we do it by weight because we are a softserve ice cream. It takes a little practice—but if you start pushing out too much product and take in too little money for it, you'll start hurting soon.

We pay a royalty fee to our area distributor, and they in turn pay something to the International. We don't pay a percentage, we pay so much per each gallon of mix that we buy. Now they've changed. With new operators, there's a flat percentage of gross sales, 4 percent or 5 percent, I think. But I've been here nine years and we send in a mix count at the end of each month, with a royalty check per gallon.

As for financing, my pension plan equity, some money from selling my old house, and a bit from my brother-in-law were the going-in funds. The man I bought the store from carried the rest. My purchase included the land, the building, everything. Some who buy today purchase the building and contents and lease the land.

I've been very pleased with the decision to come into it. Now that I've adjusted to this way of life, I like it. I'd certainly recommend a franchise to anyone who had no experience. As I said, I'm not any business person and if I had gotten into something that started from the ground up, I don't know where I'd be now. Everything here is laid out and you are told how everything is done, how everything is made, so it's relatively simple.

One of the toughest adjustments I had to make was in dealing with people and young help. Previously I had been relating to ten other men in the fire department for fourteen years. Most of my employees are high school kids, good workers and honest, but their lack of maturity takes a while to handle. So it took a few years to accomplish that adjustment successfully.

All my help is part-time and I generally have six or seven people in the summer—our good period for business. When I first got into it, our large family came in handy. My three teenage daughters were an instant help. All my daughters and now my sixteen-year-old son have worked here; they've all run through the business. I put in more time myself during the slow periods, winter and early spring, so that way I don't carry a big payroll in the off seasons. In the busy summer, I put in less time.

My wife does the bookkeeping at home. That's another thing about being inexperienced in business. We didn't know the first thing about licenses, government agencies, and the different taxes. Unless you had the knowledge, you couldn't do it yourself. Luckily I got in touch with the previous bookkeeper as soon as I took over, and he showed my wife some of the ins and outs. Today, of course, we know a lot more, but at that time it was all Greek.

We still have about six years to go and then we'll own the entire place free and clear. Now we're building up a lot of good equity and when we sell there will be a good amount coming back. In the meantime, it's been good to us. The first few years were tough; you'd wait for the money to get into the bank to pay the bills. We were just skimming along, but after a while, you get to see the daylight.

You know, when I came into this I was just a little over forty. It was a big decision to change my lifestyle from what I was doing into something so completely different. We look back on it now and we feel we couldn't have made a better decision. We are happy with it. Both of us are happy.

COPYBOY *is a printing/copying franchise. There are a number in this city, which is also the corporate headquarters. This store faces a heavily traveled major boulevard and is highly visible.*

Joseph Leaming: I've had other businesses in the past—a gift shop, a catalog store, a motel supply route, and now I have this. I definitely prefer this to working for someone else because I don't take directions well.

Before going into COPYBOY, I looked into several other franchises and many of them didn't seem to come up to the expectations that were promised. We looked into a number of them, all the way from hamburger stands to ice cream places, and others I don't remember now.

Whenever I looked at a specific franchise, I'd go and talk to two or three of the franchisees—and *not* the ones the company suggested I should talk to. I found that a lot of them, even the well-thought-of ones, were not a good buy, particularly on a resale situation. There just wasn't enough left, after all the expenses were taken care of. I also found that a lot of them had promised plenty of help, but after the early stages, this wasn't so. I feel if you're paying 7 to 10 percent royalties, you should expect to see more help than that.

As far as COPYBOY goes, I not only talked to every outlet in this city, I also checked a few other franchisees of their competitors for comparison. From what I could see this one seemed to perform the best; it looked like it gave the best support. As it turned out, any questions I have, they've always been ready to help out with the answers.

This location already existed for some nine or ten years and I purchased it. I've been here less than a year and one of the big benefits is that the headquarters is in this city. They call me at least once a week to see if there are any problems and the area representative drops in at least once a month, if not more often.

I had two weeks of training in the company store, and part of my arrangements with the previous owner was that they would stay for six weeks.

They are still on call, although I haven't needed them, but I'm still learning the business and there are plenty of people around if I need them. As far as projections go, I'm below about 20 percent, but it is coming back and I anticipate getting up to equal or above within the year. There's competition across the road there, but I think they're my best asset.

For the person who has no business experience, I think the franchise route is a way to go. Again, keep in mind that the older franchises do have a track record, but others may not. If I had expertise in the printing/copying field before I got here, I wouldn't need to pay a franchise fee, royalty, or anything. But because I didn't, then I'm still convinced I'm better off this way.

If you're going to franchise you must check with other franchisees and even those in competition. If it's a national franchise, I would check outlets in other towns because one area may have a good franchise director and another may not. It's good to get a cross-section of what's going on. One caution, however. When you're being interviewed, or someone is trying to sell you a franchise, keep in the back of your mind that he or she is a salesperson only and is paid to sell it—and you will never see that person again.

COPYBOY—*this franchisee has two outlets, both new, in another area of town.*

Paul Schwager: This isn't my first business. I've had a limousine company, an electrical contracting one, and an egg hatchery. The reason I've gone into a franchise is that I believe there's more chance for success—not less chance of failure, but more chance for success!

I didn't care what kind of franchise; it really made no difference to me. The reason I got into this one was because I was mad! I needed some printing done and I couldn't find anyone on this side of town that would take care of me. What I wanted was such a simple job, a screen background, you know, my cars just screened, and the counter person didn't know what it was and couldn't help us so I left. I said to my wife, "We've got to find someone to do it" and there were no print shops up here.

So I told my wife to call the leasing agents and see which of their shopping areas didn't have a printing store and that's how we got started. I looked at two franchisors who had local headquarters here and when I decided on COPYBOY, I interviewed *all* their franchisees—twelve of them. When it came to a location, they wouldn't sell me one here because they said this area wasn't ready. That's why the first store is over east of here. A year later, they thought this area could support an outlet, so they sold me this one.

The training period was six weeks, full-time, in town. Then they put a man in with you for the first three weeks, and then they stop in to see you twice a day for a few weeks after that. Their cooperation has been great, I really can't say enough good for them. We've been in business two years now and everything has exceeded whatever they told me. They've been good in every way except loaning you money. They don't want to talk about that. They don't advance anything, or even lease the equipment. I've had to find my own money, find it wherever I could.

Frame Factory is a do-it-yourself and custom picture framing shop. The premises are located in a fairly new, very trim U-shaped row of stores and offices.

Jack Bickel: My wife and I formerly owned a party supply store in the East for about four years. That was our only entrepreneurship. Previous to that I've always been an industrial salesman and Marilyn had been a schoolteacher.

Years ago my wife and I determined that after we reached a certain point in life, we wanted a business that we could go into together. We weren't looking for this business—it just came about through a series of coincidences. After my wife's mother passed away, we discovered a great number of photos in the basement. They weren't doing anyone any good there, so we decided to frame them. That became our Sunday afternoon project.

There was a franchise outlet of this company only a few blocks from our house, and that's where we spent our Sundays for a few months, on do-it-yourself picture framing. One afternoon I asked my wife "How would you like to have a place like this to work?" She thought it would be a great idea and a lot of fun—kind of creative and challenging also.

That was it. We agreed, and we decided to pursue it. Our first inquiry didn't get any response from the main office in Houston. Maybe it was the mail, or something. A second inquiry worked and we arranged for an interview with their vice president and area representative, near our home in New Jersey. We spent a half day with him and he questioned us in the many aspects of our background—what we had done, what we were doing now, our future plans, general outlook, and so on. He, of course, filled us in verbally about their requirements and our obligations, fees, royalties, and other details. Later they mailed us all the papers with a sample contract.

I think that initial meeting was an extensive one, because as far as I know, they are the only franchise that has *never* had a store fail! At this present time, I believe they have 170 to 180 stores over the country and are the largest in this particular field. Their two trademarks are Frame Factory and Framin' Place, and I think it will all finalize as Framin' Place.

By the way, when we got the contract we took it to our lawyer for a review. After he went through it thoroughly, he said if they would keep their part of the bargain in this, it was a very fine contract—probably one of the best he ever read. Well, I certainly felt that was a lot of points in their favor, and in a short while we went ahead.

The work we had done ourselves on those Sunday afternoons was helpful. Additionally, I would give the owner of that outlet a hand whenever her help didn't show up or they got too busy. So I got to know some of the background of the business. Then we both went to their school for three weeks, and that was very thorough in all the basics. Like any school, you can't learn everything. Every day our door opens here, there's a new challenge.

Marilyn is creative and I'm mechanically inclined, so somehow we manage to handle things. In fact, I think we're getting a reputation of being able to cope with the really tough assignments. We have one full-time person and she's a very good designer. Incidentally, the school had things set up so that it was practically a replica of what we have here. Worktables with the equipment and tools for do-it-yourselfers, prints and pictures on the walls, samples of frame sections, display units, mats in the back room, the whole works.

As far as their income projections for the rate of business growth, well, during our first and part of our second year they seemed pretty much in line. Our third year, however, hit into the economic slump and that's our basic problem, as well as, everyone else's. But there does seem to be an improvement on the way.

When it comes to follow-up assistance, they are as close as our telephone. Legal or operational problems can be discussed with the home office. If it requires more than the telephone, our area representative will try to arrange his schedule to come here in a few days and give us some input as to how we can correct the problem. He also comes about every three months on a regular visit and calls once a month to check if there are any problems.

They work very closely with their franchisees. Although we had to provide our own finances, for example, they were able to assist us with all the paperwork to get an SBA loan. Their relationships with the banks and their other outlets' track records paved the way for this loan approval. When we first opened, one of the teachers from the school worked with us. Our area representative was also here during that week. Although they felt comfortable that we could handle things after that first week, this is a creative business and new, unusual projects are always coming in. We're always learning something.

They send us lots of promotional material. Videotapes for TV commercials are also supplied to us at no charge. That's included in the royalty and advertising fees, which total 6 percent of gross sales—4 percent royalty and 2 percent advertising. We don't have to buy any of our supplies from them; we have the choice to buy from them or anyone else—it's our option.

This location was selected jointly, but they had two or three locations, including this one, for us to choose from. They did all the demographic, and marketing studies—population breakdown, income levels, and so on. We have a ten-year lease on this location and we've been satisfied with its choice. Our franchise contract is for five years and if we agree there'll be a renewal negotiation. Most of the franchisees do sign up for renewals, but we'll have to see how we feel when we get there.

Our business now is about 60 percent custom framing and 40 percent do-it-yourself. We'd like to reverse that because we like the flow of people in and out, talking with them and helping them. We found out that the people who do it themselves enjoy themselves, and they come back more often.

Would we recommend franchising to others? Yes, if people who go into it can get the franchisor's complete support, and I know that's not always true for all franchises. If you're a beginner with no experience, the franchising field makes a lot of sense.

As far as would we do this one again, the answer would still be yes. We believe we've achieved the objectives we originally set out and now all we want to do is grow. Hopefully our franchise will achieve that.

IN SUMMATION

These interviews have their own characteristics and they bear out a number of factors that were covered in the earlier chapters. One of those stands out like a real beacon in the night. It's the one we keep re-iterating—*talk* to other franchisees if you want to get specific evaluative information.

It's very interesting to note that none of those interviewed had any experience in the fields they chose as franchisees. Of course, one of the major advantages that franchisors proudly proclaim is that experience is not necessary. Is it true? Does a franchise always work out well? By talking to those already in the franchise, you can realistically discover the negatives or positives of these claims that no experience is necessary.

At the same time, you're learning a lot more than just that. Those franchisee interviews can clearly indicate the following:

- if lack of experience can be overcome quickly
- if the initial training was sufficient
- if you can catch on to the system within a reasonable time
- if the franchisor's projections are valid
- if follow-up assistance exists
- if help is available when you have problems
- if the contract is an onerous one.

You can learn about all of these aspects of a franchise operation just from talking and listening. What you're really finding out is whether the franchisor is competent, truthful, and a real partner. No colorful brochure or list of promises can tell you that—but the franchisees can!

There's a misconception that many would-be entrepreneurs have that the interviews touched on. As mentioned earlier, the acquisition of a franchise does *not* automatically put you into the money overnight. Even with the franchise identity, there was a necessary period of establishing the new outlet's presence.

What is a definite plus, however, is the satisfaction with the franchise—a really positive endorsement of this marketing and distribution system. Some have already grown into acquiring a second unit, others are looking forward to that possibility.

The training offered by the franchisors seem to range from quite adequate to excellent, according to those interviewed. And there seems to be general agreement that they received franchisor assistance when they needed it.

These positive votes relate only to the specific businesses of the interviewees. The interviews certainly do give you an idea of the kinds of information you can elicit through the process of exploring your concerns about a particular franchise with those who already own one. Don't neglect to do so!

Appendices

A

Financing the Business

Financing is often thought of as the real stumbling block for the budding entrepreneur. But is it?

Here again, awareness is the key that starts you off on your way to a solution.

At this stage you may know *what* you need. Now check this appendix about *how* to get it!

FINANCING—HOW SO?

Now that you've reviewed the ways to become an entrepreneur, it's time for the million-dollar question to rear its ugly head: "Where's the money coming from?" This is also where you must learn to develop financial awareness.

Let's go back to the very beginnings of preparation—talking and reading. Bankers, business owners, the SBA, and those conducting seminars all have valuable information to impart about this subject. Make sure you're listening! As far as reading goes, your library, bookstore, government agencies, and business organizations have a wealth of material for you to study.

Initially, the basic types of financing relate to equity financing and debit financing. Equity dollars are used for ownership of the business. They are not repaid, for they represent getting money in exchange for a piece of the business. If there are investors who supply capital in return for a share of the venture, you will have to think in terms of a partnership or corporation, rather than a sole proprietorship.

Debit financing relates to money you borrow—loans that must be repaid, usually with interest. Normally the lender receives no ownership at all. Banks, loan companies, SBA-guaranteed loans, and government agencies are the most likely source. Personal friends and relatives also may provide funding, and many an entrepreneur has found them to be his or her main fountainhead of starting capital.

HOW MUCH IS ENOUGH?

Many a future entrepreneur begins to think concretely about owning a small business when savings reach the $10,000, $20,000, or $30,000 figure.

The first big question that usually shoots to the surface is will it be enough? That's the signal to look over the earlier chapters of each book, dealing with each method of how to get started in your own business. Consider the following questions:

What kind of business?

How big will the business be?

What do you need to start off the business?

What will the operating costs be?

When you hit this stage, it's no surprise to realize that each of those questions translates itself into some form of dollar requirements. Pinning down the amount of those dollars is important in determining the yes or no of your intentions to open for business.

Certain ventures require more costly start-up cash outlay than others. Restaurants and manufacturers often require expensive equipment to begin operations. Some retailers have a mandatory need to carry large inventories, in addition to the very necessary furniture and fixtures.

Services, on the other hand, may be able to manage with a minimum until things really get rolling. Many franchises have a heavy entry fee, as well as extensive requirements for the premises. New products have a whole new set of demands that invariably require large expenditures. Do you have a handle on your specific requirements yet?

WHERE DO YOU STAND?

Knowing how much money you need is essential; determining where it comes from is equally important. Coming up with the funds, however, is the key to making the dream a reality.

Since most sources of capital will involve all kinds of conditions that will bind you to them, the first source to examine is yourself and those around you. This, of course, means your own personal resources and the resource of your family and friends, business associates, and any others you can approach.

Personal Resources

Your own capital is the least expensive in cost, the quickest to obtain, and requires the least paperwork to initiate. If personal savings are insufficient, it will be necessary to combine them with some of your other possible resources:

- stocks and bonds
- mortgage on real property
- home mortgage refinancing
- cash surrender value of insurance
- passbook loan
- credit union loan
- personal loan
- cosigner loan
- life insurance policy loan.

If you can manage to raise all the initial funds yourself from your own resources and some loans, you will be the sole owner and the firm may operate as a sole proprietorship.

Your Family and Friends

Relatives and friends are a natural source that most beginners turn to for extra financial support. If one of them is wealthy, that's all to the good. But often it's a matter of a modest contribution from a number of them, especially if they have faith in your proposed venture.

Even when the contributions are strictly loans, without active participation, make sure you write out how and when they will be repaid—

with or without interest. It is wiser to make a formal arrangement rather than a promise and a hearty handshake.

You should also be selective as to who you approach for loans. Your relationship with certain friends and relatives might come to an abrupt and bitter end if your business does not succeed and you cannot repay within a reasonable time frame. Also, you should avoid borrowing from persons who have a great tendency to get involved in areas they're not supposed to, even when the ground rules dictate against their interference.

So be careful when it comes to friends and family. If you do decide to borrow from them, make sure it's on the best of terms—both financially and personally.

Partners

If your business plans have already included partners, you will be sharing the initial costs and the ownership of the venture as well. But partners should also be considered when you discover that your financial needs cannot be met through your own resources.

In that case you will be adding to your starting capital by selling equity ownership to others, who may or may not participate in the operation of the business. Similarly, they may or may not share liabilities, depending on their status as general partners or limited partners. Partnerships can also be used to take advantage of the skills or experience, that the partners possess. As a result, you will be satisfying both your capital requirements and your personnel needs.

If you incorporate, you can sell shares to others. You will be raising equity capital, and the buyers will become shareholders, with part ownership of your business. Both the partnership and corporate forms of organization should be handled by an attorney.

HOW CREDITWORTHY ARE YOU?

No matter which option of going into business you choose, your own financial standing will have to be examined in great detail with relation to borrowing of any kind.

The initial questions aren't new: length of time employed, years at present address, loans outstanding, credit accounts, credit references, income of spouse, and so on.

The loan grantor's interest in these answers centers around your track record. Living within your income is a plus. Paying obligations on time is another plus, as is a previous history of no defaults or repossessions. Your annual income from all sources is a major gauge in determining ability to repay. Net worth will be a factor. You must show a positive financial background as the key to a good credit rating.

One type of questionnaire about income follows:

Income Statement	*For year ending –*
Earned income (salary, commission, fees)	_____
Interest and dividends received	_____
Rent received	_____
Income of spouse	_____
Other income from (list sources)	_____
Gross income:	_____
Deduct taxes paid:	
State and federal _____	
Real estate, etc. _____	
Net income:	_____

Hopefully your outgo, including savings, falls within your net income. This information is vital for a loan grantor, a seller of a business, and a franchisor. But it's also important when it comes to selling yourself. Create your own financial folder and have all the facts available, whenever they're needed, to indicate your credit status.

PERSONAL NET WORTH

Both for yourself and for those involved in supplying financial assistance you must determine your net worth. It's basically a matter of listing what you own and what you owe, or, in other words, adding up all your assets and then subtracting your liabilities. The easiest way to accomplish this is by completing a balance sheet—a simple listing of pluses and minuses, rather than a formal statement.

For many, this balance sheet evaluation is a first, and many are surprised at the size of their own net worth. Now that knowledge is just another fact sheet in your financial folder. Later, when you seek financial assistance, it will be a necessity.

Balance Sheet (as of _____)

Assets

Bank accounts—checking, savings, money market	_____
Securities—stocks, bonds, CDs, funds	_____
IRAs, Keoghs, vested pension funds	_____
Real estate—home, vacation house, land	_____
Life insurance—cash surrender value	_____
Collectibles—coins, stamps, art, jewels, etc.	_____
Automobiles	_____
Notes and accounts due you	_____
Total assets	_____

Liabilities

Mortgages	_____
Loans—auto, bank, insurance	_____
Current monthly bills (utilities, rent, insurance)	_____
Personal debts, credit card balances, charge accounts	_____
Total liabilities	_____
Total assets less *Total liabilities* =	_____
	Net Worth

PLAN, PLAN, PLAN AHEAD

Within the discussions of all three ways of becoming an entrepreneur, there has been ample warning about the need to formulate a business plan. One of the main purposes of a business plan is to help you to understand where you might be going—and to *stop* you if all the ingredients don't add up.

The focus and structure of the business plan relate to what you intend to do and how you intend to do it. When it comes to getting a loan or participation from any source—other than yourself and relatives—some kind of plan and projection will definitely be required.

The plan may only cover two or four pages. Some professional assistance regarding the financial statements may be necessary.

Because it's established, the purchase of an existing business goes a long way in supplying both the ongoing and projected income data. It also facilitates supplying information on competition, location, and marketing statistics. Working with factual information is a lot easier than research from ground zero.

As noted in the discussions of how to start from scratch, a great deal of fresh research will be required to determine initial costs, inventories, income projections, competitive conditions, and so on for a new start-up. You will have to collect and supply these facts in your plan, or no one will consider your request for financing.

The distinct advantage in joining a franchise group is that much of the required information already exists with the franchisor. Initial fees, royalties, equipment costs, cash flow, insurance, pro-forma figures, and other financial data are know and tabulated. And the franchisor may also help in other areas.

FINANCIAL AIDS

Before we tackle the bank borrowing and venture capitalists for the additional monies that may be required, let's take a look as some other more direct sources.

Although there are some who espouse the thought that you can start a business with no capital or buy real estate with no money down, the realities for most of us are another matter. Generally speaking, what you yourself possess and can borrow from others around you is the type of capitalization most of us are familiar with. This is usually the basis of the initial capital investment, and often it's just not enough.

Each method of entering the business ownership area has one or more financial pluses that should be examined with regard to financing.

In buying an existing business, for example, the seller is a key figure in enabling you to meet the purchase price. It sounds strange but it's true, and it becomes an immediate test of your negotiating ability.

Starting from scratch is a completely different kind of problem. In this case, the type of venture you choose and how *you* handle all the operational details becomes the key to easing your financial needs.

By joining a franchise group, the great potential ally is the franchisor—perhaps as a financial partner, or at the very least as a strong financial guiding hand. Here again, selling yourself will be a determining factor.

CAN THE SELLER HELP?

The purchase of an existing enterprise may often require less money than if you started from scratch. This can be true even though the established business is usually worth a lot more than the beginner unit.

If setting up a bookstore, for example, necessitates the actual cash expenditure of $70,000 for site preparation, furniture and fixtures, inventory, and supplies, you may be able to purchase an $80,000 established bookstore for a $23,000 cash down payment and $57,000 in notes (plus interest) to the seller.

That deal, of course, relates to the seller's desire to mitigate capital gain tax consequences wherein he or she must receive less than 30 percent of the total amount in the year of sale. In this type of transaction the seller is not taxed for the entire gain in the sale year and can spread the gain over the years of the remaining installment payments. The seller, however, may also be a lender for reasons other than tax consequences. Perhaps the sale has become a necessity—truly because of ill health, or retirement, or involvement with other interests. Of course, a sale based on "terms" also gives the seller an opportunity for a *higher* price.

In other cases, the initial purchase terms may call for all cash. In subsequent meetings the seller may insist there will be no deal without a total cash arrangement. Don't throw in the towel at this stage! Keep talking. Because the seller is your best source for a loan, you must try to have the seller finance as much of the purchase price as possible. Terms and interest rates will be better than any bank's loan contract.

Is the seller bluffing? Is there a real need for the cash? Try to determine where the stumbling blocks are. You or your attorney should offer to secure your note to the seller's satisfaction. Perhaps you can increase the purchase price slightly, or shorten the time period of the loan arrangement. In other words, if it's a good deal, keep trying to convince the seller to arrange a modest down payment with owner financing of the remainder.

Your seller may finally realize that owner financing, in whatever form—installment payments, mortgages, or a consultancy contract—would be the most positive way to ensure the sale within a specific time period. If that agreement can be achieved, your negotiations were worth the effort.

In any purchase of a business, your personal finances should be sparingly used for a down payment arrangement. Borrow as much as the business can afford to repay and have your remaining capital available as a backstop for those unexpected but inevitable business emergencies.

BOOTSTRAP FINANCING FOR A NEW START-UP

According to Webster's Dictionary, the adjective form of bootstrap can relate to "undertaken or effected without the help of others (a bootstrap operation)." Another familiar phrase is "pulling oneself up by one's own bootstraps."

The meaning is clear, but the idea of not needing help from others is not true. You do need trade credit from your suppliers and you will need advance payments from your customers, where that's called for.

The idea of bootstrap financing simply means using the company's internal resources to generate capital. Getting that thirty- to ninety-day credit from your suppliers is one example. That kind of extended credit is much cheaper than getting a bank loan. Unfortunately, suppliers will usually demand cash payments from a brand-new start-up. However, by meeting your suppliers directly, giving them credit references, and talking up your projections, you may be able to convince them after the first few orders. Make sure you pay for those initial orders on delivery.

Leasing equipment usually requires no down payment, and the costs are normally fully tax deductible. Often the equipment supplier may arrange for time payments, or you may consider an equipment loan from the bank. In all cases, you are not using vital start-up cash for this purpose—it will be more useful as working capital to generate profits.

As the recent father of the bride, I became fully aware of bootstrap financing via the advance payments route. The printer of the invitations, the still photographer, and the caterer each requested one-third to one-half down payments of their estimated invoices. This is a normal arrangement for any of the professions or services that require "progress" payments—the builder, decorator, upholsterer, engraver, and many, many more.

In my own business of motion picture production for corporate communications and TV commercials, the standard contract called for three progress payments. The first payment was due upon signing of the contract, before anything was undertaken. The client is supplying the financing as each stage of the order is completed. This is especially true with any type of custom sales or highly specialized orders.

Another important facet of bootstrap financing is that you, the owner, keep a tight rein on all expenditures. Spend where it's necessary, but save on waste and overpayments. Look for cost savings that won't harm the efficient operation of the business. Check them against the industry average for supplies, inventory, rent, utilities, even owner salaries. All in all, what we're talking about is good management.

If you really want to go it alone, size your operation to your own resources and then go all out for bootstrap financing. Rent your premises, lease your fixtures and equipment, build up your suppliers to the extended trade credit terms and tightly manage your costs and expenses. Cut your own salary until the business can pay what you and it can afford.

THE FRANCHISOR

A great many franchisors do supply some form of financial assistance. The what and how of their financial aid may already be indicated in their literature or disclosure statement. The assistance they offer will be in the form of debt loans, where you are repaying the loan over a specific period of time.

Equity loans, on the other hand, are not paid back but you have to give up a piece of the business instead. Most authorities, franchisors included, will tell you to back away from this kind of loan. With a franchise, you have already given up a unique portion of your ownership, because of the royalties. There's no value to dividing the business any further.

If you have done a good job with your financial folder and included a modest business plan, keep the communications with the franchisor going. They may be impressed by your in-depth approach to the field, your knowledge of their franchise, and your motivation to succeed. This may result in additional financing support, or the maximum help the company policy allows.

Where the franchisor gives very little or no assistance, your detailed approach may still result in a valuable payoff, such as an introduction and strong recommendation to financial sources the franchisor knows and does business with, or the possibility that the franchisor will act as a guarantor of a portion of the loan.

No matter what amount of capital you have to raise, it's obvious that you should approach the franchisor first. The knowledge of their own franchise system certainly enables them to judge your success potential. If their evaluation of you as a franchisee is a positive one, then the chances of obtaining assistance should be very high indeed. Therefore, get on the ball and sell yourself!

Franchisor Assistance

Some examples of franchisors that require a moderate investment have been extracted from the *Franchise Opportunities Handbook*. As noted earlier, franchisors do vary in the amount and type of their offerings.

Equity capital needed: $10,000 to $30,000. Assists franchisee in obtaining financing from local bank. Supplies merchandise for resale on a thirty-day account basis.

Equity capital needed: approximately $27,000. A total investment of $72,000 is required to open a Center. Approximately two-thirds of this can be financed for creditworthy applicants.

Equity capital needed: $40,000 minimum. The purchase price is $85,000. An initial $20,000 franchise fee pays for the franchisor services prior to opening. The franchisor has made arrangements with a leasing company for financing of the equipment package for $65,000.

Equity capital needed: franchise fee $15,000. Opening fee $5,000; inventory, leasehold improvements and operating capital are an additional $30,000–$45,000. Franchisor will carry note on portion of franchise fee.

Equity capital needed: $40,000 to $75,000. No financial assistance available. The franchisor is available for consultation with lenders.

Equity capital needed: $7,500. Partial financing to qualified applicants.

Equity capital needed: $65,000 or more. Sales and credit personnel will counsel and assist franchisee to obtain necessary assistance through local sources, or through company's own assistance programs.

Equity capital needed: $10,000–$20,000 depending upon location and size of area. Franchisor will finance 50–80 percent of the franchise fee, if franchisee has established a good credit rating.

In addition to the above, of course, there are franchisors that offer no financial assistance, and indicated finances were dependent on the franchisee's own sources.

It doesn't take much reading between the lines to note that your credit rating is one of the big keys to obtaining direct assistance from the franchisor. That also holds true for the franchisors who will help arrange financing through the local banks and/or other sources they work with. In all cases, then, your completed financial folder will be essential in obtaining assistance from the franchisor.

BORROWING TO BUY A BUSINESS

In the context of debt financing, commercial banks are the most common source of borrowed capital, which must be repaid with interest. No ownership equity or control is usually given to the lender in these instances.

With an existing business takeover, however, the bank concentrates on an income statement. The bank also looks at what in the business about to be purchased can be pledged as security. Is there real estate, equipment, or furniture and fixtures, and are they free and clear? Even with collateral, the loan officer is concerned with the new owner's management expertise and the venture's profitability. The banks are not gamblers, and they want to make sure that principal and interest will be paid.

Additionally, the banks may have you sign a personal guarantee for the loan and will also ask for your spouse's signature. This is almost mandatory for any small business loan, especially a new situation.

When buying a business, the medium-or long-term loan that is not secured by real estate or equipment has a few other requirements. It's doubtful that the bank will consider such a loan at all unless the new owner is putting up 50 percent or more of the initial takeover capital. They will also require a good personal credit rating, some sort of past managerial experience in that type of business or a similar one, and a fairly complete business plan.

The plan should relate to the essentials of the business being purchased, your own background, the disposition of the loan funds, past financial history of the venture and your future projections, and so on. Two or four pages of a business plan may be adequate for a normal loan situation, whereas much more detail will be required for any extensive or equity financing.

Consider the bank you are now dealing with, but don't be afraid to shop a few others for comparison purposes. You may have a better rapport with another loan officer. In fact, the not-impossible ideal is to find a loan officer who has been active in some prior small business, one who may have had the experience of meeting a payroll and who understands more than just the structured paperwork of standard loan agreements.

BORROWING TO START A BUSINESS

Bankers know that new business start-ups are the riskiest investment around. They are not gamblers, and they are not in the investment business. Repayment of a loan, along with the appropriate interest, is their main concern and their reason for existence.

Nevertheless, there is definite value in investigating loan possibilities with the bank loan officers and the SBA. If nothing else, you may learn where your projections may be at fault, or not thorough enough. They review hundreds of new business proposals—some just wishful thinking, others quite comprehensive. As a result, they may very quickly pinpoint sloughed-off areas or simple miscalculations. Take advantage of any guidance they are willing to offer.

Where a commercial bank does approve your loan request, it's usually for a personal loan, rather than one specifically awarded to start your venture. If you have a good credit rating that indicates prompt payment of previous obligations, the outlook for a loan is usually favorable. But when your banker knows there's a business start-up involved, he or she will also insist upon some form of collateral. Savings accounts, stocks, bonds, real property, and perhaps a cosigner or guarantor are among the accepted forms of collateral.

A savings bank passbook can generate a dollar for dollar loan without disturbing your savings. You can assign the passbook to whatever bank you choose—the one charging the lowest interest rate can help determine your choice. The savings bank will note that the account is being used as collateral, and therefore you cannot withdraw funds from it, but you can add deposits. In the meantime, those funds keep earning interest to help offset the interest you will be paying for the loan. Additionally, you will be enhancing your credit rating for any loans that may be needed later.

Where you do put up the major capital requirements from your own personal resources and you have managerial experience in the type business being contemplated, some honest consideration will be given to your request for additional funds. Even though banks are reluctant to grant start-up loans, talk to their loan officers about your particular venture.

The main point is to know your needs and the requirements of the various sources of financing, then match them up and make the approach. The worst that can happen is a turndown, usually with lots of advice. That advice can be helpful!

BORROWING TO BUY A FRANCHISE

To qualify you as a franchisee, all franchisors will want to know something about you and your potential. An initial mini-check, before any interview, would include your credit standing, your net worth, and perhaps a short résumé of your past work experience.

Not surprisingly, this is the same kind of information that would be required by any lending source you might approach for financial assistance. Most new franchisee prospects do not have all the required capital to purchase the franchise they've selected, so raising money is one of their most important jobs in becoming an entrepreneur.

The potential franchisee must know all about the costs involved in acquiring a franchise: initial franchise fee; construction or lease charges; cost of furniture and fixtures, equipment, opening inventory and supplies, and promotion expenses. What are the royalty fees and advertising fees, if any? Are these the total costs to purchase and operate the franchise?

The bank will also look at the franchise agreement and evaluate the projections made by the franchisor. If they are familiar with the franchise and think it is a good one, your chances for a loan will be much higher than if you were planning an independent start-up. If the franchise is not a familiar one, the bank will treat it as any other new venture. In that case, unless collateral or cosigner guarantors are involved, getting a business loan approval will be difficult.

The funds you are personally investing in the franchise and your business plan are important. The way you handle yourself and make your presentation is also important. Approach the bank with confidence and project the impression that you know what you are doing, that you have researched the franchise offering thoroughly and believe in its success. We're back to the importance of selling yourself. A loan officer's favorable impression of the applicant is a factor in the loan decision.

Keep in mind that a commercial bank's business relates more to loans for existing, successful ventures rather than new ones. But if the loan officer is impressed by your presentation, he or she may recommend you to another source, private or government.

If one bank turns down your loan application, go to another. Make sure you know the reason for the rejection. If your presentation is at fault, correct it before the next application. When the financing is for equipment, the bank may look for some involvement by the franchisor—perhaps a cosignature or condition in the contract that may relate to their buy-back of the equipment. Different loan officers put different emphasis on certain aspects of loan applications, so do not give up after one bank turns you down.

Where your credit-risk record and references are good and your own resources are also being invested, the potential for a personal loan is much greater, especially if you have been dealing with the bank previously and your net worth reflects tangible assets. Although the personal loan may be limited, that may be all you need to complete the initial financing.

Where a franchise building, equipment, or furniture and fixtures are being financed, however, the franchisor or its subsidiaries may institute a leaseback arrangement. Instead of laying out capital to purchase these items, the franchisee contracts to pay monthly fees for many years. Factoring companies and other lenders specialize in leasing to franchisees. The International Franchise Association, 1025 Connecticut Avenue, N.W., Washington, D.C. 20036, may be able to supply additional information on aspects of leasing.

You will often see listings of financial sources that include savings and loan associations, commercial finance companies, and many of the well-known consumer finance units. Most of these sources must relate to real estate or equipment loans, or some specific collateral. If your venture can offer that kind of security, compare the rates and regulations of these sources with those of the commercial banks.

With consumer finance companies, security may consist of personal property, cars, boats, or even qualified collectibles. If you have already been turned down by the commercial banks, the rates you encounter from other sources will most likely be higher. In any event, shop for funds the way you shop for other needs until you get the best deal possible.

WHAT ABOUT UNCLE SAM?

Although future administrative and congressional action may severely limit its activities, the Small Business Administration (SBA) is a logical source of information. Direct loans can be obtained from the SBA, but the chances are fairly slim for a number of reasons:

1. Insufficient funds are allocated for direct loans and therefore they are depleted quickly.
2. Preference is given to minorities, women, the economically disadvantaged, and the handicapped.
3. About 90 percent of SBA loan activities relate to guarantee bank loans, not direct loans.

Guarantee loans, or bank participation loans, are the most common form of financing assistance to be obtained from the SBA. Under this arrangement, the SBA is guaranteeing 90 percent of your bank loan.

You must first apply to the bank for a loan. Only after two banks turn you down can you ask the same banks to request an SBA loan—one where the bank would only have a 10 percent risk. The loan officer will then have you fill out the SBA forms, which will require the same information as the bank's.

The forms and loan request will be submitted to the SBA, and you will be notified of their decision by the loan officer at the bank. Very often the loan officer can estimate the probability of acceptance or rejection, for the SBA would also like the applicant to have a good credit rating, supply up to 50 percent of the initial capital required, submit a business plan, and have the capability to succeed. Previous experience in the same kind of business is a definite plus, but new ventures are a definite risk for both the bank and the SBA.

Since the SBA is committed to aiding small business, however, the sometimes undercapitalized and inexperienced beginner will be given consideration if the proposed business shows a good potential for success. Don't jump for joy, though, because past history indicates only a small percentage of loans to new start-ups. Most of the funds have gone to ongoing situations.

Other loan programs in the SBA are geared to the economically or socially disadvantaged minority and to the disadvantaged or physically handicapped. These applicants are considered even if they can only contribute 20 percent of their capital requirements.

Neither the SBA nor the bank, however, grants these loans arbitrarily. Both expect the probabilities of repayment to exist, as will be evident when you fill out the required forms and supply all the requested information.

In applying for a loan to take over an existing business or to request funds for expansion, a track record of sorts does exist through past performance and future projections based on previous actualities. A loan request in these cases is more likely to receive favorable SBA consideration than a loan for an operation that is starting from scratch.

The paperwork required for an SBA loan is quite extensive. It involves SBA forms and ample documentation of the venture's viability, including the following:

- loan application (SBA form)
- personal history of principals (SBA form)
- personal financial statements (SBA form)
- proposed bill of sale, with terms, asking price, schedule of inventory, equipment and machinery, furniture and fixtures
- current balance sheet (past ninety days)
- projection of income and expense for one year
- profit and loss statements of business to be purchased for previous year
- federal tax returns for previous two years
- business lease and terms
- business plan including business history, loan purpose and use, and problem areas.

Loan and equity investment applications seem to place great emphasis on the need for a thorough and detailed business plan that indicates where the business is going and with what tools this will be accomplished. At the same time, it highlights the owner's managerial abilities—the acknowledged need for that presentation and the follow-through to provide it. The professional assistance necessary in buying a business can also facilitate the preparation of a business plan, and such assistance should be utilized as needed.

Can you get assistance from the SBA when you are buying a *franchise*? Here again, after determining how much or how little the franchisor will offer in financial aid, you have to check your own resources. What do *you* own in the assets column that can be used for the franchise purchase?

Your assets and your business plan are the areas the SBA will be looking at, along with all the details and projections of the franchise outlet you have selected. Fortunately, the franchisor may be able to offer professional guidance in these categories.

Although there are many who doubt the probability of ever getting a loan from the SBA, the records do show the opposite. Many millions of dollars of loans to franchises in the areas of fastfood, gas stations, ice cream, and auto dealerships have been made. Unfortunately, too many borrowers have defaulted on these loans.

Whether or not this makes the SBA gun-shy with relation to franchise outlets, it's still worth approaching the SBA through the bank-participation loan program.

In the future, the SBA will be trying to have the franchisor shoulder some of the risk involved in the loan to the franchisee. If this becomes a requirement, it may lead to more loan approvals and more franchisor participation in the loan applications.

Another SBA program that you may apply for is a lease guarantee. This is a program wherein an insurance policy pledges that rent payments on the lease will be paid. The policy is issued by a private insurance company and is backed by the SBA reinsurance agreements.

As indicated earlier, the choice of a bank is extremely important, especially when it comes to an SBA bank participation loan. For example, there are some banks that encourage loans under the loan guarantee program. At such a bank, the loan officer would be thoroughly familiar with all the program's intricacies. If you're applying, that's the kind of player you would want on your team.

In addition, the personal relationship and rapport that you can achieve with the loan officer will result in valuable support and guidance for your business. So try to select *both* a banker and a bank that are on your side.

The SBA has listed more than 250 banks that are qualified in a new program that simplifies the guaranteed loan procedures. Check your regional SBA office for this information, or write SBA, Public Information Office, 1441 L Street, N.W., Washington, D.C. 20416.

The Small Business Administration may very well be the entrepreneur's single meaningful ally for lower-interest loans and the oft-needed managerial assistance in the art of running a business.

Deficits, budget crunches, and some kind of congressional action will affect the SBA in the very near future. Keep your eyes and ears open and stay in touch with your local or regional SBA office to know how and if the changes will affect your proposed venture.

Other government agencies and federally funded agencies can be approached for financial aid in special situations. They include state and local development companies, the Environmental Protection Agency, the Veterans Administration, the Bureau of Indian Affairs, the Commodity Credit Corporation, the Federal Housing Authority, the Farmers Home Administration, and many others. If you think the shoe fits, check the applicable requirements with your regional SBA office, which may be able to guide you to the right source.

The SBA's financing activities also relate to other areas and include arrangements with state and local communities, as well as venture capital firms. In most cases, these relationships are for the purpose of providing aid to small business. In others, the funding is targeted to the venture that can provide an economic benefit for the community.

STATE AND LOCAL DEVELOPMENT COMPANIES

The Small Business Administration is also authorized to lend funds to the state and local development companies for use in financing small businesses. Here, the criteria have a different emphasis. The primary purpose is to promote the economic welfare of their communities. Therefore the entrepreneur who applies for financing must be able to show that substantial benefit to the community will be one of the results of the venture.

For example, a manufacturer who needs financing to buy or lease a plant, which in turn will bring employment and tax revenues to the community, may be a favorable applicant. Many states are organizing development corporations or industrial foundations specifically to promote the establishment or expansion of businesses in their areas.

In some instances, longer-term loans or more favorable amounts than would normally be available from the banks are a possibility with these organizations. Managerial and technical counseling services may also be forthcoming. If the business you intend to purchase can fit the necessary requirements, check to see if there is an established local development company in your area. Your SBA regional office may also have that information.

MINORITY BUSINESS DEVELOPMENT AGENCY (MBDA)

Formerly known as OMBE, the Minority Business Development Agency wants to help the minority entrepreneur. Assistance can be obtained through a nationwide network of local offices that are funded by the MBDA. These local offices are known as business assistance centers, and their services encompass helping minority business people overcome many of the handicaps they may come across in owning and operating their own business.

General business counseling, management and technical assistance, new business starts and expansions, franchises, technology opportunities, and so on are all part of their program. If you are a member of a minority group, they can offer a helping hand regarding a business purchase.

The MBDA business assistance center will help in preparing loan applications, obtaining credit lines and applying for other forms of capital assistance, such as equity participation and federal loan guarantees. A listing of all centers can be found in the "MBDA Funded Organizations" booklet or the Franchise Opportunities Handbook. Check the phone book for your region's Department of Commerce office, under federal government listings, which may be able to give you the information necessary to order these publications. The publications may also be available for study and photocopying in the Department of Commerce office's library.

VENTURE CAPITAL

Venture capital is a source of financing that is often touted to the beginner as if it were a magic spigot of unlimited funds, just waiting to be turned on. Nothing could be further from the truth!

First of all, private venture capitalists are usually professional investors who look for experienced management and/or a unique product. High-technology situations, energy, electronics, growth industry profiles, and essential services are more their cup of tea. Pure start-ups and retail operations are practically zero in their books, but if your venture fits what they're looking for, give them a try.

Once involved with you, venture capitalists will acquire a good percentage of ownership for their equity investment. Without question, you will now have a partner! Stock ownership is the usual route to their participation, so your venture will have to be incorporated to take advantage of this type of equity financing.

Along with their money, however, you can gain a good deal more. Your venture capitalists will take a keen and active interest in your operation. They will provide guidance in marketing and product development, additional financing, and general management consultation. Their investment in the initial growth and development stages of your venture can prove invaluable to its success. From their own point of view, it's risk capital targeted toward a key objective of high capital gains. Their participation, however, is no guarantee of success, and no matter how selective they are, many of the investments just don't make it.

Nevertheless, there is ample equity capital available for those ventures with the right combination of ingredients, such as things unique, essential products or services, high-tech products, fast-growth industries, superior management, or futuristics with exceptionally high-growth characteristics. It's the venture with great expansion potential that attracts them, not the modest, stable, normal product or service venture.

Accordingly, there may be a conflict of operational philosophy between you and the venture capital organization. You want to own and build a business that will throw off a substantial income. They, on the other hand, want to make a lot of money, and their best way to accomplish this may be to sell out within four to seven years. Therefore, their emphasis may relate to anything that will enhance the short-term growth of the venture. This may be a definite conflict with your own outlook and direction.

But if you think you have what venture capitalists want and you need their financing, get some professional assistance and go after it. Be aware, however, that in most cases the private venture firms tend to search out the best and most viable opportunities themselves. They have also listened to and acted upon recommendations from bankers, accountants, and others in their professional circles.

Perhaps, as a viable alternate, the better place to go may be the federally funded venture capitalists. These are privately organized, privately managed firms that make their own investment decisions but are pledged to provide venture capital only to small, independent businesses. They are licensed and financed by the Small Business Administration for the purpose of providing equity capital and long-term loans.

Known as SBICs and MESBICs, their formal designations are Small Business Investment Companies and Minority Enterprise Small Business Investment Companies. In the past twenty-two years, they have made over fifty thousand loans and investments to small ventures. Although all SBICs will consider applications from socially and economically disadvantaged entrepreneurs, MESBICs normally make *all* their investments in this area. These minority entrepreneurs include blacks, Hispanics, Indians, and Eskimos.

For minorities, the MESBIC's provide financial services for small ventures. The investments or loans must go to businesses that are more than 50 percent owned by minority individuals.

The SBA office nearest you can supply additional information on these small business investment companies, as well as on their own loan programs.

As to the type of financing, each SBIC investment is a highly individual situation that you and SBIC will negotiate. The arrangement may involve buying shares of your stock or simply a long-term loan. They, like the private venture capitalists, are interested in generating capital gains, and they will also provide active management counseling.

Because these organizations are federally funded, do not make the mistake of thinking they are more lenient in judging the viability or potential of an applicant than private financial sources. Like all investors, they require complete information and, again, the business plan presentation is crucial.

The National Association of Small Business Investment Companies (NASBIC) publishes a directory of over three hundred SBICs and MESBICs. That number represents approximately 90 percent of the industry's resources, with locations throughout the nation. Of great importance is the code designation of each listed firm to denote their investment policies, industry preferences, and financing limits. This enables you to target the SBIC that would be most interested in your specific type of venture. For their twenty-eight-page directory, send $1 to 1156 Fifteenth Street, N.W., Washington, D.C. 20005.

B

Reviews and Checklists

No matter how one chooses to enter the field of entrepreneurship, it's a gamble.

Professional gamblers will always study the odds involved. Since *winning* is their goal, they prepare accordingly.

If you have the same goal, review the following lists to see how well you have prepared:

- personal characteristics
- buy an existing business
- new business start-ups
- franchise evaluation.

ONCE MORE, WITH FEELING

When it comes to interviews, seminars, or class study, the question most frequently asked is: "What is the greatest cause of failure for new businesses?" Not so strangely, the answer is usually the same—lack of preparation. That's really the core reason for Dun & Bradstreet's statistic that "managerial incompetence" accounts for 92 percent of the small business failures.

Of course, managerial incompetence covers the whole spectrum of fundamentals that apply to entrepreneurship, not just personal traits and capital requirements, but some management practices, buying, pricing, and clearly identifying the market for your product or service—whether that market is large enough to return a reasonable profit and whether your product or service fulfills a definite need. Reread the pertinent sections of this book for specific details that apply to these and other basic areas of small business.

Preparation, by itself, won't make you a successful owner-manager overnight. It will, however, definitely stack the odds in your favor, and it will cushion both the surprises and realities that are sure to come your way. Most of your final entrepreneurial polish and experience, however, will come from on-the-job actualities.

If you've definitely decided to go ahead and become an entrepreneur, to take the risk and put it all together, this may be the time to go over it all once more. The following series of checklists are brief condensations of evaluative steps that should have already been filtered through your decision-making process.

Personal Characteristics

Are you the type to operate your own business? There are many characteristics that help make an owner-manager a successful entrepreneur. These have been identified and are incorporated in the questionnaire that follows. Try for an honest self-appraisal. Be objective in determining the level that comes closest to your feeling about yourself in each area.

We all have strengths and weaknesses, and it's important to identify them in yourself, for you are your venture's most valuable employee. Use the scale of 1 to 5 below, where 1 represents a real strength and 5 a real weakness, and 2, 3, and 4 represent the range in between. The lower your score the better, but don't circle the lowest number unless that category is one of your real strengths.

Energy level:　　1　　2　　3　　4　　5

Energy is one of the key characteristics of a successful small business owner. Good health and drive are subcategories in this area. If you tire easily, lose interest quickly when things don't go smoothly, and lack any great need to achieve, circle the high number; you have problems! Hard work and long hours are essential to running your own business, as is stick-to-itiveness.

Self-starting ability:　　1　　2　　3　　4　　5

Many people find it difficult to get going on their own. Others can keep things moving. As an entrepreneur you are on your own all the way, so it's vital to initiate actions without waiting for anyone else's directions. If you often handle things your own way and don't need anyone nudging you, the low numbers may categorize you best.

Risk-taking: 1   2   3   4   5

Your own small business is a high-risk venture. It's a scary one for any banker, but even more so for you. Do you usually play it safe? Do you approach most things with great caution? Are your investments generally conservative? Do you need guarantees before committing yourself? Imprudent risk is just as dangerous as extreme caution, but where do your normal feelings lie? If you are generally conservative, will you be able to handle the everyday risks inherent in a small business? Rate yourself carefully on this one.

Making decisions: 1   2   3   4   5

One entrepreneurial action you will be doing quite often, is making decisions. Do you normally require lots of time to make decisions. Are you always vacillating? After making a decision, do you remain apprehensive? If you've made decisions in a hurry, were they usually right or generally acceptable? Do you have confidence in your decisions? Would you rather have others make the hard decisions because you're afraid you might foul things up?

Relating to others: 1   2   3   4   5

Getting along well with people as customers, suppliers, and employees, will affect your venture's potential for success. Do you generally like people? Have you had difficulties communicating with others? Do you have leadership abilities? Would you be able to guide and train employees and replace them when necessary? Does "the customer is always right" as a traditional business principle really frustrate you? Do you listen?

Organizational talent: 1   2   3   4   5

Do you take the easy way and let things develop naturally? If problems occur, do you panic or immediately take hold? Are you a planner, setting up schedules and strategies ahead of time? When problems arise, do you seek logical solutions that will eliminate future repetitions? If a quick-fix is necessary, do you treat it as a temporary stop-gap and then look for a better resolution? Do you seriously evaluate suggestions from others?

Learning ability: 1   2   3   4   5

Since most of your entrepreneurial skills will come from the actuality of on-the-job training, the ability to learn from experience is vital. In the past, when confronted with new ideas or applications, were you able to absorb them quickly and easily? Was it too much of a hassle? Do you recognize opportunities somewhat faster than others? If things don't work out one way, do you try another? Is your memory retention good? Are you impatient with in-depth study and exploration? Is your attention span fairly good, and can you concentrate, when necessary?

Your Ratings

Energy level	_____
Self-starting	_____
Risk-taking	_____
Making decisions	_____
Relating to others	_____
Organizational talent	_____
Learning ability	_____

The total score isn't as important as the individual categories. This is where you can discern your strengths and weaknesses. In some cases, a weakness can be compensated by a partner who is strong in that area. Or it may be taken care of by hiring the correct employee.

Additionally, there are other questions you can ask yourself that relate specifically to the venture you may already be contemplating. In that case, it shouldn't be too difficult to identify what added personal characteristics are required.

Although these ratings don't constitute a final evaluation to determine if you are the type for entrepreneurship, they do help point the way if you're not. Where the total of these categories indicates a very high score, it would be best not to go ahead with your own business. It can only mean that you have too many deficiencies in the characteristics that are necessary for a successful entrepreneur.

Buying an Existing Business

Many things must be considered when you buy a business, and neglecting just one or two vital areas can lead to disaster. Although no checklist can cover everything, the following may aid greatly in not overlooking some significant areas. Obviously, every question may not apply to your particular situation, but most will have some relevancy. With this list, the more "yes" answers, the better.

Have you understood the advantages and disadvantages in buying a business?   _____

Do you know the type of business you intend to buy?   _____

Have you taken your experience, skills, hobbies, and major interests into consideration?   _____

Is your business choice in a growth or expanding field?   _____

Are current conditions good in the field you are selecting?   _____

Do you know the real reason the present owner wishes to sell?   _____

Have you checked the firm's reputation with suppliers, employees, and the nearby business community?   _____

Did you verify the quality and extent of the competition?   _____

Have you researched all aspects of the business *location*—community demographics, area stability, parking facilities, rent and taxes, potential for expansion, lease provisions?   _____

Has the present owner defined his or her market, the type of customers, and present advertising efforts?   _____

Were suppliers, product costs, and pricing strategies reviewed?   _____

Did you discuss the present bookkeeping system and methods of inventory control?   _____

If personnel are a part of the business, were you able to get a rundown of each employee's experience, longevity, and contract arrangement, if any?   _____

Did you ascertain insurance requirements and present coverage?   _____

Are the equipment and fixtures in good condition and not outdated?   _____

Is the inventory current and well balanced? Has it been evaluated by age?   _____

Have you had an accountant review all the financial papers and analyzed the past and present figures?   _____

Have both you and your accountant estimated future sales and profits for the next few years?   _____

Do the various ratios of the industry approximate those shown in this business?   _____

Have sales and profits been increasing in the past few years?   _____

Has net worth been professionally appraised and goodwill carefully evaluated?   _____

Is estimated rate of return better than what you would earn in other investments?   _____

Has the seller's asking price been negotiated with relation to the future profit potential of the business?   _____

Did you compare the purchase price with the costs of starting the same type of business?   _____

Have you taken all this knowledge and formulated a simple business plan?   _____

Have you determined your total costs to purchase this business and the methods of payment? Do you know where you will obtain the required capital?   _____

Did you engage a lawyer to finalize a contract and has he or she checked for liens, validity of title, present lease provisions, and what licenses are required to do business?   _____

Has your attorney also included a noncompete clause, an escrow fund arrangement, and a seller's warranty for your protection?   _____

Each of the listed questions is only a *condensed* overview of the steps you should complete for the process of evaluating and buying an existing business. The present owner's sales effort, for example, should relate to the type of media in advertising, the percentage of sales that was spent on advertising, the increase or decrease in the past five years, and so on. Customer profiles could include approximate income breakdown, rate of community unemployment, types of employment, family structures, and age groupings as they relate to the products or services offered.

"Yes" answers to all the questions relevant to your particular venture will indicate that the vital steps were carried out and evaluated before final purchase. A slough-off in these areas could cost you your entire bankroll.

New Business Start-ups

New business start-ups are the riskiest of entrepreneurships—mostly because too many are started without any great degree of preparation.

There is always plenty of enthusiasm, that's for sure, but little experience in management practice is par for the course.

The failure record indicates that poor planning is the major contributor to the demise of new business start-ups. This checklist is a review of the areas you should think about and then follow through with appropriate action if you select this method of becoming an entrepreneur.

Have you thought of a business to start?   _____

Is the business based on your present skills or work experience?   _____

Does the business relate to a hobby or major interest?   _____

Do you know the field?   _____

Should you get more knowledge by working for someone else?   _____

Will you need a partner whose skills will complement your own?   _____

Will you be a manufacturer, distributor, wholesaler, retailer, or services supplier?   _____

Is there a need for your product or service?   _____

Is your product or service a unique idea or a variation of something existing?   _____

Does your idea have a marketable advantage over existing situations?   _____

Have you in any way tested the need or advantage of the proposed idea?   _____

Have you identified the specific market, the categories of buyers?   _____

Do you know your supplier sources?   _____

Do you know what method of distribution you will use?   _____

Have you researched the specific field involved by checking the competition, the growth potential, trade sources, and general business conditions?   _____

Have you selected a general location—town, city, rural area, farm or industrial community?   _____

Did you review your initial plans with an experienced adviser— businessman, banker, SBA, consultant?   _____

Did you estimate your money requirements to get started?   _____

Did your money estimate include working capital and living expenses for three to six months?   _____

For the first year, do you have an outside income to supplement the minimal return from the business? ____

Do you have the required capital to open for business? ____

If you need additional capital, do you know where the rest is coming from? ____

Have you decided what type of business organization you will choose—sole proprietorship, partnership, or corporation? ____

Have you outlined a preliminary business plan, with an economic projection? ____

Did you check the trade sources for typical operating ratios that would apply to your business? ____

Do you know if this business requires any special licenses, permits, or zoning variances? ____

Did you research the industry and trade associations for guidance as to realistic estimates of your initial sales volume? ____

Does there appear to be a real potential for profit, taking estimated sales volume and subtracting all estimated costs? ____

If you've put in the heavy preparatory time needed to accomplish most of what's in this review list, then you should be pretty confident about going on with your business plans. In that case, *finalize* the following:

1. Determine the type of business, the capital required, and the business structure.
2. Select a business name and register it.
3. Set up a separate business checking account and banker relationship.
4. Pick a location—shopping center, suburban, city, or rural area; store, office, or building.
5. Select a lawyer to handle your legal needs and help with the lease negotiations.
6. Obtain all necessary licenses and permits.
7. Arrange for furniture and fixtures, remodeling if necessary.
8. Order all utilities and a security system, if needed.
9. Consult an insurance broker to determine immediate coverage.
10. Select an accountant to set up and initial bookkeeping system and file for an employer identification number.

11. Purchase stationery, business cards, order forms, and invoices.

12. Arrange for immediate cash requirements as indicated on your projections of sales, costs, cash flow, and fixed expenses.

13. Establish terms of credit, if possible, with suppliers. Tell them your plans.

14. If personnel are required, set up specifications and arrange interviews. Check references and make final selections.

15. Order and set up inventory, equipment and supplies.

16. Determine operating procedures regarding credit, markups, inventory control, and personnel.

17. Set up your distribution system—mail order, retail, wholesale, distributors.

18. Plan the opening promotional and ad campaigns, based on your marketing area and the type of customer you wish to reach.

19. Be determined to stay aware of the specific characteristics of your market, your consumers, the local competition, your trade associations, your suppliers, and your own business objectives.

20. Set an opening date!

Once again, if you've completed this type of preparation, the odds for success will be on your side. These areas should be researched and evaluated before you don the entrepreneur's hat. This kind of preparation is especially essential when the start-up venture is your first business. As noted earlier, awareness of the business fundamentals is more than half the battle. No one expects you to be a professional at the start, but the more you can become familiar with beforehand, the better.

In the meantime, don't forget to keep alive and well your initial enthusiasm and confidence. They are both absolutely essential!

Franchise Evaluation

In some ways, buying a franchise as a method of entry into the small business world seems the easiest to evaluate. Unfortunately, that's just the kind of thinking that frequently has resulted in the superficial investigation of a prospective franchisee opportunity, often with disastrous results.

One of the best checklists for those interested in franchises was published many years ago by the SBA. About the only current comment that could apply to it now is the many new franchises that have emerged in recent years. Their track record as franchisors isn't very extensive. You will have to check their record as an independent business prior to franchising, and their reputation, expertise, growth, and financial backing.

The checklist, from the SBA's booklet, "Starting and Managing a Small Business of Your Own," by Wendell O. Metcalf, is reproduced in its entirety.

Questions To Answer Affirmatively Before Going Into Franchising

check if
answer
is "yes"

The Franchisor

1. Has the franchisor been in business long enough (5 years or more) to have established a good reputation? _____

2. Have you checked Better Business Bureaus, Chambers of Commerce, Dun and Bradstreet, or bankers to find out about the franchisor's business reputation and credit rating? _____

3. Did the above investigations reveal that the franchisor has a good reputation and credit rating? _____

4. Does the franchising firm appear to be financed adequately so that it can carry out its stated plan of financial assistance and expansion? _____

5. Have you found out how many franchisees are now operating? _____

6. Have you found out the "mortality" or failure rate among franchisees? _____

7. Is the failure rate small? _____

8. Have you checked with some franchisees and found that the franchisor has a reputation for honesty and fair dealing among those who currently hold franchises? _____

9. Has the franchisor shown you certified figures indicating exact net profits of one or more going operations which you have personally checked yourself? _____

10. Has the franchisor given you a specimen contract to study with the advice of your legal counsel? _____

check if
answer
is "yes"

11. Will the franchisor assist you with:
    a. A management training program?   _____
    b. An employee training program?   _____
    c. A public relations program?   _____
    d. Obtaining capital?   _____
    e. Good credit terms?   _____
    f. Merchandising ideas?   _____
    g. Designing store layout and displays?   _____
    h. Inventory control methods?   _____
    i. Analyzing financial statements?   _____
12. Does the franchisor provide continuing assistance for franchisees through supervisors who visit regularly?   _____
13. Does the franchising firm have an experienced management trained in depth?   _____
14. Will the franchisor assist you in finding a good location for your business?   _____
15. Has the franchising company investigated *you* carefully enough to assure itself that you can successfully operate one of its franchises at a profit both to it and to you?   _____
16. Have you determined exactly what the franchisor can do for you that you cannot do for yourself?   _____

The Product Or Service

17. Has the product or service been on the market long enough to gain good consumer acceptance?   _____
18. Is it priced competitively?   _____
19. Is it the type of item or service which the same consumer customarily buys more than once?   _____
20. Is it an all-year seller in contrast to a seasonal one?   _____
21. Is it a staple item in contrast to a fad?   _____
22. Does it sell well elsewhere?   _____
23. Would you buy it on its merits?   _____
24. Will it be in greater demand five years from now?   _____

check if
answer
is "yes"

25. If it is a product rather than a service:
    a. Is it packaged attractively? _____
    b. Does it stand up well in use? _____
    c. Is it easy and safe to use? _____
    d. Is it patented? _____
    e. Does it comply with all applicable laws? _____
    f. Is it manufactured under certain quality standards? _____
    g. Do these standards compare favorably with similar products on the market? _____
    h. If the product must be purchased exclusively from the franchisor or a designated supplier, are the prices to you, as the franchisee, competitive? _____

The Franchise Contract

26. Does the franchise fee seem reasonable? _____

27. Do continuing royalties or percent of gross sales payment appear reasonable? _____

28. Is the total cash investment required and the terms for financing the balance satisfactory? _____

29. Does the cash investment include payment for fixtures and equipment? _____

30. If you will be required to participate in company sponsored promotion and publicity by contributing to an "advertising fund," will you have the right to veto any increase in contributions to the "fund?" _____

31. If the parent company's product or service is protected by patent or liability insurance, is the same protection extended to you? _____

32. Are you free to buy the amount of merchandise you believe you need rather than being required to purchase a certain amount? _____

33. Can you, as the franchisee, return merchandise for credit? _____

34. **Can you engage in other business activities?** _____

35. If there is an annual sales quota, can you retain your franchise if it is not met? _____

36. Does the contract give you an exclusive territory for the length of the franchise? _____

37. Is your territory protected? _____

38. Is the franchise agreement renewable? _____

39. Can you terminate your agreement if you are not happy for some reason? _____

40. Is the franchisor prohibited from selling the franchise out from under you? _____

41. May you sell the business to whomever you please? _____

42. If you sell your franchise, will you be compensated for the goodwill you have built into the business? _____

43. Does the contract obligate the franchisor to give you continuing assistance after you are operating the business? _____

44. Are you permitted a choice in determining whether you will sell any new product or service introduced by the franchisor after you have opened your business? _____

45. Is there anything with respect to the franchise or its operation which would make you ineligible for special financial assistance or other benefits accorded to small business concerns by Federal, State, or local governments? _____

46. Did your lawyer approve the franchise contract after he studied it paragraph by paragraph? _____

47. Is the contract free and clear of requirements which would call upon you to take any steps

check if
answer
is "yes"

which are, according to your lawyer, unwise or illegal in your state, county or city? _____

48. Does the contract cover all aspects of your agreement with the franchisor? _____

49. Does it really benefit both you and the franchisor? _____

Your Market

50. Are the territorial boundaries of your market completely, accurately and understandably defined? _____

51. Have you made any study to determine whether the product or service you propose to sell has a market in your territory at the prices you will have to charge? _____

52. Does the territory provide an adequate sales potential? _____

53. Will the population in the territory given you increase over the next 5 years? _____

54. Will the average per capita income in the territory remain the same or increase over the next 5 years? _____

55. Is existing competition in your territory for the product or service not too well entrenched? _____

YOU — The Franchisee

56. Do you know where you are going to get the equity capital you will need? _____

57. Have you compared what it would take to start your own similar business with the price you must pay for the franchise? _____

58. Have you made a business plan — for example:

   a. Have you worked out what income from sales or services you can reasonably expect in the first 6 months? The first year? The second year? _____

   b. Have you made a forecast of expenses including a regular salary for yourself? _____

check if
answer
is "yes"

59. Are you prepared to give up some independence of action to secure the advantages offered by the franchise?   ____

60. Are you capable of accepting supervision, even though you will presumably be your own boss?   ____

61. Are you prepared to accept rules and regulations with which you may not agree?   ____

62. Can you afford the period of training involved?   ____

63. Are you ready to spend much or all of the remainder of your business life with this franchisor, offering his product or service to the public?   ____

Conclusion

In conclusion, franchising creates distinct opportunities for the prospective small business owner. Without franchising it is doubtful that thousands of small business investors could ever have started. The American consumer might well have been denied ready access to many products and services. The system permits these goods and services to be marketed without the vast sums of money and number of managerial people possessed only by large corporations. Therefore, it opens up economic opportunities for the small business.

But not even the help of a good franchisor can guarantee success. You will still be primarily responsible for the success or failure of your venture. As in any other type of business your return will be related directly to the amount and effectiveness of your investment in time and money.

Index